SPACE AND MOBILITY IN PALESTINE

PUBLIC CULTURES OF THE MIDDLE EAST
AND NORTH AFRICA

Paul A. Silverstein, Susan Slyomovics, and Ted Swedenburg, *editors*

SPACE AND MOBILITY IN PALESTINE

Julie Peteet

Indiana University Press

Bloomington and Indianapolis

This book is a publication of

Indiana University Press
Office of Scholarly Publishing
Herman B Wells Library 350
1320 East 10th Street
Bloomington, Indiana 47405 USA

iupress.indiana.edu

The paper used in this publication meets the minimum require-
ments of the American National Standard for Information
Sciences—Permanence of Paper for Printed Library Materials,
ANSI Z39.48-1992.

Manufactured in the United States of America

Library of Congress Cataloging-in-Publication Data

Names: Peteet, Julie Marie, author.
Title: Space and mobility in Palestine / Julie Peteet.
Other titles: Public cultures of the Middle East and North Africa.
Description: Bloomington : Indiana University Press, 2017. |
    Series: Public cultures of the Middle East and North Africa |
    Includes bibliographical references and index.
Identifiers: LCCN 2016024513 (print) | LCCN 2016040105 (ebook) |
    ISBN 9780253024800 (cloth : alk. paper) | ISBN 9780253024930
    (pbk. : alk. paper) | ISBN 9780253025111 (ebook)
Subjects: LCSH: Palestinian Arabs—Social conditions. |
    Israel—Boundaries. | Israeli West Bank Barrier. | Space—Social
    aspects.
Classification: LCC DS113.6 .P48 2017 (print) | LCC DS113.6 (ebook) |
    DDC 305.892/74—dc23
LC record available at https://lccn.loc.gov/2016024513

1 2 3 4 5   22 21 20 19 18 17

Contents

Acknowledgments

THE IDEA AND PASSION for this book project was launched at a conference at Bir Zeit University in 2004. A special thanks to Sari Hanafi for organizing the conference and inviting me to participate. Lena Dallasheh is to be commended for her wonderfully informative and intense tours of the wall, which were, in significant part, the inspiration for this book.

This book could not have been written without interlocutors from many walks of life in Palestine. As always, they provide the bedrock upon which ethnographies are written. There are too many to name individually, and many prefer not to have their names made public. Warm welcomes and the willingness to share their stories have been consistent features of my experience as an anthropologist among the Palestinians. My heartfelt thanks to people in Bil'in, Iskaka, Zawiya, and Jenin for their generous welcome and for the inspiration to bring this book to completion. The gracious hospitality I received from Palestinians in the West Bank is another chapter in many years of ethnographic work among Palestinian communities in Lebanon and the West Bank.

In Palestine, friends and colleagues provided support, friendship, insight, and much-needed background information. I was lucky to have the close friendship and never-flagging support of Wassim Abdullah and Um Ghassan, who always had an open door, a great meal, and wonderful stories. Sadly, she passed away before the publication of this book. Both SHAML directors, Sari Hanafi and Awad Mansour, welcomed me and provided an affiliation and office space. I am honored and thankful to have had input as well as inspiration from Sanabel Harwani, Caroline Abu-Saba, Awad Mansour, Fadwa al-Labidi, Maha Samman, Sonia Nimr, Nadera Shalhoub-Kevorkian, Penny Johnson, Salim Tamari, Issam Nassar, Rema Hammami, and Lisa Taraki. Anne Meneley, Ted Swedenburg, Shira Robinson, and Chris Toesing provided companionship during part of my fieldwork. As the director of Palestinian American Research Center (PARC) during my PARC fellowship, Hadeel al-Qazzaz was a valued colleague, and a fount of knowledge on Palestine. A special thanks is extended to Kathy Bergen, former American Friends Service Committee (AFSC) director of the Ramallah Friend's Meeting House, for her wonderful hospitality and for sharing her knowledge of the area. To Jean Zara, clerk of the Ramallah Friend's Meeting, and the staff at the Ramallah AFSC I extend my gratitude for their time and for helping me to understand what daily life is like under occupation. Sonia and Louay were invaluable friends and a source of many stories and much help in traveling in the West Bank.

Parts of this book have been presented at conferences in Beirut, Athens, Cyprus, Norway, New York, Cincinnati, and Palestine as well as at meetings of the American Anthropological Association and the American Ethnological Society. The feedback I received from participants at those meetings was invaluable in preparing the manuscript.

Over the past decade, funding for research has been generously provided by a research fellowship from PARC, a senior research fellowship from the American Center for Oriental Research in Jordan (ACOR), and by the University of Louisville. A Bunting fellowship at the School for Advanced Research (SAR) in Santa Fe provided me with a wonderful opportunity, as well as a very peaceful and supportive site, to plow through pages of fieldnotes, dozens of recordings, and files of photos as I wrote a rough first draft of the manuscript, and to share ideas in an atmosphere of collegiality and intellectual exchange.

In Jordan, ACOR fellows Anne-Marie Pederson and Chris Tuttle and I became fast friends as well as colleagues, and they provided much-needed encouragement to carry on with this project. Over the years, Barbara Porter, director of ACOR has consistently offered a warm welcome and good company when I am in Jordan. ACOR head librarian Humi Ayubi was an invaluable source of references and assistance in locating sources. I have a profound appreciation of Nasreen al-Sheikh, for her friendship, hospitality in the best Arab tradition, and abiding interest in this project. Elena Corbett and Sally Bland provided intellectual friendship, moral support, and encouragement, and deep knowledge of the region and Palestine.

To Susan Slyomovics, Ted Swedenburg, and Paul Silverstein my most heartfelt gratitude for bringing this book to Indiana University Press. Without their unwavering support, this book would not have seen the light of day. IUP editor Dee Mortensen deserves the sincerest thanks for enthusiastically taking on this publication, as do Nancy Lightfoot, Paige Rasmussen, and Charlie Clark for taking this book through production. To Ginny Faber—thanks for your judicious editorial pen and attention to detail that made this a better and certainly more readable book.

My colleagues Shawn Parkhurst and Yvonne Jones were always ready to discuss areas of uncertainty and help me reach clarity. To Omar Attum, a biologist, goes a pointed thanks for alerting me to funnel-traps. A special thanks is extended to the students who have been research assistants over the past decade—Brett McGrath, Claire Gervasi, Anna Mallory, Amanda Yee, Irene Levy, and Anna Brashear—for all their help in assembling this book and their diligence in finding resources and tracking references. I can only hope they acquired new and useful skills in research and writing that will serve them well in their future careers.

SPACE AND MOBILITY IN PALESTINE

Introduction

Space and Mobility in the Time of Closure

Perched on a large boulder, on the dry, hilly edge of the West Bank Palestinian village of Bil'in, Ahmad and I are observing the weekly Friday protest unfolding in the surrounding olive groves. Prevented from entering Israel to work by its policy of closure, Ahmad has been working in his family's olive grove, and we are watching the olive trees being uprooted by weaponized bulldozers flanked by Israeli soldiers and police. They are carving out the route for Israel's separation wall and for the expansion of the colony on once well-cultivated, now confiscated, village lands, and Ahmad's family is one of those losing substantial tracts of land to this effort. We can see the occupation forces throwing tear-gas canisters at the unarmed villagers as they, and their Israeli and international supporters, protest peacefully. This sends the protestors running through the fields, and Ahmad turns to me and says glumly, "This is the third stage in our dispossession." His words capture the spatiality, temporality, and topography of the nationalist settler-colonial project in Palestine, yet they are uttered amid a protest against this very progression of history, an attempt to disrupt the continuity of past, present, and future.

As anthropologist Patrick Wolfe (2006, 388) reminds us, "Invasion is a structure not an event." Ahmad's life trajectory illustrates particular moments in a logical and sequential, rather than disconnected, set of displacing actions that have unfolded in the context of settler colonialism. Born under occupation, he has known no other way of life. Domination by and the expected show of deference to the Israeli settlers and military are routine, as is imprisonment for political activism. Ahmad was formerly employed in a Tel Aviv restaurant, without benefits or the right to live or sleep overnight in Israel. Ahmad began working his family's olive grove when Israel reduced its reliance on Palestinian labor. The expansion of the Israeli colony next to Bil'in has left Ahmad's family in precarious economic straits.

I had my first sight of the behemoth separation wall in spring 2004, when I traveled to the West Bank to attend a conference. Apart from its visual impact, the wall separates and immobilizes, engenders economic chaos, imposes discipline and punishment, appropriates Palestinian resources, and, by ostensibly quelling resistance, gives the Israelis a sense of security. In Palestine, violence has become part of everyday life. Later, Ahmad sighed, "The Israelis are masters in thinking up new ways to torment us."

I position mobility as key to the elaboration and affirmation of place—place as the site of particular configurations of power, identities, and meaning in a modern settler-colonial context. In this book I examine the intersection of mobility and space, looking specifically at how access to space and thus to mobility devolve from racialized categories of ethnicity, religion, and nationality. Israeli policies of closure and separation and the associated physical structures and bureaucratic requirements and procedures—the wall, checkpoints, identity cards, the road system, and permits—dramatically constrain Palestinians' mobility, impeding their ability to construct and give meaning to place. Indeed, closure and separation are critical to opening up space to be reconfigured along new lines of sovereignty and affiliation. In this active relational geography of inclusion and exclusion, managed chaos has become a modus operandi of daily life in Palestine. Mobilities are positioned here as relational, as sedimented in a system of interdependencies, however asymmetrical; the flip side of Palestinian immobilization is the far less encumbered, high-speed mobility of the Israelis through a contiguous and seemingly secured space. How Palestinians comprehend, experience, narrate, and respond to spatial fracturing and immobilization is detailed here. Several processes and practices are at play: a colonial occupation with a complex set of regulations governing mobility, the imposition of calibrated chaos, punishment and rule through the construction of spaces of disorder, and the application of technologies of surveillance and monitoring to control mobility and velocity. All rest on the elaboration of social categories of difference along which the partitioning of (and access to) space is organized. As lived, embodied experiences, these processes foster fragmented and spatially bound habitus; perhaps habitus in the plural would be more appropriate. A politically grounded geography of mobilities, the differentially allocated scope and speed of movement and access to space, opens a way to carry forward the concept of habitus in a time of high-speed and unrestrained mobility for some and constricted mobility for others. Further, as Palestinians traverse different spaces, each with particular configurations of power, habitus shifts and adjusts, foregrounding its plurality.

That first sight of the separation wall sparked my interest in exploring these spatial dynamics and the structural mechanisms that render Palestinians at once mobile and immobile, visible and invisible, and subject to both ordering and disordering practices. Indeed, with the wall, the spectacular has been built directly onto the environment and into the routines of everyday life. Its overpowering presence is a stark and unmistakable declaration of separation and exclusion. Indeed, this book is an ethnographic effect of the wall.

Settler Colonialism in Palestine

Wedged between the Jordan River to the east and the Mediterranean Sea to the west, Palestine has for the past century been dismembered and reconstituted politically, demographically, and discursively. Envisioned in Zionist ideology as part of the territory of a Jewish state, the demographic weight of Palestine's indigenous Arab population posed a challenge.[1] The conundrum of two ethnic/ national groups simultaneously occupying the same space suggests several possibilities, ranging from forced removal or ethno- or genocide, as in the Americas, to apartheid-like segregation and restricted interaction to the regulated intimacy of the household in Dutch Indonesia (Stoler 2002). Whether based in custom or law, degrees of separation are related to demographics, economics, resistance, and culture: the number of settlers vis-à-vis the number of natives, the labor requirements of resource extraction, the elaboration of cultural differences, and indigenous acquiescence.

Over the course of a century, as Jewish colonization proceeded apace, Palestinians faced diminishing access to land and water resources. Historical maps of the area show the 1947 United Nations Partition Plan; Israel at the end of the 1948–49 war; the 1967 conquest of the West Bank, East Jerusalem, and Gaza; and the present configuration of land control in the West Bank. Zionism's time-space trajectory is marked by the watershed dates of the 1917 Balfour Declaration, the 1948 establishment of the state, the 1967 occupation of the remainder of Mandatory Palestine, and the post-Oslo period.[2] How has the Zionist project acquired the bulk of Palestinian land without the Palestinians? First, by denying the return of those who were expelled or had fled during the 1948–49 war. Then the Israelis enacted laws, such as the Absentee Property Law of 1950, that enabled them to confiscate the land of Palestinians that was now outside the new state's borders. Other legislation denied Palestinians access to land and transferred land to Jewish Israelis, including the Development Authority Law (1950), World Zionist Organization–Jewish Agency Status Law (1952), the Jewish National Fund Law (1953), Land Acquisition (Validations of Acts and Compensation) Law (1953), and the Prescription Law of 1958.

The fairly consistent components of the Zionist project have included diluting and dispossessing the indigenous population; fragmenting and isolating their villages, towns, and cities; warehousing Palestinians in refugee camps and immobilizing them in enclaves (Peteet 2016); steady Jewish colonization, the expansion of Israel's sovereignty, and the control of borders and air space, along with a strategy of separation. Ahmad's third stage of dispossession suggested a spatiotemporal formulation of local history characterized by mass displacement in 1948, punctuated and furthered by the 1967 conquest of the West Bank and the

Gaza Strip, the final remnants of Palestine, and now nearing its end in the new millennium. Palestinians keenly grasp the continuity between the past and the present, from 1948 to 1967 to the current set of policies and practices designed to further dispossess and render them politically impotent and effectively preclude a geographically contiguous Palestinian territory, and draw an eastern border.[3] In short, the past, present, and future are conceptualized as intimately and purposefully linked. Colonies in the occupied Palestinian territories (OPTs) following the 1967 war, for example, are understood as a continuation of the Zionist settler movement from the pre-1948 period.

In 2005, when I traveled across the Allenby Bridge from Jordan to the West Bank, Israeli claims to sovereignty and jurisdiction were unmistakably inscribed on the landscape. Israeli occupation authorities handled security, immigration, customs, and visas at the Jordan–West Bank border, and the ubiquitous blue and white Israeli flag, the signs in Hebrew, Israeli currency, and the presence of military personnel at all entry and exit points were hard to miss. The first question the young Israeli women who were screening travelers asked was, "What is the purpose of your visit to Israel?" Then, "Do you know any locals? And if so, who are they, what is their address and phone number, and where do they work?" Ahmad once sarcastically commented after we had passed through a checkpoint together, "They are gods and we are animals," underscoring the omnipotence of the Israeli and animality of the Palestinian. In short, since the beginning of the occupation, the territory between the Jordan River and the Mediterranean has been ruled by one sovereign state. And although Palestinians live within the Israeli state, they are not of the state. Their daily lives and mobility are governed by an occupier that by and large considers them an obstacle to expansion and a threat to its existence.

The conceptualization of Zionism as a form of settler colonialism in which land and water resources are expropriated for the exclusive use of the colonial population, and the indigenous population is slated for removal and replacement or, at least, for containment rather than incorporation as a labor force, gained traction over the last two decades and is now a standard academic formulation.[4] Locating Zionism in a family of colonial histories works to counter claims of Israel's exceptionalism and forges beyond the impasse of nationalist frames of analysis. Most significantly, the settler-colonial paradigm calls forth such terms as *the indigenous, colonies, colonists,* and *decolonization.* Now that settler colonialism is a fairly standard term of reference, it is time for a shift in English from "settlements" to "colonies" and from "settlers" to "colonists." I use the terms *settlements* and *colonies* interchangeably, as part of an ongoing shift in terminology in the academic scholarship on Palestine-Israel. *Settlement* usually implies making population inroads in one's own territory into an uninhabited frontier and the maintenance of ties with and support from the state. A *colony* includes these features but also points to a territory not under state sovereignty and to moving the home country's population into it.

In his powerfully evocative novel *Waiting for the Barbarians,* South African writer J. M. Coetzee masterfully depicts settler colonialism as a modular project, bound neither by time nor place but universally characterized by resource extraction, exploitation, cruel domination, and dehumanization.[5] Its modularity is akin to Wittgenstein's (1953, 32) "family resemblances" with an "overlapping of many fibers." Zionist settler-nationalist colonialism is more akin to the displacement of indigenous populations, by the United States, by the British in North America and Australia, and by whites in South Africa. By any stretch of the imagination, Palestine could hardly have been classified as *terra nullius,* the seventeenth- and eighteenth-century doctrine that holds that if land is not owned in ways recognizable in Western property law, and if it can be put to more profitable use, then those who do so can legitimately claim ownership (Pateman and Mills 2007). Yet Palestine was often imagined as devoid of an Arab population with rights and attachments to the land; when the Arab presence was acknowledged, it was not as its rightful owners or occupants. Zionism also bases its claims on a biblically inspired mythico-history of a Jewish linkage to the space of Palestine, which has been transposed into a modern conception of exclusivist rights and citizenship.

While spatial confinement and constrained mobility are central features of settler-colonial projects, each project is a "distinct historical formation" (Piterberg 2011, 46). For example, the settler plantation seeks the native's land and labor and thus has more "porous" social boundaries than the "pure settlement colony" with its "dichotomized" settler/native relations (ibid., 6). Land and demography have been central imperatives in the Zionist project. Like most forms of settler colonialism, it embodies an eliminationist logic. Accordingly, in 1948–49, Zionist forces cleared Palestine of its majority Arab population. Through a combination of expulsion and flight, the majority of Palestinians (700,000–800,000) were displaced and subsequently denied the right of return to what became Israel.

Twenty years later, the 1967 occupation of the West Bank and Gaza Strip brought all of Mandatory Palestine under Israeli rule, marking the second stage in the endeavor to create the land of Israel in Palestine. In 1967, forcible expulsions were not so easily undertaken without arousing international media attention and widespread opprobrium; still, from 100,000 to 250,000 Palestinians were displaced to Jordan. Occupation brought over 1.5 million Palestinians under Israeli rule. Contravening international law, Israel has constructed over one hundred settler colonies and moved over a half million of its citizens into the West Bank and East Jerusalem, with military assistance and protection and generous state subsidies. Critiques of the assumption that reason and rationality direct colonial governance make room for recognizing other tactics of colonial governance, in this case, ambiguity, disorder, and pervasive uncertainty (Stoler 2009, 57–58). The early colonial movement in the OPTs was largely improvised, somewhat chaotic, and driven by colonists with their own political rivalries (see Zertal and Eldar 2007; Weizman 2007, 91–95). A more coherent approach to colonizing the OPTs begin to crystallize with Likud's 1977 assumption of power, although the state continued to claim that the colonists were beyond their control. To Palestinians, a clarity of purpose and strategy was evident: the fragmentation of space, land expropriation, demographic dilution, immobilization, and the obstruction of Palestinian national politics. Closure and the permit system compel the question, how did ambiguity take shape as a form of rule and what did it mean for Palestinian subjectivity?

The late 1970s "Master Plan for the Development of Settlements in Judea and Samaria," drafted by the World Zionist Organization Settlement Department (Drobles 1980), set out a comprehensive reordering of Palestinian space against the backdrop of a "race against time," given that a peace treaty between Israel and Egypt was in the works. Space was to be strategically dotted with settlements that would constitute "facts-on-the-ground," and thus the issue of their dismantlement would be off the table in any negotiations with the Arab states. The Israeli settlements were to be situated between areas with concentrated Palestinian populations, so that the Palestinians "will find it hard to create unification and territorial contiguity." They were to occupy the high ground, giving them a panoptic view of the nearby Palestinian villages.

The location of the colonies is intended to forge the geospatial parameters of the state, as Israeli sovereignty extends to them and their Jewish inhabitants. Closure and separation have for the most part been driven by the realization that if Israel's rule over millions of disenfranchised Palestinians continues, Jews will cease to constitute a significant majority in the territory over which Israel exercises sovereignty. Although Israel refuses to define the state's final borders, the official Israeli maps, and those in school textbooks and for tourists, include the West Bank, with the Jordan River forming the eastern border. For example, a map accompanying an Israel Land Fund (ILF) advertisement, with the tag line "Guarantee Your Share in the land of Israel now!" depicts the Jordan River as Israel's eastern border, as does the ILF map logo.[6] Interestingly, Israeli maps incorporate the West Bank, and Israel's official population statistics include the Jewish colonists there, but not the Palestinian population (Kruger 2005, 7), reinforcing a demographic imaginary of space devoid of Palestinians. Israel's maximalist geographic vision works with its demographic uncertainty.

A strategy of willful ambiguity about borders has been a consistent feature of Zionism. Israel's Law of Return stipulates that Jews anywhere in the world have a "right of return." Although Israel excludes from the political body the majority of the Palestinians in the territory it governs, it extends its "limitless sovereignty" to people outside the state (Bowman 2007, 127). The offer of citizenship to Jews anywhere in the world extends the state boundaries based not on territory and borders but on religious/ethnic affiliation. Thus, "if Israeli sovereignty is extensible to anywhere Jews exist, then there are in effect no borders at all" (Bowman 2007, 132; see also Yiftachel 1998). A Palestinian right of return is recognized internationally, yet denied by Israel. In the Zionist project, there is room for only one return and one exile. For the most part, the Palestinians' idea of a return is a reconfigured modernist vision of state, society, and citizenship.[7]

Israel has encouraged and supported the colonial enterprise in the West Bank financially, politically, militarily, and in international diplomacy, regardless of whether the Labor or Likud parties were in power. More importantly, West Bank infrastructure (water, electricity, and telecommunications) is a state-run endeavor. This "intertwined" colonialist-state relationship has been neatly summed up by Idith Zertal and Akiva Eldar:

> The expansion of the settlements would not have been possible without massive aid from various state institutions, without legal sanction, and without the expedient and affective ties woven between the settlers and the military. The settlements flourished not only with the authorities' seal of approval but also with official encouragement and at the government's initiative (Zertal and Eldar 2007, xvii).

Colonies are central to Zionism's endeavor to settle the land and expand Israeli sovereignty. Historian Tony Judt (2009, 1) wrote presciently of their location in narratives and images of the state that circulated abroad: "Israel needs 'settlements . . . they are intrinsic to the image' and its 'neo-collectivist frontier narrative' of a state engaged in perpetual self-defense. The image is 'profoundly misleading' as the largest settlements are urban concentrations such as Maale Adumim with a population over 35,000, covering 30 square miles. In a highly urbanized Israel, 'the settler myth' has been transposed somewhere else." Jewish colonies may be the single most diagnostic feature of Israeli intent and policy. During an ostensible "settlement freeze," their numbers doubled, providing indubitable evidence of Israel's unwillingness to relinquish territory. As colonies proliferate, Palestine fragments and shrinks. The colonies Maale Adumim in Jerusalem and the quasi-urban Ariel in the central West Bank occupy large swaths of land running west to east that cut the West Bank into noncontiguous areas. Composed of planned, well-laid-out and neatly arrayed, often red-roofed symmetrical buildings surrounded by neatly manicured gardens and lawns, these gated communities are a stark contrast to the Palestinian villages, with their asymmetrical layouts and lack of architectural uniformity, in whose midst they sit. With their expansive boundaries and the bypass roads, they constitute nearly 50 percent of the West Bank (Falah 2005). A perimeter around them is held in reserve for future settlement expansion, bringing the total land in historic Palestine held by Israel close to 70 percent (Dolphin 2006, 7). Palestinians occupy just 12 percent.

Colonial regimes have conceptualized, governed, and interacted with native populations in a variety of ways that are closely related to how the populations fit into the overall scheme of resource extraction and territorial control, which in turn is intimately bound up with the labor requirements of the colonial economy, resources to be extracted and the labor necessary to do so, and the demographic ratio of colonialists to the indigenous. Zionist colonialism is distinct in several respects. Temporally, the sheer rapidity with which the majority of the indigenous population was removed from heavily populated areas in 1948–49 distinguishes it from Australian and early American colonialisms. In another departure, Zionism did not demand that Palestinians subscribe to Zionism or enter into its cultural orbit; there has been no civilizing mission, nor did the Zionists initially envision profiting by putting the natives to work. Instead, Zionism engaged in the territorial conquest and showed little concern for winning hearts and minds. The logic of displacement, population replacement, and resource acquisition prevailed over that of exploitation. With the 1967 occupation, Israel added over a million disenfranchised Palestinians to the territory it controlled. The cheap, captive Palestinian labor force was soon utilized. But because they were considered interlopers, and ethnically/religiously unsuited for full and equal citizenship in a Jewish state, there was little imperative to invest in shaping their subjectivity as potential citizens. Using brute force and draconian administrative and bureaucratic measures, however, the occupation regime did attempt to fashion a *new* Palestinian subjectivity, basically that of a quiescent population unable to slow down or reverse the expropriation of its resources. Moreover, there was an imperative to subject Palestinian bodies and mentalities to a new organization of space. Israeli colonialism differs in another respect from that in the Americas, Australia, and South Africa: settlers in those communities eventually clamored for political autonomy and independence.

Ahmad's third phase of colonialism is difficult to name or label because there has not been a discrete or identifiable moment in time like the watershed years of 1948 or 1967, although "post-Oslo"[8] and the "second intifada" are possible contenders. In the post-Oslo years, Israel undertook a slow-motion project to thin the native population. Voluntary migrants are easier to contend with than refugees with international legal claims. Exploring Ahmad's third, or late-stage, settler colonization of Palestine, throws Zionism's central paradox into relief: Israel claiming nativeness in an already inhabited territory made it necessary to erase the indigenous population narratively and physically, and the Palestinians who remained had to be controlled to ensure their exclusion from the state and to mitigate the potential security risk they represented. Paradoxically, Palestinians in Israel are immobilized through a bureaucratic system of classification and confinement and the physical mechanisms of incarceration and immiseration that, it is anticipated, make choosing to leave Palestine a practical response. In essence, Palestinians inhabit a prison from which they are encouraged to escape.

The field of difference between Arab and Jew is an artifact of power, and the Zionist construction of difference is, as in most colonial projects, cultural and racial (see Shamir 2005; Shohat 1999; Willem 2010) and encompasses internal Jewish difference (Lavie 2014) as well. In the time of closure, bio-social profiling, integral to the Israeli security apparatus, assesses threat and risk and collapses the social into the biological (Abowd 2014; Fassin 2001; Willem 2010). Difference is inscribed on the body, in particular, through discerning behavior. Rather than try to define phenotypes, the governing apparatus concentrates on cultural differences, which, in elaborating difference, can be as pernicious as race, leading to what Erik Erikson referred to "as 'pseudo-speciation' . . . the human tendency to classify some individuals or social groups as less than fully human" (quoted in Scheper-Hughes 2004, 370).

Even as it excludes Palestinians from the state and segregates Jews and Palestinians, Israel penetrates Palestinian society and sharply contours its daily life. In this setting, closure and separation are a means of inclusion through exclusion— Palestinians are excluded from the state but subject to a primordial hierarchical allocation of rights and mobilities. The logic in the seeming paradox comes into focus if we understand this as a settler-colonial setting, *replacing* one population with another, and discerning temporality in the slow-motion ethnic cleansing. In this demographic orbit, mobility is calibrated to manage, control, punish, and reward.

Legal distinctions have generated and solidified ethnic-national categories in Israel-Palestine. For example, Israel extended its laws to Israeli citizens settled in the OPTs, but governed Palestinians through a series of over two thousand military orders and military courts. The absence of a moral imperative militated against extending the colonizer's law to the occupied, as did the desire to avoid acquiring millions of new Arab citizens. The legal arena operates not to assert Israeli civilian law over the colonized or to convince Palestinians that Israel's law is impartial and just, but to rule them, acquire their resources, and squelch resistance. With little ambiguity, this occupied/occupier distinction, embodied in law, further consolidated distinct political identities. Political identities take shape around state formation and its categories of distinction and belonging (Mamdani 2001, 22). These distinctions form the basis for structuring mobility and access to space.

In the aftermath of the Oslo agreements, Israel launched a concerted project of unilateral separation (*hafrada*) and creeping closure. To safeguard the Jewishness of the state, concretized distinctions, between insider and outsider and citizen and noncitizen, became imperative. Initially a project of the Labor movement, the rightist Likud Party quickly perceived the territorial benefits of separation. In closure, *hafrada* was given spatial expression resting on a tripartite system of checkpoints and bypass roads, the wall, and the permit system, which confines, immiserates, and immobilizes the native population.

Launched in March 1993, the policy of *closure* refers to Israeli restrictions on the movement of Palestinian goods, labor, and people into Jerusalem, in and between the Gaza Strip and the West Bank, and between them and Israel. For Palestinians, closure and separation have resulted in fragmentation, economic devastation, social fracturing, and a deep sense of isolation and abandonment. A crude strategy, closure combines both high and low technologies; the former ensure surveillance, while the latter, for example, the checkpoint, are public, tangible, and tactile, declaring domination and demanding submission. To be effective, the colonized must know that they are being watched, monitored, and separated; low-tech devices such as the wall are highly visual and visceral.

Closure separates Israelis and Palestinians, denying a mutuality of both time and space. It crafts spatiotemporal zones, where predictability, vital for the smooth functioning of daily social life, is a scarce resource. Palestinians understand these policies as an attempt to continue diluting their presence in historic Palestine. Former Israeli prime minster Ariel Sharon's declaration that the first decade of the twenty-first century is the second half of 1948 hardly fell on deaf ears. Indeed, Palestinian experiences articulated with Sharon's vision. "We are like a bird in a nest, and they are destroying the tree!" is how a Palestinian farmer in the village of Zawiya described life in his enclaved village in 2009. Closure *removes the land* from the Palestinians. For example, the agricultural lands of the towns of Beit Sahur and Beit Jala, just outside Jerusalem, were expropriated, but not the towns themselves and their inhabitants. With Israeli settlement and the extension of sovereignty, the land can then be repopulated and re-landscaped as exclusively Jewish space. Palestinian resistance, international opprobrium, and Jordan's determination not to accept more refugees make the sweeping transfer of the indigenous population, as occurred in 1948, less feasible. Thus, the state may anticipate that this temporarily drawn-out, multipronged spatial strategy may lead to increasing numbers of Palestinians moving to enclaved urban areas, such as Ramallah or Bethlehem, as well as seeking to emigrate. Urban areas in the West Bank have increased dramatically (over 100 percent). Given the weak pull factors (jobs) in West Bank cities, such as Ramallah or Nablus, "push factors" (isolation, lack of jobs) from rural enclavization are driving urbanization. Ultimately, the goal may be to create voluntary migrants engaged in "self-deportation," rather than refugees with an international legal status and presence.

Closure was cemented by the Oslo Accords's spatiotemporal contours and aggressively advanced in the wake of the 2000 al-Aqsa intifada and growing concerns over Arab-Jewish demographics. Counterinsurgency practices, in which population control is the center of gravity, were ramped up, severely restricting Palestinian mobility. I weave together counterinsurgency practices that revolve around mass incarceration, decelerated mobility and motility, spatial constriction, and new surveillance technologies to render Palestinians visible, legible, and containable. Mechanisms of control, such as the wall and checkpoints, work in tandem with colonists' and soldiers' violence and cultivated indifference to subjugate the occupied population.

Palestinians bitterly compare closure to living in an open-air prison. In an age of mass incarceration and expulsions (Sassen 2014), surveillance technologies and forms of policing and confinement constantly mutate to visualize, immobilize, and contain surplus people displaced by both late capitalism and modern settler colonialism. These processes are not unique to Palestine/Israel but have parallels in contemporary formations of inequality across the globe (see Alexander 2010; Sassen 2014). Perceived as a security threat, Palestinians have faced mass incarceration and "rightlessness." In the first decade of the twenty-first century, the number of young males incarcerated was about 69,000. In over four decades of occupation, around 650,000 Palestinians have been arrested (Rosenfeld 2011, 3–4). By 2014, the number of incarcerated had risen to 800,000, including 8,000 children arrested since 2000. Given the small size of the Palestinian population in the OPTs (1 million in 1967 and about 4.5 million in 2012), this is an exceptionally high rate of arrest, detention, and incarceration. Carceral politics in Palestine have relied heavily on technologies that compel visuality and a built environment that constrains mobility and spatially isolates and confines. Thus, the prison is now accompanied by the wall, checkpoints, and the permit system that imprison Palestinians. The term "open-air prison" cleverly captures the way closure mimics the space of the prison.

The scaffolding and logic of Israel's policy of closure—aptly dubbed a "matrix of control" (Halper 1999)—comprises overlapping layers, from the spatial to the legal and bureaucratic. In the matrix, victory comes not by defeating or decimating enemies but by immobilizing them. The first layer is spatial, the on-the-ground control of space and key nodes through the location of Jewish colonies and their bypass roads, military bases, checkpoints, closed military areas, and above-ground air power. The second layer, bureaucratic and legal, refers to the permit and planning systems with their tangled web of restrictions, which severely constrain Palestinian mobility and limit construction in their areas. Both layers are accompanied by vivid displays and the ever-present threat of violence. For example, colonist attacks on Palestinians and their property reached an all-time high between 2006 and 2011, increasing by 315 percent (Munayyer 2012, 2). Again, the supposition is that these unbearable conditions will compel voluntary migration, clearing the land gradually. The Israeli government's talk of dismantling colonies has triggered the vandalism of Palestinian property and religious sites, the signature "price tag" being scrawled on torched mosques, churches, and cars. While these actions have fostered a hypervigilant, angry, and anxious population, Palestinians continue to adapt, and to cobble together the means to live from day to day in a state of precariousness.

Cartographies: Regional and Local

The regional geopolitical context for this book was marked by a new regional-colonial cartography and relations, epitomized by the US war on Iraq, and locally by the post-Oslo period and the second intifada; my research ended in 2012 in the midst of the Arab Spring. The local context was closure, separation, and intensified colony building, a compliant and corrupt Palestinian Authority (PA) heavily dependent on donor aid, and the eruption of a second intifada. The dual lenses of space and regional reordering bring into relief the continuities and connections among events in the region and work to locate Palestine in a broader regional context.

In the first decades of the new millennium, Iraq, Syria, Afghanistan, Palestine, and Lebanon were engulfed in conflict. In the midst of the 2006 Israeli assault on Lebanon, then US secretary of state Condoleeza Rice stated baldly, "These are the birth pangs of the new Middle East." Situating Palestine in a regional and broader perspective of the War on Terror (WoT) provides a lens through which to view the extraordinary whirlwind of violence that accompanies separation and closure and the geographic imaginary propelling it. In Palestine, the vision of the "new Middle East" entailed spatio-political remapping and a corresponding reterritorializing of populations.

Fragmentation and demographic upheavals have figured prominently in the region's new colonial cartography (Khalidi 2004). The twentieth century opened with the crumbling of the cosmopolitan world of the Ottoman Empire, in which Muslims, Christians, and Jews comingled in many aspects of social life (Campos 2011), and gave way to the 1916 British and French Mandates, and, eventually, to the formation of nation-states of varying forms of political inclusion and citizenship. In the early to mid-twentieth century, the Zionist presence in Palestine intensified as independent states were forming in the region, and both secular Arab nationalism and local nationalisms were prominent forms of political consciousness and organizing. Indeed, Israel has consistently rejected the notion of a secular, democratic state of its citizens, a central component of the initial Palestine Liberation Organization (PLO) charter. By the mid-2000s, it was not uncommon to hear the War on Terror (WoT) referred to as an attempt to fragment and reorder national spaces, borders, and structures of governance and reinvigorate ethnic and sectarian affiliations and identities. These crises of the first decade of the new millennium evoked 1916, when the region was carved into mandates. Sadly, the twenty-first century ushered in the attempted dismembering of Iraq, assaults on Lebanon, the disintegration of Syria, and the final push to acquire maximum Palestinian territory and consolidate Israeli sovereignty.

In Iraq, US actions laid the groundwork for a sectarianism in which each ostensibly bounded group occupies its own geospatial niche, and political power and representation are apportioned by sect. Spatial fracturing and imposed divisions that separate and transform landscape and place-population relations are crucial to implementing and reproducing a hierarchy of access to natural resources, sovereignty, and human rights. In the West Bank, Iraq, and Syria the inscription of a new cartography has dramatically respatialized ethnicity and sect, and thus national landscapes. Regionally, access to space is increasingly distributed along ethnic and religious lines.

On a regional level, spatial practices in the West Bank bear a resemblance to those of Lebanon's civil war (1975–91) and then to Iraq and Syria. Brutal campaigns of sectarian violence drew deadly boundaries across Beirut and Baghdad and checkpoints controlled movement. During Lebanon's civil war, and in post-invasion Iraq, the identity card could be a pass to mobility or a death sentence at checkpoints; in Palestine it determines the scope and speed of mobility. In Iraq, concrete blast walls demarcated sectarian enclaves, along with violent ethnic-sectarian cleansings, transforming erstwhile "mixed neighborhoods" into more homogenous enclaves (al-Mufti 2006).

In the Arab world, memories and narratives of past external interventions frame interpretations and understandings of contemporary events. For example, the US occupation of Iraq resonated with Iraqis' collective memory of the thirteenth-century Mongol invasion, as well as of the 1917 British occupation. The 2006 Israeli invasion of Lebanon evoked those of 1978 and 1982. Palestinian narratives locate the beginnings of their displacement and occupation in the British Mandate's promise to create a homeland for Jews in Palestine. Algerians were under French control for a century. These occupations and those of the contemporary era are not unconnected events; indeed, for many in the region, they are conceptualized as part of a long history of unequal relations with the West (see Khalidi 2004). Evoking an Arab-Islamic collective memory, a middle-aged Palestinian Jerusalemite shopkeeper, whose family has lived in the city for over a thousand years, said about the stepped-up property confiscation that was paving the way for new Jewish colonists: "This city has been occupied many times. The Crusaders were here for a hundred years, and Jerusalem was eventually liberated. We lived as a pluralistic and tolerant city for hundreds of years under Muslim rule." Memory, whether historically accurate or nostalgic, nuances the cultural parameters of current militant opposition.

Memory also plays a role in constructing moral and communal boundaries. When the Crusaders conquered Jerusalem in 1099 after a forty-day siege, there ensued a massacre of thirty thousand of the city's Arab Christians, Jews, and Muslims (Maalouf 1984). When Saladin liberated the city in 1187, Christians and Jews practiced their religions, and synagogues were rebuilt. Under nearly eight hundred years of Sunni Muslim rule, Jerusalem enjoyed unparalleled religious pluralism and tolerance. Israel's 1967 occupation launched a sustained policy of demographic and cultural Judaization. To de-Arabize the city, Palestinian property has been confiscated, and legal obstacles to residency enacted, while Jewish colonists settle the Old City and East Jerusalem (Abowd 2014). The Palestinian economic sector has faced severe restrictions, and since the early 1990s, West Bank and Gazan Palestinians' access to the city has been severely restricted.

The first two decades of occupation were punctuated by the first intifada (1987–93), a popular, mass uprising and campaign of civil disobedience protesting the land confiscations, settlement construction, house demolitions, curfews, and arbitrary arrests and detention, as well as torture and a lack of civil and political rights. As the intifada slowly wound down in the early 1990s, it was followed by the Oslo negotiations resulting in the 1993 Israel-PLO Declaration of Principles. The newly established PA, a proto-state formation, was tasked with limited powers of self-government in areas from which Israeli forces were to withdraw. Palestinian critiques of the Oslo agreement argued that it legitimized continued occupation and outsourced Israeli security to the PA in a shift to indirect rule. The core issues of refugees, the right of return, water, borders, and Jerusalem were postponed until the final status talks. In summer 2010, an elderly faculty member at al-Najah University described the results of Oslo:

> We were recruited to be Israel's security force. The international community gives us funds as long as we protect Israel by smashing local resistance. Negotiations are a waste of time! They are adamant that we will have no rights. The EU and the US finance us as long as we agree to their conditions. So much money goes to secure Israel! Our prisons are full of Palestinians who have resisted Israel. The US and Israel want peace—but an imposed peace—on their terms. Donor money from the West is to get us to concede our rights.

On the ground, the realization set in that Oslo had garnered Palestinian acquiescence to colonization and was ultimately an agreement to buy time so that Jewish Israelis could further populate the West Bank. As part of indirect rule, the PA would work to contain Palestinian militancy and insure Israel's security, relieving some Israeli military personnel from the brutalizing violence of occupation.

"I am not against peace. Peace is against me. It's going to destroy me. Erase my culture," raps the Palestinian group DAM in the song "Who Is the Terrorist?"

A close look at the peace process illuminates the relationship between time and colonial territorial expansion. For example, US proposals to initiate Israeli-Palestinian peace talks are often followed by an announcement of the building of new colonies or the expansion of housing units in the West Bank or East Jerusalem. In effect, the peace industry stretches time and opens temporal space for colonial expansion while paying lip service to the "peace process." For peace, in this case, always begins with contemporary time and space rather than address historical grievances and injustices, or root causes. It is itself a perpetual beginning. "Peace" is a shell game or busy work that buys time. There is an info-gram by a Palestinian NGO titled "20 Years of Talks: Keeping Palestinians Occupied."[9] The double entendre captures the irony and duplicity of a process in which Palestinians are "occupied" by the fig leaf of peace talks and handshakes, while occupation and colonial expansion proceed apace.

In this post-Oslo political orbit, the buzzword "conflict management" and separation, not peace, highlighted a shift in the nature and operation of power from discipline to control, or predatory and "repressive" peace (Sivaramakrishnan 2005, 321).[10] Rather than the seeking of long-term political solutions, steady, low-level conflict became sustainable. Indeed, peace was no longer a prerequisite to economic development and growth. Israel realized it could enjoy remarkable economic growth and continue the occupation. Instability, once deemed detrimental to investment, was not necessarily negative for the market. Israel is a prime example of the Davos dilemma: "an economy that expands markedly in direct response to escalating violence" (Klein 2007, 428). Occasional eruptions of violence could coexist with administrative and disciplinary mechanisms of regulation and pacification. Intermittent flare-ups, such as the assaults on Gaza in 2008–9, 2012, and 2014, were referred to as "mowing the lawn" or "cutting the grass," metaphors that capture the maintenance involved in protracted conflict.

Oslo was premised on the neoliberal assumption that markets, deregulation, free trade, and foreign investment would generate prosperity as well as some measure of quiescence. The Oslo Accords can be situated in Israel's neoliberal restructuring of its economy and desire to enter the world market as the "Middle East's free-trade hub" (Klein 2007, 429). Concomitantly, Israel's interest in Arab markets waned as it traded the possibility of peace for a high-tech, security-oriented economy in a global marketplace. In the wake of 9/11, the arms and high-tech security industries mushroomed. Israel's arms industry positioned itself as a "shopping mall for homeland security technologies" (ibid., 435) boasting an expertise based on years of dealing with local "terrorists" and a living laboratory in the OPT. Israeli filmmaker Yotam Feldman's 2013 documentary *The Lab* is a stark look at the arms industry, in which Palestinians provide a stage set for experimentation in military technology innovations. In a seminal article on Palestine as a critical node in imperial and counterinsurgency campaigns, Khalili

(2010) sets out the "*horizontial* circuits" by which security techniques, personnel, legal frameworks, population control, training, and doctrine move from locale to locale across space rather than in a unidirectional, top-down fashion. In this equation, Palestine is a "critical node" in a horizontal chain of transmission. Consequently, by the late 1990s, security had become more lucrative than peace. Marketing Israel as an experienced player in the global WoT was highly profitable. Thus separation and closure coincided with the rise of Israel's high-tech security industry and a booming economy.[11]

Other salient factors in this intersection of global, regional, and local forces were the colonies and Palestinian labor. In violation of the Oslo agreements, by the early 2000s, the number of colonists in the OPT had increased, from 140,000 in 1996 to 200,000 by 2001. By 2012, the number of settlers (incuding those settled in Jerusalem) had doubled, to over 500,000. Palestinians' realization that this was a sign of Israel's unwillingness to withdraw was pivotal in igniting the second intifada. The number of Palestinian laborers who, post-1967, had worked in Israel in low-paying manual jobs gradually went from an estimated 115,000, or one-third of the Palestinian labor force in the OPTs in the early 1990s to less than 50,000 (less than one-tenth of the Palestinian labor force) by 2004 (Kruger 2005). By the mid-1990s, Israel had turned to foreign migrant labor to reduce its reliance on Palestinian labor, bringing in between 200,000 and 300,000 temporary replacement workers from South Asia, mainly the Philippines, Thailand, China, India, and Sri Lanka; Africa; and East Europe (Kruger 2005, 10–11), who had little investment in local politics (Willem 2010, 269).

Now excluded from the economic benefits of Oslo, except for a sector of the Ramallah-based PA and employees of foreign-financed NGOs, and with the Israeli market for their labor shrinking, thousands of Palestinians found themselves unemployed and quarantined by closure. The word *quarantine* is semantically freighted. It refers to bodily pathologies that require separation and isolation. Israelis do use the biologically inflected word *sterile* to connote areas cleansed of Palestinians. Once the mutual, though lopsided, economic dependency collapsed—Israel on Palestinians for cheap flexible labor and Palestinians on Israel for jobs—Palestinians joined the growing global ranks of surplus, disposable populations.

By 2000, Palestinian frustration had exploded into the second intifada. Lightly armed Palestinian forces and civilian stone throwers were pitted against the Israeli military. Palestinian suicide attacks against Israelis proceeded apace, as did Israeli assassinations of suspected Palestinian militants. Israeli forces escalated their assault on the West Bank in 2002, targeting the Palestinian infrastructure of telecommunications, educational facilities, PA ministries, police stations, and a multitude of nongovernmental organizations (NGOs) for destruction, portending the Dahiya doctrine later deployed in Gaza and Lebanon.[12] Closure tightened as checkpoints proliferated and roads to and from the villages were blocked, further fragmenting the road system.

With the OPTs neither officially annexed nor the population uprooted en masse, as had happened in 1948, it became an unwanted, surplus population. What happens to a population that no longer produces a profit as cheap labor, whose land and water are coveted, and that engages in persistent opposition? Extending official, formal sovereignty to the OPTs would render Israel, in effect, a state where the half the population is non-Jewish and unenfranchised. Over fifty years of occupation, the Israeli state has faced several choices. First, it could have formally annexed the OPTs and extended Israeli citizenship to the Palestinian population thus making Israel a state of its citizens. Or, it could have annexed and extended sovereignty without granting citizenship to the Palestinians, thus formally resembling an apartheid state and society. Alternatively, it could have withdrawn from the OPTs in a negotiated settlement and remained a Jewish state. Or, finally, it could have annexed the OPTs, extended sovereignty, and diluted the native population, as it had done in 1948. However, this option was not as doable as it had been in 1948. Palestinians had learned from experience what happens when fleeing armed conflict. In addition, International Law is in effect, to some extent, and the modern media do check, however minimally, such massive population movements and violations of human rights; and neighboring host states' capacity and willingness to absorb more refugees is questionable.

Closure: Distinction, Order, and Chaos

I met Munira, a twenty-seven-year-old nurse working in a local medical clinic, and the mother of two young children, a few days after a particularly distressing experience at the checkpoint she crossed each day to get to work. Over coffee in her office, she explained her understanding of closure:

> I think they have what I call a "misery committee." I envision a group of Is-
> raelis sitting around and devising well-organized forms of misery to inflict on
> us. We are either killed or we rise above the misery. The situation is so bad, I
> don't know how we don't all go crazy. For example, I have to pass through the
> Bethlehem checkpoint every day to go to work. Last week they wanted to strip-
> search me and I refused. Do you know, they made me wait at that checkpoint
> for twelve hours without food or drink or anyone knowing where I was. They
> were waiting for me to submit to a strip search. They finally let me go after
> twelve hours. The genius of the misery committee is to operate through the
> smallest details that then obscure the larger picture. It is amazing the way they
> think up ways to humiliate us and make our daily lives miserable.

What Munira refers to as a "misery committee" is a fairly cohesive set of Israeli civilian and military units that wield power over the Palestinians: the IDF, border police, the General Security Services (Shin Bet), the Civilian Administration, and over a half million Jewish colonists. Closure is a pronounced spatial expression of bio-power, targeting the fabric and rhythms of daily life. Munira's "smallest details" impose unpredictable delays and irreparable harm and humiliation. The daily obstacle course of going to and from work was taking a toll on family life. She was exhausted from what had become a laborious and unpredictable commute. The consequences of closure reverberated among her children, husband, extended family, and neighbors, who were on call in case of delays.

In Palestine, the mobility, order, and security of one population is maintained through the imposition on another population of a punishing immobility and confinement, on one hand, and disorder and chaos, on the other. The policy of closure reverses noted political scientist James Scott's (1998) notion of states' planned, geometric formulations of space in order to control and rule by making the natives simultaneously (selectively) visible and invisible, cultivating relative mobilities and speed, and rendering the now-fragmented landscape illegible. The order/disorder formula generated by closure recalls the creative destruction of "disaster capitalism" (Klein 2007) and Condoleeza Rice's "birth pangs."

Closure visually and experientially spatializes the distinction between Palestinians and Jewish Israelis and generates a type of order, territorial contiguity, and land for new Jewish colonies. Closure's main mechanism, the eight-meter-high concrete wall snaking deep into Palestinian territory, draws a unilateral border that includes large blocks of colonies on the Israeli side, prevents a territorially contiguous Palestinian state, and separates Palestinian villages from their agricultural lands and from each other. In other words, closure fragments and miniaturizes Palestine and facilitates stringent control over access to the space of Palestine by Palestinians.

Although closure routinizes confinement and subdues resistance, it is equally about rule through the imposition of calibrated chaos. This book argues that choreographed conditions of seemingly incommensurable chaos and unpredictability operate hand in hand to create an atmosphere of anxious anticipation. Disorder ensures a measure of order inside the state and points to the mutual constitutiveness of spaces of disorder and order. An "essential paradox" of colonial rule is the conflation of the rational and the absurd. For example, the simultaneous order and pandemonium that greets those crossing the Allenby Bridge underscores that paradox in "its capacity to be ordered yet incoherent, rational yet absurd . . . to elicit compliance and contestation, discipline and defiance, subjection and insurrection sometimes all at once" (Comaroff 1998, 340, quoted in Feldman 2008, 11). Munira, like many Palestinians, wakes up every day to a maze of obstacles as she tries to make her way to work, school, the doctor, or simply to visit family. It is hard to predict from one day to the next whether one will encounter the same set of obstacles, or whether they have been rearranged to present a new set of challenges. Yet within the chaos, a swirl of patterns that structure daily life and hint at things to come is discernible. "Order is what is not chaos; chaos is what is not orderly. Order and chaos are *modern* twins" (Bauman 1991, 4) in which the objectification of order is a hallmark of modernity, its absence signifying the premodern threat lurking at the edges. National Religious Party leader and retired IDF Brigadier General Effi Eitam succinctly voiced Israel's self-conceptualization as an ordered, healthy space—in which Palestinians are a "cancerous tumor destroying the ordered host" (quoted in Graham 2002, 647). This biomedical metaphor implies wild, unrestrained, and destructive growth, a tumor that threatens the whole, and suggests the need for aggressive surgical or nonsurgical measures to excise it or shrink its size.

Palestinians do discern a logic and meaning in the capriciousness of movement. As Ahmad bluntly put it, "Closure is punishment—and a means to make us so fed up we see leaving as the only way to have a normal life." At checkpoints, for example, the regulations governing passage can change every day, on the same day, or at periodic intervals, so that just when one gets used to a certain pattern of movement, it changes. Standing in a checkpoint line several hundred deep for hours in the blistering heat in summer 2009, with no movement and the soldiers' refusal to provide an explanation or a time when the checkpoint would open, the chaos was palpable. Palestinians milled about, or sat on the ground exchanging complaints and grumbling about tasks unaccomplished and visits not made. Unpredictability, humiliation, and the omnipresent anticipation of violence are the only sure things. As I saw it, calibrated chaos was crafting spaces of disorder that were themselves a form of rule.

Anthropologist Lori Allen (2008, 475) writes that Israeli occupation and colonialism "are congeries of forms of discipline, domination, and brute force"; they cannot be characterized in a Foucauldian fashion in which power is imprinted on and thus fashions a disciplined body and is replicated throughout the social order. She argues that "the social and spatial instabilities that result from physical violence make any particularly precise organization of the body through space impossible, which is the anti-discipline of the occupation" (ibid.). I would amend this slightly by noting that discipline is operative but that it derives from calibrated chaos. Discipline and anti-discipline are partnered to simultaneously produce visibility and invisibility, chaos and order, predictability and unpredictability, a Palestinian body that must switch gears constantly, undercutting planning and sociality—a body perpetually on edge.

Anthropological analyses of power confront attributions of intent and discern "inner states" (Rosen 1995, 3). Discerning intent can be vexing because successive Israeli governments have not legislated segregation as was done in Apartheid South Africa or Jim Crow America, where there was discernable congruence between discourse, law, and intent. In part, intent can be read in effects, but that would assume congruence between intent and effect, and reality does not always unfold so neatly. Statements by political leaders and policies and their enactment, in particular the colonies and closure, may provide some indication of Israel's intent; openly advocating "Judaization," for example, leaves little doubt. Not surprisingly, Palestinians read Israel's intent in its actions on the ground and the effects of those on their daily lives and future. For example, the Israeli practice of home demolition has been analyzed as part of the strategy of "quiet transfer" (Schaeffer and Halper 2012, 1). Checkpoints are understood to immobilize and strangle daily life and the infrastructure foundational to civil society and political life, economic activity, education, and health, as well as social networks. Along with land expropriation, and a past history of mass displacement and denial of return, they read Israel's current actions as continuing colonization.

One can map an interlocking domain of power and practices that produces a temporal order of speed, on one side, and delay, waiting, uncertainty, and an emptying landscape, on the other. Israeli minister of labor Shlomo Ben Azri announced that the use of force against Palestinians was intended to "convert the life of Palestinians into hell" until they leave (quoted in Allen 2008, 474) or, I would contend, remain but in a state of concentration and confinement. Samir, a university student I met during a long wait at the large Qalandia checkpoint, and with whom I later shared a taxi, explained:

> Israel doesn't really care if we leave or not. They want those of us who are here to be enclosed and fend for ourselves. Jordan has tightened up the bridge. To cross, one has to have a certification that a family member on the other side will receive you and they have to show up at the bridge with these documents. There is an agreement between Jordan and Israel to keep Palestinians inside.

If Palestinians leave "voluntarily," where are they supposed to go? Jordan has already received hundreds of thousands of Palestinians, in 1948 and 1967; several hundred thousand people fleeing or expelled from Kuwait during the first Gulf war; and more recently, hundreds of thousands of Iraqis and Syrians. It has now put in place administrative mechanisms to obstruct entry from the West Bank, signaling its unwillingness to be the designated holding pen for more displaced persons, or as one East Bank Jordanian woman told me, "We don't want to be the dumping ground for the region anymore." This statement was uttered, not against any particular group, but to underscore the extent to which Jordan has become a regional refugee-receiving state and that the expectations it can continue to serve as such are unrealistic.

Ultimately, closure and separation address a fundamental paradox. Since 1967, Israeli sovereignty has extended to the Jordan River, placing millions of Palestinians within the territory of the state. Israel posits itself as a "modern democratic state," a term often associated with a more inclusive conception of citizenship. Yet Palestinians reside in a territory over which an occupying state exercises de facto sovereignty, but as noncitizens without the benefits and protections of citizenship. Oslo, which sealed the deal for closure and separation, divided the West Bank into Areas A, B, C (see map I.1) and later H1 and H2. Areas A and B are under nominal Palestinian control, whereas Area C is under complete Israeli control. In Area A, about 17 percent of the West Bank, comprising urban concentrations such as Ramallah, Jenin, Salfit, Nablus, Tubas, Al-Bireh, Jericho, Bethlehem, and Qalqiliya, the PA has legal and security privileges. Israel forbids its citizens to enter these areas (see figure I.1). In Area B, comprising mainly Palestinian towns and villages, Israel maintains the right to conduct military incursions in the name of security. In Area C, about 60 percent of the West Bank, Israel maintains full control of land management, security, and civilian affairs (see Weizman 2007). Palestinians are forbidden entry without a permit. In 1997, Israel divided the town of Hebron into H1, which is under the PA, and H2, under Israeli military control. Through the division of the West Bank into discontiguous enclaves and by devolving a certain level of internal autonomy to the PA, Israel can avoid Palestinian claims for integration into the state. The enclaves form a "mock sovereign" (Falah 2005, 1343). In other words, there are multiple sovereignties in the territory occupied by Israel.

Thus Oslo marked a shift from direct rule to indirect rule to a repressive peace of closure and separation. In this reconfigured occupation, Palestinian land and water sources remain under Israeli control as it continues surveillance and control over Palestinians' mobility yet bears no responsibility for them. The PA assumed the responsibility of providing basic health care, education, and municipal services, and of policing the population and squashing resistance (Gordon 2008) in the areas under its nominal control. The Israeli military was given the power to enter these areas (A and B) for security purposes. Closure and separation were the beginning of a "politics of death," a term Gordon uses to frame the increasing Palestinian death toll. With closure and separation couched in a pervasive discourse of security, Palestinian areas became arenas of perceived threat and thus, increasingly, targets of enhanced state and colonist surveillance and violence.

The Mantra of Security

Terrorist is often a generic term for Palestinians, whose violence is always anticipated, its potential read in their bodies, movements, and gestures. Israeli securitization does not necessarily cohere with an actual threat but, rather, has slid into "security theology" (Berda 2011, 45) in which the Palestinian poses an existential threat to the state. Hypercriminalized, the Palestinian requires constant surveillance and control. In this topsy-turvy world, language and reality often

Israeli-Occupied West Bank
June 2010

Legend

Separation Wall
— Existing
---- Planned

Oslo Agreement
☐ AREA (A)
☐ AREA (B)
☐ AREA (C)
☐ Israeli Declared East Jerusalem
☐ No Man's Land

Jenin
Tulkarm
Tubas
Qalqiliya
Nablus
Salfit
Jericho
Ramallah
East Jerusalem
Bethlehem
Hebron

Lebanon
Syria
Mediterranean Sea
West Bank
Gaza Strip
Israel
Jordan
Egypt

Data: ESRI. OpenStreetMap.
Humanitarian Data Exchange.
United Nations OCHA.
Cartography:
Donald J. Biddle
University of Louisville
Center for GIS

Kilometers
0   10   20   30   40

N

Map I.1 Map of Israeli-Occupied West Bank, the Oslo Agreement, and the Separation Wall. Source: DJ Biddle, University of Louisville, Center for GIS.

דרך זו מובילה לשטח A
בשליטה הרשות הפלסטינאית
הכניסה לישראלים אסורה,
מסכנת את חייכם
ומהווה עבירה פלילית

(1) هذه الطريق تؤدي الى منطقة
التابعة للسلطة الفلسطينية
الدخول للمواطنين الاسرائليين
ممنوعة وخطرة على حياتهم
وتشكل مخالفة جنائية في حقهم

This Road leads To Area "A"
Under The Palestinian Authority
The Entrance For Israeli
Citizens Is Forbidden,
Dangerous To Your Lives
And Is Against The Israeli Law

Figure I.1 Sign forbidding Israeli entrance into Area A. Photograph by the author.

collide: victims are aggressors, aggressors are victims; the natives are foreigners, and foreigners are natives. In some respects, the threat narrative and securitization are discursive practices in which the other is filtered through the lens of risk and national security. A host of practices masquerade as security measures. For example, invoking security has advanced the expropriation of Palestinian land. Land is declared a "closed military area" for security purposes, and cleared of Palestinians, whose rights to the land are nullified; soon thereafter, colonists arrive. In this atmosphere, the Palestinian violence generated in response to these practices is called terrorism, requiring a military response.

Ethnographic observation at checkpoints, framed as a necessary precaution in the face of Palestinian violence, and statements of the Israeli government are revealing. Once, moving slowly through the line at the crowded Qalandia checkpoint, I spotted a teenage boy pushing a rickety wooden cart laden with cigarettes and small notions. He parked his cart off to the side of the line, slipped a pack of Marlboros into his right hand, positioned his arm against his thigh, and walked through the checkpoint. He chose a moment when the soldiers were goofing around and flirting with each other. His eyes darted around quickly to make sure no one was watching. He didn't have to use the pack of cigarettes as a bribe—he was not stopped. A few days later, a stout elderly woman, clad in a heavily embroidered Palestinian dress, deftly balanced a large box of fruit on her head. Looking around quickly to make sure no one was checking that lane, she adopted an air of nonchalance and walked through at a steady but not fast pace. Another time, a young soldier ordered people to pass through the two creaky metal detectors and to place their belongings on an adjacent table. She then cursorily rummaged through each bag and waved a hand-held detector to check for explosives residue. In the line I was in, an elderly man cut to the head of the line, despite the grumbling of others. Pleading age, he walked up to the table and strained to heave his two bulging bags of fruit and vegetables onto the table for inspection. When he entered the metal detector, the alarm went off. He backed up and passed through again; it sounded again. Sheepishly, he pointed to his belt buckle. She waved him through. These incidents confirmed what I had heard about laxness and bribery at the checkpoints, for as little as a pack of cigarettes. A 2002 Israeli State Comptroller's report confirmed that bomb-carrying Palestinians had crossed checkpoints, "where they underwent [a] faulty and even shoddy check (quoted in Lagerquist 2004, 19). Like all borders, the checkpoint is a site for exchange, however unequal, and articulations of relations of dependence. So much for security, I wrote in my notes.

These ritualized performances of security, inscribed in everyday encounters and framed as prophylactic and punitive measures, do become routine and mundane.[13] They feed into that anticipatory sense of danger and violence from a population deemed suspect and threatening in the aggregate. Yet "security" does something else as well. By "invoking fear," the state "designated an enemy, defined themselves in opposition to threatening others, and reinforced a narrative of Jewish Israeli suffering" and, most significantly, "harnessed fear to bind themselves to the state" (Ochs 2011, 68). Performing security for both an internal and external constituency continually "generates Israeli identity and state authority" (ibid., 42); security as a discursive formation and set of ritualized practices is a glue or a gravitional force holding the country together (Nelson 2008). Repetition and display of security checks by young, gun-toting soldiers normalize and inculcate danger and fear on the part of ordinary Israelis and position the state as the guardian of their security and protection. In this atmosphere of fear and anticipation, unmonitored and unencumbered Palestinian mobility is conceptualized as a threat to national security and the lives of individual Israelis, requiring constant monitoring for signs of potential violence. One elderly man told me in exasperation, "First they put up a checkpoint for the security of a settlement, then they put up a checkpoint for the security of the wall and they had to uproot all these trees. And now for their security, we are not allowed to use the roads. For their security, they change the roads and who can use which roads. They are destroying our lives for their security." Security has become a fetish of sorts, endowed with near-magical qualities, as well as an impressive exchange value as Israeli security industries market their expertise and products.

A capacious term that often sidetracks serious debate, analysis, and critique, *terrorism* embodies a potency whose ambiguity deflects questions and analysis of the causes of conflict.[14] Assaults on Palestinians civilians are rarely dubbed "terrorism"; instead, they are acts of self-defense, appropriate responses to Palestinian violence. Redolent of Tannen's (1998) "verbal inflation," the rhetoric of terrorism has been likened to a "black hole" in which things "collapse and disappear," a "magical term able to absorb any and all content" (Esmeir 2004, 3), and to an "enveloping cloud" in which all logic vanishes (Said 1984, 37). Open-ended and rarely explicitly defined, this highly expansive term alludes to all manner of things that are assumed to be self-evident. Within this linguistic orbit, *security and terrorism* have become a mantra, repeated endlessly in an almost sacred, ritualistic fashion, evoking emotional as well as violent responses.

If security and terrorism continue to dominate the discursive field of Israel-Palestine, this is challenged by the open discussion, across the Israeli political spectrum, of the "demographic problem" the wall can resolve. A common response to the branding of the wall as a security measure has been the question, why not build it on the Green Line instead of deep inside occupied territory?

Demographic Anxieties: "The Ticking Time Bomb"

As we walked along the path that was bringing us closer to the wall in the al-Ram suburb of Jerusalem, in 2004, Suha, a young activist who is gathering data on the wall's impact, stated flatly what I soon observed was common thinking among Palestinians: "What the Zionists are really thinking about is demographic security, and they don't hide it. And for this to be realized, the Palestinians will have to leave." Later that day, I listen to Suha's friend Nadia, a student visiting from Jordan, describe her trip across the Allenby Bridge. "This young Russian woman at the border asked me, 'Do you have family in the West Bank?' When I replied, 'No,' she continued, 'Is your mother Palestinian? Is your father Palestinian? Are you married to a Palestinian? Do you have children? Do you have any cousins who are Palestinians? What about your grandparents? Are they Palestinians? Do you have any uncles or aunts here?'" After Nadia had answered no to each question, the soldier repeated them. "This went on for over an hour—the same questions—the same answers. I don't know what she wanted. Finally, she asked who I was going to see, why did I want to see them, where did they live, what is their phone number, and who else did I know here? She also demanded to know,

'What areas are you planning to visit?'" The subtext of this obsessive genealogical inquiry is demography. Will Nadia stay in the area, marry, and have children, adding to the Arab population?

Israeli geographer Elisha Efrat (2006, 110) writes, "It must be understood that the security rationale is not the primary case for the fence. Far more important is the demographic rationale." Separation does have a security component, but it is more about achieving security through numerical superiority. Anxiety about a potential Palestinian demographic majority intensified after the 1967 war, when nearly 1.5 million (now around 4.5 million) Palestinians came under Israeli rule. The demographic "ticking time bomb" issue emerged. How can a state be Jewish if only half the population and citizenry are Jewish? Occupation has left Israel ruling over a near-majority Palestinian population, largely noncitizens, raising the specter of an apartheid-like state. This conundrum is at the heart of the policy of separation. Nationalism, of whatever stripe, is concerned with demography, but Israel's "political arithmetic" "heightens this obsession, as well as its consequences" (Kanaaneh 2002, 28). A full-page ad in the *New York Times* with the tag line "Separation from the Palestinians is a Must" called for a demilitarized Palestinian state, or face the following demographic in Israel:

2015: 52 % Jewish
2020: 49% Jewish
2030: 44% Jewish

The accompanying map depicted a Palestinian state in the OPTs and Israel within its 1967 borders.[15] The 2005 unilateral redeployment from Gaza, which removed a million and a half Palestinians from direct Israeli rule, was, in part, driven by demographic concerns.[16]

After the fall of the Soviet Union, about 800,000 Russians (Jews and non-Jews) immigrated to Israel, temporarily alleviating demographic concerns, as did the arrival of Ethiopian Jews in the 1980s and 1990s, who today number around 85,000 (Kruger 2005, 3). At the 2002 Herziliya Conference, participants cautioned that the Jewish population could dip below 50 percent in the space controlled by the state. Since Palestinian citizens of Israel comprise slightly more than 20 percent of the population, with another 4.5 to 5 million Palestinians living in territories controlled by the state, Israel would appear to be on the road to becoming a binational state in which citizenship is the preserve of Jews (aside from the Palestinians who obtained citizenship in the wake of 1948). Seen through this lens, separation and closure appear to be attempts to halt this looming "demographic problem."

In a speech on Army Radio, former military commander Effi Eitam aptly summarized the dilemma, "We will have to expel the great majority of the Arab presence in the OPTs. It is impossible with all these Arabs, and it is impossible to give up the territory" (Khoury 2006).[17] The platform of the Yisrael Beiteinu party of Moldavian immigrant and politician Avigdor Lieberman calls for annexing the West Bank and transferring its population as well as the Palestinian citizens of Israel. The now-defunct Moledet party advocated denying Palestinians work to compel emigration or voluntary transfer propelled by immiseration. Still promoted by some right-wing nationalists, the idea of "Greater Israel" has been superseded to some extent by a demand for unilateral separation. Separation consolidates Israel's control over more than 50 percent of the West Bank, closely following the post-1967 Allon Plan.[18]

Effi Eitam's statement on expulsion captures the conundrum of an exclusivist Jewish state in an area heavily inhabited by an indigenous, non-Jewish population and intimates a possible solution. Around half the world's Jews (around 7 million) live in Israel. Immigration has slowed, and there is a high-growth rate among Palestinians: Israel's crude birth rate is 2.1, with a fertility rate of 2.9 (higher among the Orthodox) compared to a Palestinian crude birth rate of 3.3 and a fertility rate of 4.2. Separation and closure are responses to creeping demographic imbalance. By including massive settlement blocs on the Israeli side, and anticipating slow emigration by the Palestinians from now isolated towns and villages, Israel can maintain Jewish demographic superiority in a fortified state that extends deep into the West Bank and includes the Jordan Valley.

Israeli geographer Arnon Soffer, the Cassandra of the impending demographic implosion and an outspoken academic advocate of the "fence" (the wall), takes credit for influencing the Israeli decision to unilaterally withdraw from Gaza. He is, in fact, generally credited as the intellectual grandfather of separation. Soffer (2005, 32) argues that separation will ensure Jewish demographic dominance. He proposed a fence that would locate the "maximum number of Jews on one side of the border and the maximum number of Palestinians on the other" (ibid.). Then demography ceases to be a problem (ibid., 36). When queried by the US State Department as to how much of the separation is related to security and how much to demography, Soffer replied, "One hundred percent demography" (Galili 2002, 4). Palestinians will "return to the negotiating table, not for peace . . . but for reasonable arrangements . . . for the good of their own wretched people" (ibid., 37). In an interview in the *Jerusalem Post*, Professor Soffer linked separation and the peace process:

> In the 1970s . . . I began to say publicly that Israel's days were numbered . . . the demographic clock is ticking, and that unless we made courageous decisions, Israel's countdown would begin. . . . There is going to be a clash of civilizations. In the Middle East, there is going to be the highest Arab birth rate in the world. . . . Time is passing and Palestinian women are getting pregnant . . . We have to separate . . . when 2.5 million people live in closed-off Gaza, it's going to be a human catastrophe. Those people will become even bigger animals than they are today, with the aid of an insane fundamentalist Islam. The pressure

at the border will be awful. It's going to be a terrible war. So, if we want to remain alive, we will have to kill and kill and kill. All day, every day. . . . The Palestinians will be forced to realize . . . we're here and they're there [and] . . . ask for "conflict management" talks—not that dirty word "peace." Unilateral separation . . . guarantees a Zionist-Jewish state with an overwhelming major- ity of Jews. . . . Between 1948 and 1967 . . . 400,000 people left the West Bank voluntarily. This is what will happen after separation. I believe there will be movement out of the area (Blum 2004).

Soffer and Bystrov (2005, 10–11) argue that "a solution for this demographic crisis is an initiated separation" that "entails the establishment of two states along a demographic border." The key phrase is "demographic border," which means the retention of large blocks of Jewish colonies in the West Bank—precisely what the serpentine wall does. They concede that a full-scale frontal transfer is "hardly applicable" in the present" (ibid., 10–11). Their figures show that the "Jewish pop- ulation in all the territories of the Land of Israel amounted to 49% in 2003, and it is expected to fall to some 40% toward 2020" (ibid., 13). They recommended a withdrawal from Gaza, ceding some areas of the West Bank, and a separation fence. The fence is also positioned as a response to high poverty rates and Pal- estinian attempts to "penetrate" Israel in search of work (ibid., 14).[19] Professor Soffer's blustery rhetoric of fear, doom, and violence is written with aplomb and seemingly little fear of recrimination. He acknowledges that with immiseration, "there will be movement out of the area," or voluntary transfer.[20]

A final word on demography—in 2002, the Israel Council for Demography met to "encourage the Jewish women of Israel—and only them—to increase their child bearing" (Levy 2002). "Democracy has to be subordinated to demography," said Major General Shlomo Gazit of the Jaffee Center for Strategic Studies (Galili 2002, 6). The demographic threat is not just that Palestinians now constitute 20 percent to 22 percent of the population of Israel within its 1948 borders; it is, more significantly, that Palestinians constitute 35 percent of the Israeli population under twenty years of age (Warschawski 2006, 50). A more recent demographic development concerns Jewish colonists' high rate of natural growth. In the wake of the second intifada, the number of Jewish Israelis opting to settle in the West Bank declined, but natural growth more than offsets this decline. In 1991, 9,000 Jews immigrated to the West Bank (excluding East Jerusalem), and 2,600 were born there. By 2012, the relation had been inverted: 3,600 Jews immigrated to the West Bank, while 10,800 were born there" (Gordon and Cohen 2012). Orthodox Jews tend to have a higher birth rate (6.5) than the overall Jewish population (3.0).

Researching Palestine

Methodologically, my research project (2004–2012) integrated participant- observation, informal conversations, semistructured interviews, and media sources. I read the press stories, interviewed Palestinians in villages and towns, observed protests, constantly engaged in discussions about mobility experiences, and had recourse to secondary published material. It was imperative to simply move around the area to simultaneously observe and participate in a regime of re-stricted and surveyed mobility. Accordingly, on numerous occasions I rode around the West Bank on public transportation, the ubiquitous buses or vans, sometimes alone, oftentimes with Palestinian interlocutors, to observe and acquire a feel for the techniques of closure and how they are experienced, navigated, and under-stood. What follows is an exploration and analysis of how separation, closure, and regulated mobility are lived experiences with far-reaching consequences.

Early in this project, Aymen, a shopkeeper I saw frequently, asked about my research. After I explained the purpose of ethnographic research, he jokingly warned, "Don't drive yourself crazy looking for patterns. The only pattern is to keep us off balance and take our land." The anthropologist seeks meaning in the patterns as well as in the contradictions of social life. Clarity and consistency do come into focus and work alongside chaos and ambiguity. Palestinians un-derstand a pattern of finely tuned ambiguity and chaos as a strategic weapon to engender uncertainty and manufacture immiseration.

Participant-observation takes on heightened significance in Palestine where few written orders govern passage at a checkpoint. Verbal orders, subject to change daily, are given to checkpoint staff, who then modulate an atmosphere of arbitrariness and unpredictability. The lack of transparency "makes it difficult to determine when the regime began, or important milestones in its development" (B'Tselem 2004, 9). When the immediacy of separation and closure are so perva-sive in everyday life, it can be difficult to grasp what to hone in on. I did not con-duct ethnography among Israelis or on the state; the fundamental focus is on the Palestinian experience. The policies, intent, and actions of the occupying author-ity are refracted through the everyday experiences and voices of Palestinians.

At times, words have failed me in trying to convey the complexities of sepa-ration and closure and to work through their ambiguities. The lacework spatial frame laid over the West Bank is, at times, beyond our vocabulary in the anthro-pology of space and mobility; at times, it seems almost unrepresentable. A bio-medical analogy does come to mind: closure and separation's deep incisions in the landscape are like a kind of surgery intended to slowly kill the patient but appropriate the body.

In 1990–91, I did research in a West Bank that was in the throes of the first intifada. A return visit in 2004 set this book in motion. In the years in-between, the landscape had been profoundly transformed; I could not figure out where the roads were or easily navigate once familiar neighborhoods. It was as though the pieces of a puzzle had been rearranged with vast and sinuous spaces between them. Although this analogy captured my confusion, it did not quite capture the logic of transformation and fragmentation of the landscape. This reorganization of space was, indeed like a puzzle, unfathomable at first; however, over time, the patterned logic of isolation and strangulation of Palestinian space and mobility crystallized. The incrementally shrinking space of Palestine and the concomitant expansion of Jewish-Israeli space, coupled with mechanisms of confinement and immobilization, define the parameters of this contemporary stage of colonization.

In the 1990s and the 2000s, Palestine was filled with researchers anxious to produce knowledge of an envisioned postcolonial transition to statehood. However, as soon became apparent, the Oslo Accords had inaugurated a new colonial relationship. What is the role of the anthropologist in the colonial present? Our role, I contend, is twofold: first, to compile an ethnographic archive of ordinary everyday life under a settler-colonial occupation and, in doing so, to challenge the official story, which has long silenced and marginalized a Palestinian narrative; and second, to provide theoretical analysis of how contemporary forms of colonial power operate through fast-changing spatial parameters that intertwine with ever-changing rules, at once unpredictable and comprehended viscerally in a violence-saturated environment.

This book is organized thematically around space, surveillance, mobility, and time to explore closure's impact and how Palestinians make sense of and proceed with daily life under constraints most people would find unbearable. Chapter 1 explores separation and closure and their spatialization in the built environment. A scar on the landscape, sometimes described as a gaping wound, its two sides have distinct aesthetics. The chapter poses a series of questions about surplus populations. Chapter 2 situates mobilities as controlling tools in the arsenal of war and governance. It explores the regime of mobility and its structuring of space and relates it to state expansion. This chapter details the macro-social taxonomy that produces and is produced by separation. I then lay out the technologies that monitor and drastically constrict mobility: the complex permit system governing mobility and the segregated road system. Continuing with mobility, chapter 3 details the surveillance system and the checkpoints that govern mobility; it also details the experience of being filtered and funneled through space. The cultural parameters that inflect mobility, such as age, gender, and class, are fleshed out; also explored is the way the once taken for granted becomes unfamiliar and objectified. As the material and experiential space of memory is reconfigured, it is anticipated that memories of past spatial formations will gradually fade. What new memories will take shape in their absence? The matter of time in a colonial setting—its appropriation, commodification, and deployment as a technique of rule and control—is taken up in chapter 4, which examines the impact of closure on the rhythm of daily concerns: health, education, kinship and intimacy, and sociality. This chapter also explores how spatial fragmentation and constriction are replicated in the temporal domain and addresses Palestinian subjectivities as they are structured by closure and separation. Chapter 5 elaborates on resistance to the colonial present with particular attention to the localization of politics. Within these shrinking political spaces, direct action, joint protests, and international solidarity actions came to the fore during the research period.

Conclusion

A strategy of managing and controlling a captive population through immobilizing and incarceratory policies and practices carves out sites where a particular form of power is wielded and a vision of the ethnic-sectarian and national composition of space is enacted. The Zionist state-making project is constructed around distinction and, more recently, consensus that unilateral separation from the Palestinians is vital for security and to to decelerate and contain an impending Palestinian majority. Separation and closure fix Palestinians in labyrinthine spaces of entrapment and facilitate the unequal allocation of rights and resources.

A complex palette of spatial and bureaucratic strategies in Palestine has generated physical and social distance and facilitated resource acquisition. Through these optics, spatial tactics and structures on the built environment limit Palestinian mobility and render visible and tactile the social hierarchy of a colonial occupation. Separation and closure are pivotal to this instance of contemporary colonial rule, inscribing on the landscape tangible and visceral lines of order/disorder and inclusion/exclusion. Closure is understood by Palestinians as a means to immobilize and immiserate them in anticipation of their eventual emigration. Most significantly, it is understood to ensure the impossibility of a contiguous Palestinian state. The morbid description of an environment "tightening around them like a noose" (Weizman 2007, 5) is equivalent to the Palestinian's common metaphors of the "open-air prison" and "suffocation." Morbid biomedical metaphors capture the process of dismemberment, control of circulation, the paralysis of mobility, and gradual strangulation of the Palestinian economy and sociopolitical body.

New, exclusionary inscriptions of place may eventually color new memories and dilute previous ones. If place acquires definition and meaning through the social activities and relationships that unfold in them, then Palestinians are increasingly constrained in their place-making capacity. They can only craft and give meaning to place in delimited areas through acts of memory, resistance, and simply staying put.

With Israel's discernable shift from conflict resolution to management, along with a decline in the need for Palestinian labor, the Palestinians are at risk of remaining under occupation, with minimal self-government, in the midst of an expansionist state that covets their resources. Although Palestinians are perpetually visible and legible, they have become a disposable or abandoned people left to their own limited means and that of the international donor community. Initially, closure was cast as a temporary measure, much as the settlements were over forty-five years ago. With occupation now ending its fifth decade, this book turns to the lived reality of life on the frontier of an expanding state. It is a life with little predictability and the ever-present threat of violence.

1 "Permission to Breathe"
Closure and the Wall

I WAS STANDING AMID the debris of an uprooted olive tree, on land belonging to the villagers of Iskaka, on a sweltering summer afternoon. In the hot, still air, the only sound was the whirring of the two Caterpillar bulldozers that were busily yanking dusty olive trees out of the neatly terraced soil. Clumps of fresh soil clung to the trees' gnarled roots, which had been tossed aside to rot in the open air. Hundreds of villagers, and their local and foreign supporters, were making their way over the rock strewn landscape to the orchard and the path being cleared for the wall. Two Israeli soldiers stood guard over the bulldozers, automatic rifles at the ready. And then a woman dropped to her knees, waving her arms in the air, and screamed, "We are in a prison. Everyone talks about Abu Ghraib—we—here—we are in prison."

As I approached the now teeming crowd gathering in the orchard, I caught sight of Um Salim, a middle-aged mother of four in a long, black dress. She was standing in front of a still-rooted olive tree, tearfully yet defiantly waving her white scarf in a gesture of mourning. Then she picked up a broken olive branch, flailing it as she angrily wailed, "They can come from Poland, they can come from Russia, they can come from America, and they can come from Ethiopia, but this will always be ours! This is Palestinian land!" Pointing to different trees, she exclaimed, "This one feeds my children breakfast! And this one, dinner! How will I feed them? What will I feed my children!?" Her words carried a palpable place-based sense of history and belonging, of life itself. References to sustenance, the rhetoric of feeding the next generation, ran deep among this once largely peasant population.

Um Salim's angry cries captured the relentless march of late-modern settler colonialism, with its rapacious destruction of natural resources and callous indifference to indigenous lives. Israeli military and civilian personnel, hand-in-hand with armed colonists, exercise a substantial measure of control over the daily lives of several million Palestinians. With Israel's superior military weaponry and ability to quickly call in reinforcements, two or three soldiers could ensure the bulldozers' ability to carve a destructive path through village lands, as Palestinians stood watching.

Back in Ramallah a few days later, I was enjoying a leisurely lunch in an office full of young Palestinians. Twenty-five-year-old Selma, articulate and assertive, exclaimed half-jokingly but with unmistakable bitterness: "I want to live a normal day just once in my life. I have never had one. I want a sweet morning, a peaceful afternoon and a quiet evening—a whole day where one doesn't think about this mess. What would it be like to live a normal life?" When one of her colleagues scoffed, "It would be boring!" Selma ignored the comment and continued, "I visited Amman and Cairo and I saw young people and how they live. I was so envious. Youth here are frustrated and feel hopeless. We want to lead a normal life—the kind we see on TV."

As people drifted back to work, Selma and Jihan, another employee in this office, sat in the kitchen and continued the conversation over coffee. "I have never had a normal life," Selma said. "My father was in prison most of my childhood because he gave a sack of grain to a poor man in need who was later arrested for being a security threat. My mother worked and I had one brother and one sister. Those with larger families really suffered because the eldest had to help take care of the kids. At least we were just a few children." Palestinian subjectivity is conditioned by multiple contexts, including age, gender, religiosity, and family, among others, but the occupation looms large: life in a contested space, the protracted violence of everyday life under occupation, chronic insecurity and unpredictability, and an acute consciousness of and desire for another way of life, the normal life that Selma dreams of.

Talking about the multiple checkpoints she must pass through on her way to work, Jihan complains, "Soon we will need permission to breathe," capturing the suffocating physicality of immobilization. The West Bank has been carved into zones, many of which are off-limits to Palestinians. There is a well-honed regime of surveillance and control over the individual and aggregate body. Jihan's "permission to breathe" and Selma's desire for "a normal life" are recurring refrains about colonialism's encroachment on daily life that illuminate the particular politics of subjectivity in Palestine. Both are bitingly poignant, for the act of breathing indicates life, its absence signals death. "Permission" evokes Palestinian subordination to the occupation's domination over life and death. "Normal life" calls attention to both the immediate and prolonged effects of closure.

In Palestine, a shift to spatial forms that monitor and entrap a surplus population is apparent. This chapter explores segregation/separation, closure, and immobilization by exploring two of its main pillars: the wall and the enclaves. Chapters 2 and 3 detail the other mechanisms: identity cards (*bitaqat hawiyyaat*), permits (*tassrihaat*), roads, surveillance, and checkpoints. Under segregation/ separation, populations are assigned to different spaces and are constrained in their access to other spaces. Thus segregation aptly describes the situation in Palestine. Life behind the wall and in the enclaves sheds light on the intricate, often twisted relationship between space and subjectivity. As a dynamic arena, space is productive of subjectivity. French philosopher and sociologist Henri Lefebvre (1991, 143) contends that a primary purpose of spatial formations is to "produce subjects obedient to spatial rules." Thus this chapter asks: What is it like to inhabit the spaces of closure? What do closure and spatial fragmentation look like on the ground?

A blight on the landscape, the mammoth wall simultaneously produces order and disorder, drawing an unmistakable line of inclusion and exclusion. On the Palestinian side, a cruel dystopia has settled over a landscape of increasingly disconnected and isolated enclaves. These are spaces of despair, where time has slowed, patterns of sociality are disjointed, and the future appears bleak. The wall is both a counterinsurgency technique to maintain control and squelch resistance and a massive land grab. Along with checkpoints and the division of Palestine into Areas A, B, and C, the wall has engendered a new spatial form in Palestine: the enclave and the sequestered subject.

An inescapable backdrop to daily life, the wall, or the fence in some areas, is at once taken for granted and yet a constant part of conversation. When I visited Um Salim a day after the protest, her house was packed with neighbors and relatives talking animatedly about the previous day's demonstration and the tear gas that drove many protesters to seek first aid in the village's small clinic. When I had trouble following the multiple strands of conversation, she laughed heartily and said, "We are all storytellers now. Every Palestinian has lots of stories, and everyone tells stories all the time. Our lives are a series of stories about how we went from here to there, what happened along the way, and who has land and can make a living."

Separation and Closure

Closure is touted as a security measure to prevent militant attacks on Israelis. Under international law it is a form of collective punishment. Separation and closure complicate the standard observation that expanding frontier and colonial populations meet and interpenetrate colonized societies in networks of economic exchange and sociality, however skewered the power relations between them (Brooks 2002). It is worth remembering that in building the wall, Israel made a statement about its detachment from the region and positioned itself westward. Some Israeli scholars argue that Zionism has produced an inward-looking, parochial, and xenophobic subject with a siege mentality. This ostensible Jewish "return to origins in the Middle East" and the establishment of a state "ideologically and politically oriented almost exclusively toward the West" (Shohat 1999, 7) is paradoxical. Israelis have "an inherent tendency . . . to associate themselves and their collective project with a 'cultured Europe' . . . often played out through disassociation" from the Arab world (Rabinowitz 2001, 44). As an "extension" of Europe, Israel is "in," but not "of," the Middle East (Shohat 1999, 14). The wall keeps Palestinians out and cuts off any direct link with the Arab world; in so do- ing, it lets Israel imagine itself as part of the West. This is an instance of "selective cosmopolitanism" (Mandel 2008, 14), of being open to the world but not to the other in their midst. However, the separation is not airtight. Indeed, it has some porosity, especially as concerns work permits. Israeli employers still manage to obtain permits for needed Palestinian workers.

Separation has a genealogy traceable to early Zionist notions of exclusivist land and labor and the imputation of cultural difference. It derives from a ranked classificatory scheme "perceived as the norm" in Zionist ideology (Warschawski 2006, 47), which distinguishes Jews and Arabs. With the consolidation of the Israeli state and the *nakbah*, the 1948 Palestinian catastrophe of defeat and exile, the multiethnic and multireligious space of Palestine gave way to an impulse to carve out seemingly homogenous spaces. In the process, historical narratives and memories of past coexistence were gradually marginalized, if not silenced (see Shohat 1988, 2003; Campos 2011), obscuring a historical past and a memory of pluralism as well as Israel's own internal social complexity. The Palestinians in Israel constitute between 20 percent and 22 percent of the population, while Jews of Arab ancestry (*Mizrahim*) constitute about half of the Israeli Jewish popula- tion.[1] Thus Israel has always been more ethnically and religiously plural than its dominant narrative and self-image might suggest.

The campaign slogan used by Israeli Labor politician Ehud Barak in his 1999 run for prime minister, "Us here, them there" (quoted in Gordon 2008, 197, 282), epitomizes these socio-spatial categories. Central to human cognition and mean- ing making, classification is deployed to effect a hierarchical social order. The essentialized categories of Arab and Jew constitute the parameters of ordered relations and the assignment of space and political-legal rights. The ostensibly homogeneous spaces, Jews here and Arabs there, are separated socio-legally and physically. Between closure and the wall, the categories become literally ce- mented in space.

Following the 1967 occupation, there was little commingling of communi- ties, and certainly little intermarriage. It was in the realm of labor, and the un- equal economic relations it entailed, where interpenetration was most clearly at work. Although the Green Line blurred as Palestinians and Israelis traversed it easily until the early 1990s, residential segregation remained prevalent. Contem- porary Zionism's separatist impulse, captured by Prime Minister Yitzak Rabin in 1994, when he declared, "We have to decide on separation as a philosophy" (Makovsky 2004, 52) was consolidated by Oslo.

States often hold "categorical identities" as a kind of trump card over fluid ethnic, religious, and national lines of distinction (Calhoun 1994, 26–27). How are these categories constructed and around what putative differences are they organized? Akin to sociologist Charles Tilly's (1998, 6) "distinctly bounded pairs," classificatory categories "do crucial organizational work." Separation (*hafrada*) operates through and simultaneously reifies categorical difference, and in Palestine/Israel, these lines of distinction are unabashedly spatialized. For example, the concept "legal unidirectionality" characterizes land ownership. Once land has been transferred to the Jewish National Fund, whether it was expropriated or bought, it belongs to world Jewry and cannot be sold to or owned by non-Jews (Yiftachel 1998). Law provides another example as well. The colonists brought their legal system into the Occupied Palestinian Territories, providing rights and protections for themselves that don't extend to the occupied population. Thus, within the area ruled by the state, two legal systems prevail. Israeli citizens, including those residing in the OPT, enjoy legal rights not available to the noncitizen Palestinians.

State-generated identities and the classifications of space they configure, for example, Israel, Gaza, West Bank, Jerusalem, Areas A, B, and C, and H1 and H2 are both products of and artifacts that accomplish the work of separation. The materiality of categories "appears always and instantly" (Bowker and Starr 1999, 3) as they work to maintain boundaries of rights to citizenship and mobility. In other words, a host of rights and restrictions flow from these categories. For example, Palestinians' passage through checkpoints depends on their having the correct identity cards and/or permits. East Jerusalem Palestinian residents can enter Israel and reside in Jerusalem, whereas Palestinians with West Bank and Gazan identity cards cannot enter the city without a permit.

Although Tilly (1998, 7) notes that "completely bounded categories are rare," separation and closure are attempts to impose just such boundaries and "lock categorical inequality in place" (ibid., 7–8). Classification and ordering fix a segregated and increasingly absolutist sense of space and national belonging: Jews in Israel and its colonies enjoying fairly unhindered mobility and West Bank Palestinians immobilized in multiple, noncontiguous enclaves. Israel classifies those under it rule, citizens and noncitizens, by more than a simple binary. An examination of the varied identity cards carried by those under its rule bears witness to a generalized Jewish/non-Jewish binary within which a monothetic logic can be discerned. Lines of distinction are first and foremost ethnic, religious, and national, but among the Palestinian population in the OPTs, there are multiple categories of Israeli-issued identity cards, color-coded for quick and easy assessment of risk and the holder's rights to mobility and residency. This suggests that separation and closure are not just about distinctions between Arab and Jew but also the imposition of different legal identities on Palestinians. The occupation has divided Palestinians into multiple categories: holders of Jerusalem residency cards, West Bank residents, those with Gaza identities, and those with Jordanian passports. There is "a multiplicity of hierarchically stacked citizenships" that includes citizenship extended to Palestinians who remained in Israel after 1948, albeit with "curtailed" political rights, and the potential for automatic citizenship made available to Jews anywhere through the Israeli Law of Return based on descent and religion (Shafir 2005, 55).

Within the framework of global neoliberalism(s), separation and closure join other forms of structural and spatial management of racialized inequality and expulsion. The new era of immobilization and incarceration takes many forms—from the US prison system and its military prison at Guantanamo Bay to the wall in Palestine. In Palestine, physical separation mimics and carries forward the distinction between ruler and ruled, citizen and noncitizen, Israeli and Palestinian, as the wall concretizes identities. Separation resembles Jim Crow America: the dominant sector of society is unable to imagine life in which the other is equal, and the other inhabits a world hedged with restrictions and boundaries whose transgression can elicit a swift and violent response.[2]

Closure's most immediate effect has been to obstruct Palestinian mobility and access to employment, education, health care, political organizing, commerce, and family and social relations. Most significantly, closure disrupts the notion of a schedule, or trust in a daily temporal rhythm. In trying to grasp this lived reality ethnographically what came to mind for me was the notion of "calibrated chaos." Chaos began to crystallize as a planned, observable, and lived pattern. After one particularly long wait, over an hour, to pass through the Qalandia checkpoint, a delay that had no discernable reason except that the checkpoint personnel were chatting and horsing around, seemingly oblivious to a long line of cars waiting to pass, I complained to the driver, a friend with a Jerusalem identity card, who said, "The soldiers have told us chaos is their policy—sometimes when I joke with them about why it is so chaotic—they laughingly tell me this." Control through the creation of calibrated chaos, the changing of rules and procedures with no warning or explanation, is enacted daily at checkpoints and in applying for permits. Intermittent and prolonged curfews punctuate these measures.[3] Unpredictability is the new norm. The common expression *inshallah* (God willing) has political resonance; its utterance in the context of this unpredictability makes it much more freighted than usual.

On a late spring afternoon, I met Muna, an elegant woman approaching her seventies, for lunch. I ask, "how are you?" and she replies, "*'aisheen*" ("We are living" or "We are still breathing"). Muna's collective use of "*'aisheen*" points to an unlivable life in which breathing, the state of being alive, is hedged with an uncertainty that underscores a subjectivity characterized by a profound awareness of the simple, yet life-sustaining, act of breathing. This brings to the fore the questions: What is it like to live in a state of exclusion and confinement? What are the implications of this for shaping subjectivity?

From her apartment in the East Jerusalem neighborhood of Abu Dis, Fatima Fayyad, a twenty-six-year-old engineer by training, cannot avoid seeing the wall, just twenty or so meters from her house. For Fatima, her husband, Hasan, and their three young children, its looming shadow blocks the natural sunlight that once warmed their home. Most of their relatives live on the West Bank side. When I visited her on a dreary, rainy winter morning, she summed up the meaning of separation and the wall:

> The idea of the wall has been there for a long time. Some Israeli writers and politicians used to say the best thing is to put the Palestinians behind walls so the new generations will have no images of Israelis and thus they will be afraid of them—the enemy—we will be afraid of them. The new generation would not be as strong as the generation who fought in the intifada and struggled for years. So what can Palestinians see now? They don't know Jerusalem; they don't know the West Bank—only their own village or area. They live in terrible economic and social conditions and the situation is deteriorating every day. So these people—it is easy to deal with them, it is easy to destroy them or kill them or perhaps they will kill each other. So, this is what they want, I think. They, the Israelis, always feel they are living in a state of war, that they are targeted so they are always afraid. They are afraid from inside. Perhaps, some of them, they know they have done something wrong and that this land is not theirs and that is why they have to act strongly to keep what they have achieved. So for them it is a good idea to put us behind walls and then they can forget about us. But I don't think this will work. I don't think walls will work in our world now. It is a different world. If the wall were built in 1967—perhaps. But now it is different. The world is so small. You can easily talk and what you say reaches everybody in the whole world via the internet.
>
> They are always worried about demographics because we have more children and that is why they can never dream of allowing the refugees back. That is why they have these strategies of getting people to leave. If you don't have a place to live, and you can't rent, can't visit your family, and you do not have a job—you will easily go abroad. If you are educated and you can't find a job here and you can work in Abu Dhabi or Dubai, why not go? Or even Jordan, although Jordan doesn't allow it anymore. Wouldn't you go? It is a very difficult choice. But many people would go—people educated in Europe or the US will never come back.

Fatima laments closure's immiserating effects and the sense of estrangement it imposes, which are, she believes, intended to compel emigration. Her assessment points to the Israeli fear of those they have dispossessed and Palestinian trepidation about the future—intertwined subjectivities revolving around immiseration, privilege, and empowerment.

Fatima says of her life under closure, "We are getting used to it because it has been gradual—it has happened over a period of years—first they put up checkpoints around Jerusalem in 1991, then plastic barriers on the roads in the West Bank, then small piles of stones here and there, then the fence in some places, and now the wall. If it had appeared suddenly perhaps we would have resisted more. But we do find ways around each obstacle put in our path."

In closure, Palestinian subjectivity is colored by the suspension of time, a shrinking of space, perpetual anxiety, and estrangement from the once familiar. Ordinary excursions such as a family visit or a trip to the doctor engender anxiety and a heightened state of alert. Rania, whose family lives in Beit Jala, complained, "You can't plan your day. It is too much sometimes. I am always nervous and crying because I want to see my family. I want to be in touch with them, to be able to come and go to them. To live like normal people live. But checkpoints and the wall have made visiting my family so difficult." Rania has lost control over one of the most basic elements of daily life and yearns for normality. What makes the situation so troubling is not just its lack of transparency; it is the unpredictability: a checkpoint can suddenly close, and questions about what is going on are usually met with a gruff "shut up" or a shrug of the shoulders from the guards. This unpredictability fosters a conscious and verbalized state of anxiety, nervousness, and depression. It is the acute consciousness of their embodied dispositions that so clearly departs from formulations of habitus as a largely unconscious process, such as sociologist Marcel Mauss's "go without saying" (Bourdieu 1990, 66–67). From Bassam, who runs an old, family-owned pharmacy, and several of his colleagues, I learn that they are filling more prescriptions for antidepressants and anti-anxiety medications than ever before.

Separation and closure have spawned a distinct dystopian landscape. I use the word *landscape* to refer to the meaning imputed to an environment sculpted by human interventions and its inscription with meaning, as well as the narration of space. After a trip to visit family in Bethlehem, Fatima lamented, "The landscape is so different now. I don't remember what it looked like before. I try to remember. Every time I go to my family's house in Bethlehem, I have to ask which way I should go because it changes without warning." When landscapes are erased and then reconstituted, they can become an unfamiliar terrain. Social disarticulation (Button 2009) and cognitive disorientation are precisely what closure accomplishes. Social networks and community are disrupted, and memories of place and familiar routes begin to recede, replaced by a circumscribed space of everyday life.

The building of the wall as a manifestation of the impulse to separate and miniaturize the space of Palestine has had a temporally attenuated sequencing, a methodical progression that was less a sudden singular event, and more a creeping along in fits and starts. As a key component of the "matrix of control" (Halper 1999), its consequences have been catastrophic.

The Wall, or "Fences Make Good Neighbors"

In making the case for the wall to the administration of George W. Bush, Israel's prime minister Ariel Sharon quoted from the last line of Robert Frost's poem "Mending Wall": "fences make good neighbors." He might have noted the first line: "Something there is that doesn't love a wall." Begun in the north in 2002, the winding, now iconic, wall dominates the skyline, blocking out the sun in places. Its monotone concrete slabs severely constrain any sense of social possibility and commingling. "I am afraid that after the wall is completed around the West Bank, next will come the roof. They even own the sun, you know. It belongs to them as well," remarked Bassam as he showed me the wall. Bassam's cynicism is justified: the wall abuts his home.

Although Palestinians and Israelis live in geospatial proximity, the wall renders them distant. With the colonies on high ground and the watchtowers interspersed along the wall and looming over checkpoints, a regime of "visual dominance" (Weizman 2007, 81) gives Israelis, especially the colonists and the military, a visual autonomy and power (Mirzoeff 2011, 2) that keeps the Palestinians in sight but at a remove. As Fatima noted, a generation of Israelis and Palestinians in the time of closure is growing up with little first-hand contact with each other, except for those Palestinians who still work in Israel or in the colonies. Palestinians rarely see Israelis other than soldiers or bureaucrats, cogs in the wheels of a colonial bureaucracy governing the issuance of permits and passage at checkpoints.

As early as 1995, an Israeli commission was discussing creating a physical barrier of separation. The idea lay dormant until 2002, when then Prime Minister Ehud Barak decided to start building the wall.[4] The wall marries architectural simplicity, hi-tech surveillance, and a disregard for aesthetics. Israelis refer to it as a "fence," "the security fence," or "the separation barrier." Palestinians refer to it as "the wall" (al-jidar), the "separation wall," or the "apartheid wall," or, more bitterly, apropos its incarceratory nature, "a prison without a roof." At eight- meters high (nearly twenty-five-feet) and an estimated seven hundred kilometers (434 miles) long, it is higher and longer than the 3.6-meter-high (12 feet), 106-kilometer (66-mile) Berlin Wall and more than double the length of the 315-kilometer (195-mile) Green Line. Prefabricated concrete slabs stand upright, forming an ominous cement barrier that snakes through cultivated farm land and populated areas, punctuated by tall, circular watchtowers and firing posts every three hundred meters (nearly a thousand feet), or so. In some areas, the wall is made of metal fencing and razor wire; closer to colonies, it is more likely to be concrete. Running parallel to the wall is a thirty- to ninety-meter-wide (100 to 300 feet) buffer zone that often includes a well-maintained dirt road used by military patrols to track movement, as well as trenches, lighting, remote sensors, cameras, and coils of barbed wire. The wall is being built in stages. There has been a modicum of flexibilty in the routing and rerouting of its path, as various groups—colonists, lobbiests, real estate interests, religious parties, Israeli environmentalists, and Palestinian committees—have brought to bear their particular interests (Weizman 2011; 2007, 167).

The wall curves around blocs of colonies, incorporating them into Israel. In places, it extends as much as twenty-two kilometers (fourteen miles) into Palestinian territory, dissolving the West Bank into a multiplicity of discontiguous enclaves. When the Jerusalem colonies are included, up to three-quarters of all colonists reside in spaces contiguous with the state. Constructing the wall and the buffer zone has meant that thousands of acres of Palestinian agricultural land have been confiscated, and tens of thousands of trees have been uprooted.

By 2012, there was little doubt that the wall was a unilateral declaration of a border. The few small Jewish colonies beyond the wall are the ones most likely to be ceded in negotiations. Israel has not annexed the West Bank, as it did East Jerusalem and the Golan Heights. Doing so would force it to address the question of Palestinian citizenship. For all intents and purposes, the wall separates citizens from noncitizens. Aside from in the seam zone, the area between the wall and the Green Line, there are few West Bank Palestinians on the Israeli side of the wall. The wall furthers the state's long-time strategy of acquiring maximum land and minimum Palestinians.

In the third millennium, the United States and Israel are erecting walls, one to ostensibly deter "terrorists," the other to contain the flow of "criminals," drugs, and undocumented workers crossing the border from Mexico. Both have recourse to the discourse of security, criminality, and terror to exploit fears of the demonic other. Are walls becoming the *nomos* of the new century, part of the "production of (political) order through spatial orientation" (Brown 2010, 45)?[5] Paradoxically, economically advanced countries are building low- and hi-tech, and increasingly modular, physical structures.

Long used to separate peoples, control population movement, claim ownership, defend territory and "civilizations," and quell resistance, walls are hardly a historical novelty. Precedents abound. Over five thousand years ago, the Middle East was full of walled settlements. China's two-thousand-year-old, 6,700-kilometer-long (over four thousand miles), eight-meter-high (twenty-five feet) Great Wall, running east-west, was built to prevent invasions from nomadic Huns from the north and to forge national unity. And, indeed, Israel sees itself as a bulwark, providing "civilizational dimensions," against the violent barbarian East (Warschawski 2006, 47). At 117 kilometers (seventy-three miles) long, and four- to four-and-a-half meters high (thirteen to fifteen feet), the nearly two-thousand-year-old Hadrian's Wall in England, once a potent symbol of Roman power, was also built to prevent "barbarian" incursions. Both are now UNESCO World Heritage sites. Interestingly, on the south side of Hadrian's east-west wall were an earth mound, a ditch, and a small road running along its length. On the north side a deep trench obstructed the scaling of the wall. Castles with turrets, or lookout points, where soldiers were stationed, dotted the wall, and gates facilitated north-south passage through the wall. The layout of today's West Bank wall bears noteworthy resemblances. It is as if a low-tech (by today's standards) but spectacular mechanism with origins in ancient history has been resurrected with hi-tech accoutrements to manage modern-day inequalities.

More recent devices of separation to maintain local and global hierarchies run the gamut: the fence in Libya built by the Italians to defend against national resistance to the Italians' efforts at colonization; the Polisario wall; the Berlin Wall; Checkpoint Charlie; the buffer zone between the Greek and Turkish Cyprus; Belfast's "peace walls"; the ghettos in East Europe; the Mandelbaum Gate, which once divided Jerusalem into east and west; the "shouting hill" between the occupied Golan Heights and Syria; and the wall along the Mexico-US border. Beirut's Green Line was less a physical structure and more a line that divided the city between warring factions during Lebanon's 1975–91 civil war. Blast walls in Baghdad separated Sunni and Shia neighborhoods in the 2000s. A 1,126-kilometer (700-mile) line of control divides Pakistan from Indian-controlled Kashmir. In spring 2012, Israel began construction of a four-meter-high (thirteen feet) wall along the border with Lebanon.

It is worth noting that a state's protection of its citizens is expected to comply with international humanitarian law (IHL); in other words, the response to perceived security risks must be proportionate. In July 2004, the International Court of Justice (ICJ) ruled fourteen to one that the wall represented collective punishment and the acquisition of land by force, and that it violated the prohibition on changing status in occupied territory and thus violated IHL and human rights law. Under the Fourth Geneva Convention and the 1907 Hague Regulations, which specify the obligations of an occupying power, Palestinians are "protected persons." As an occupying power, Israel is obliged to ensure freedom of movement, an adequate standard of living, as normal a life as possible, access to food and medical care, and protection from collective punishment. In its 2004 ruling, the ICJ declared that the wall was illegal, caused disproportionate harm, must be dismantled, and that residents whose land had been taken were to be compensated. Yet no sanctions against Israel were forthcoming from the United States or the international community.

At an estimated cost of nearly $3 billion, and subcontracted by the Israel Ministry of Defense to over twenty private contractors, the wall serves as a marketing device for Israeli firms, such as Elbit and Magal, which, as Naomi Klein (2007, 439) wryly observes, "don't mind the negative publicity that Israel's wall attracts around the world—in fact they consider it free advertizing." The global politics of securitization and the fortressing of countries and communities and the militarization of domestic policing and urban space presented Israel with an opportunity to increase its exports of new security technologies. For example, parts of the wall on the US-Mexico border are being built by Boeing and its Israeli subcontractor Elbit. US immigration agents working on the Mexico-US border took training courses from the Israeli Golan Corporation (ibid., 438). The website weneedafence.com defines the problem: "illegal immigration" and offers the solution: "we need a fence," noting that Israel's wall is the "state-of-the-art in border security." And the cost calculations are similar—from $1 million to $3.7 million per mile. They combine the latest surveillance and detection technologies with low-tech, old-fashioned concrete walls.

Enclavization

Maysun and Sahar, twenty-year-old girls from Jenin, came to Ramallah to attend a conference of the NGO they worked for. They had left Jenin at three o'clock that morning. I asked if that was because they anticipated waits at checkpoints, and they responded, almost in unison: "Yes, it is now a long trip, but also we left so early because we want to enjoy every minute we are out of Jenin. We want to refresh ourselves by seeing other people and places. We want to breathe!" They sought to enjoy every minute out of their enclave. In the enclaves, they are hemmed in by the wall, a network of Jewish-only bypass roads, more than five hundred checkpoints, and more than one hundred colonies that encircle the Palestinian population centers. Like Native American reservations and South African Bantustans, the enclaves reflect the power of one party to spatially enact its interests. Within Areas A and B, and between the major west-east division of the West Bank that has been staked out by the large colonies Maale Adumim and Ariel, there are over 160 enclaves; many are actually enclaves within enclaves. The large urban enclaves correspond loosely to Palestinian towns or regions: Jenin, Nablus, Qalqiliya, Ramallah, Jericho, Bethlehem, and Hebron, areas now cut off from their traditional hinterlands. Clusters of villages form enclaves as well. Fenced-, walled-in Gaza resembles a geographically singular holding pen, the West Bank an archipelago.

Juxtaposing the dystopia of the enclaves with spaces of order replicates a global distribution of space, mobility, and power in an intensifying, segregated neoliberal world order. The wall secures a perimeter that keeps out the Palestinians. "Open-air prisons" is an apt metaphor for the enclaves, which mimic prison conditions and, like prisons, contain the marginal or those who are expelled from the social order. Not only is space carved up and for use by parties of vastly unequal status, but the mobility between spaces is controlled and surveyed. Indeed, life in the enclaves resembles that of the prison in another way: although the administrators and guards may be significantly outnumbered by prisoners, they are always in control.

In 2007, John Dugard, United Nations special rapporteur for human rights in the OPTs told the UN General Assembly that the wall in East Jerusalem is "an exercise in social engineering, designed to achieve the Judaization of Jerusalem by reducing the number of Palestinians in the city. It cannot conceivably be justified on security grounds" (quoted in Barghouti 2009).

So what did daily life look like for Palestinians in the Jerusalem area in the summer of 2004? The wall's path was marked by the shiny new metal barriers on the road erected to demarcate the coming wall's route, and progress was rapid in the al-Ram neighborhood. At the top of the main street, where al-Ram meets the Qalandia checkpoint, the cement foundations for each slab of concrete were in place. Piles of shiny barbed wire coils were stored where the taxis had once lined up. A ten- to thirty-foot zone had been cleared on each side, eating up most of the main street, and making me wonder how cars would get out of their driveways. The street was still lined with bakeries, sweet shops, a supermarket, several small groceries, a gas station, a bank, a tile shop, kitchen and bath shops, carpenter shops, and quite a few apartment buildings and detached houses. Bulldozers, with bars around the drivers' windows, were busy tearing up the middle of the street. Soldiers guarded the construction site. The residents stood amid the dust and the ear-splitting noise, watching with stunned looks as their world was literally cut in two. I stopped in a grocery store to buy a drink, and a man came in and plaintively asked, speaking to no one in particular, "How are we going to get around, go to different places?" People just shrugged and suggested alternative roads. I asked the owner if he thought there would still be a road in front of his shop and he said, "Yes but it will be very narrow and cars will have to use one lane to go both ways. It will block the sunlight from most of these buildings as well." Later I met up with Raja, a young man whose family owns a pizza shop. We walked along the freshly dug up earth and popped into the deserted pizza shop. His younger brother, who was working the oven, complained angrily, "We are losing our business. The wall is going up right in front of our shop. We have no more customers! Bills have to be paid. There is no work. This wall is killing us! I am thinking of migrating to America."

Raja's neighbor, Maher, a handsome, curly-haired man in his early twenties, lives with his parents and younger siblings in al-Ram, where his family owns a stationary store on the main street. On the day I visited him in the shop, the noise of the bulldozers was deafening, and dust swirled in the hot air, choking passersby and seeping into the shops. Cement block by cement block, the wall was effectively splitting al-Ram in half. Maher explained that business had come to a near standstill because people could no longer cross the street to get to the shop, and parking was nearly impossible because of the construction. Maher and I watched a crane lifting the concrete slabs, each one another nail in the coffin of closure. Then he turned to me and said, in a voice filled with desperation:

> This is not just about identity, about how Palestinian identity is being destroyed. You lose your belief in yourself and you hate that. In university, we read about the experience of being colonized. Now it is happening to us in a very obvious way. People don't like themselves anymore. They don't like being Palestinian anymore. When I see this wall coming down the road, I feel we are cursed because we are Palestinians. You feel that they are taking everything away from you, not just the land. Your very existence here—we can no longer move beyond our immediate neighborhood. I feel dehumanized by all of this.

The next day I took the long, circuitous route to Abu Dis to try to begin to get a sense of the scale of the wall in Jerusalem. About five kilometers from the center of Jerusalem, Abu Dis was until 1967 classified as a village in the East Jerusalem District. Israel quickly expanded the municipal boundaries of Jerusalem, annexing seventy square kilometers, encompassing East Jerusalem and over twenty-five Palestinian villages. The northwest part of Abu Dis became part of Jerusalem. Residents of Abu Dis have an array of identity cards: some have a Jerusalem identity, some a West Bank identity, and some still carry Jordanian passports.

The wall that separates West Bank Palestinians from Jerusalem in Abu Dis winds through a densely populated and heavily built-up area, abutting homes, shops, mosques, and al-Quds University (see figure 1.1).[6] As I walked along the wall, a man came out of a shop to talk to me. He was a thirty-year-old carpenter, with two children and one on the way, and he was out of work because of the wall. His lamentation revealed the relationship between immiseration, despair, and contemplation of emigration:

> All my life, I have lived in Bethany and Jerusalem but I don't have a Jerusalem identity. So now I can't enter the city. But people from Russia—from anywhere—can come and live here. They don't want peace. They want power. A wall is not peace. I will not live this way—we are thinking about leaving and going to America. God sees the wrong that people are doing. Why does he let them do these things?

Over the next couple of weeks, I visited extensively with Lena, mother of two young children and a long-time Abu Dis resident. She told me:

> My children attend the YMCA summer program in Jerusalem. It should take about ten minutes by bus to reach the Y. With the wall, it takes one to two hours to go around the wall and pass through the checkpoint back into Jerusalem, but we do not have Jerusalem identity cards anyway. Before the wall,

Figure 1.1 The wall in Abu Dis. Photograph by the author.

Abu Dis was a part of Jerusalem. Our schools and doctors are there and so are many of our relatives. Now Abu Dis is divided by the wall and we are on the West Bank side, so we can't enter Jerusalem unless we have a Jerusalem identity card. So I take my children to the jump point everyday so they can go to school and now in the summer attend the Y program. This summer I hesitated to send them, but then I thought they should have a summer break and some fun like other children. They jump over the wall coming and going to their program. My best friend lives on the other side of the wall. Her children go to the same program so she picks up my kids from the jump point and takes them to the Y and then returns them to the jump point in the late afternoon, where I wait for them.

I accompanied Lena and her children to the jump point each day for a week and also spent some time there on my own. One of the few remaining crossing points between Abu Dis and Jerusalem, this *bab* (door or gate) had become what Lena called the jump point (see figure 1.2) Indeed, when I traveled between Ramallah and Abu Dis, often I would go through the *bab* to avoid taking the longer circuitous route eastward around Maale Adumin. The *bab,* really just a short section of wall, is a barricade of cement blocks, about ten feet high and fifty feet long,

Figure 1.2 The "jump point" in Abu Dis. Photograph by the author.

buttressed by a multistoried apartment building on one end and a large, fenced convent on the other. As construction of the wall reached the edges of East Jerusalem, it encountered heavily built-up areas, where considerable land is owned by a variety of churches. Instead of crossing through this land, the wall stops and starts in small stretches between properties. One of these properties was the convent, whose iron gate opened to the Jerusalem side of the wall. Sometimes the nuns left the gate open so that people could walk across the convent grounds and slip into Jerusalem. Occasionally, Israeli police would force the nuns to close it, which meant one had to climb over the wall.

Climbing the short wall or bab required clambering up a small pile of stones to reach the uneven yet quite slippery, narrow ledge that was only about six or seven inches across and about two feet long. Holding onto a cement slab, people maneuvered their bodies around the cement block. Slipping or falling into the stone patio of the building—about a twelve-foot drop—could cause serious injury. Children sometimes balked, crying that they were afraid of falling. Upon reaching the other side of the short wall or barricade, they had to scramble down another pile of stones. People lined up on both sides of the wall or barricade to wait their turn, since only one person at a time could cross. If two people tried to cross from opposite directions at same time, one of them had to back down. Women, many carrying heavy bags as well as children, hitched up their *jalabeeb* (long coats) and cautiously made their way across. The risk of falling while carrying children and bags often elicited a call from the crowd. "Help her!" usually spurred quick assistance from young men, who then passed infants, toddlers, and bags across the wall. Economic exchanges transpired, as well, particularly by shopkeepers on the Abu Dis side, who were now cut off from their suppliers on the Jerusalem side. Building materials were handed over the wall. One day, window frames, complete with the glass panes, were handed across. Another woman crossed back and forth carrying heavy boxes of ceramic tiles from the Abu Dis side to the Jerusalem side. Nonbreakable packages were sometimes tossed over the cement blocks rather than carried across, or passed by hand. Quiet murmurs of *ya latif* or *ya allah* (Oh, God) could be heard as people waited, crossed, and observed others do so. On the West Bank side, a small market had appeared to service the crowds that gathered; a vendor hawked baby chicks from a cardboard box, and another peddled cold soft drinks from a portable cooler.

The wall can be scaled at either end, though most people used the one just described. The left side had a very small opening, a slit really, and one had to hoist oneself up the sharp stone wall of the convent and then squeeze through, a feat accomplished only by the very thin, intrepid, and agile. It took a certain amount of arm strength to lift oneself up and then jump down on other side. With the agility of youth, and absent the cultural requirement of modesty, young boys displayed their bravado by blithely crossing back and forth, nimbly scaling the rocks.

Sometimes, without warning, the Israeli Border Police would pull up in their jeeps and take up position on the Jerusalem side of the wall where buses and taxis dropped off and picked up Palestinian passengers. I observed one occasion when a jeep with four or five border police loudly raced up, parked in the small area in front of the wall, and began checking those coming over the jump point to make sure they had Jerusalem identity cards. The process of selection seemed random; some were stopped; others quietly and nervously kept walking. Two young women were kept waiting for half an hour before they were allowed to proceed. At the same time, young men leaving through the convent door were not stopped. At other times, the police just sat in the jeep and shouted instructions in Hebrew through a bull horn hooked up to an amplifier that almost no one could decipher over the loud and scratchy sound system. Sometimes Arabic obscenities spilled forth. Lena explained to me that people were sometimes ordered to meet with the Israeli Intelligence Service (GSS), where they were alternately enticed and threatened to collaborate.

When school was in session, children and their parents lined up by the dozens to cross. If the Israel Border Police happened to be on the other side, they could and did send children caught without a Jerusalem identity card back. Knowing the wall would soon be sealed and thus crossing would be impossible, Lena and other parents were facing the fact that their children would have to find a new school. Medical care was also affected. Two main hospitals in Jerusalem served the residents of Abu Dis: Maqassed, at the Mount of Olives on the Jerusalem side, and another just up the street from the convent. Palestinians from Abu Dis or the West Bank who needed to go to the hospital had to apply for a permit to enter Jerusalem; or, they could cross at the jump point and risk arrest and a fine for being in Jerusalem "illegally"—that is, without a permit. Those who obtained a permit nevertheless had to go around the wall, traveling east nearly to Jericho, in the Wadi al-Nar (Valley of Fire), and then back up to Jerusalem passing through multiple checkpoints. Since many Abu Dis residents do not possess a Jerusalem identity card, it is illegal for them to be enter the city, which severly limits their access to doctors, clinics, and hospitals. One day at the jump point, I spoke with elderly blind people, crossing to go to appointments at St. John's Eye Hospital, and women with newborn babies, trying to cross the ledge to take them to see a doctor in Jerusalem. Some women in the early stages of labor were crossing as well. Both signified the depravity of indifference.

When I returned to the jump point in the summer of 2007, it was sealed. Not knowing this at the time, I took the bus to Abu Dis thinking I would avoid the Qalandia checkpoint. I had an appointment to visit the Fayyads on the Jerusalem side of Abu Dis. I barely recognized the site when I saw it. I walked the length of the wall for a while, trying to find a way through. A couple of young men were looking for a way over as well. Eventually, I gave up. As I took a bus back to Qalandia checkpoint, I left them still searching for a sliver of an opening they could crawl through. At Qalandia, I crossed on foot, took a bus to Jerusalem, and then a taxi to the Fayyad's house. When I finally reached their house—more than two hours late for our appointment—I realized I was only about a hundred yards from where I had started on the other side of the wall.

Both Hasan and Fatima were university graduates employed in professional jobs, he with a NGO in Ramallah and she in Bethlehem. Their daily lives provide insights into the way closure impacts work and family. When I first met Fatima, she was on maternity leave. Her Jerusalem identity card enabled her to "reside" in the city, while Hasan, who carried a West Bank identity card, resided "illegally" in his own home and the city of his birth. He and his mother, father, and siblings held West Bank identity cards as well, even though all had been born in Jerusalem's Old City. Hasan's family now lived on the other side of the wall in Abu Dis. In 1967, when the occupying Israeli forces conducted a census to determine who would receive Jerusalem residency, Hasan's family was staying in Azzariyya, about five hundred meters from Hasan's current home in Abu Dis, so they were not given residency. For Fatima to keep her Jerusalem residency, she had to reside within the city limits. I heard countless stories of Jerusalem residents who had married and were living outside the city's municipal limits, who subsequently lost their residency because of it. Revoking residency is a way to winnow out the Palestinian population and is a source of extreme anger and frustration for Palestinian Jerusalemites who are forced out, whereas Jews from anywhere in the world can live in the city. The Fayyads had applied for "family reunification" status, so that Hasan could acquire a Jerusalem residency and thus live legally in the city of his birth, but had been repeatedly rejected. Finally, after five years of appeals, he was given a permit to live in Jerusalem that had to be renewed every six months. His first application for renewal was rejected. Hasan said, "It is so difficult when you have lived all your life here, and suddenly you have to have a permit to live in your own home and it is denied. You are used to coming and going to your own home and work, and then suddenly that right is taken away. It was such a shock. I had a hard time." On top of structural obstacles and the permit bureaucracy, he also experienced the randomness of closure:

> At checkpoints, the soldiers don't always recognize their own laws and permits. During the last month of my six-month permit, at some checkpoints, they wouldn't accept the permit and turned me back. Why? Who knows? It is just like this! It can depend on their moods. Or, perhaps they have orders to deny access to permit holders on that particular day. One never knows from day to day what the rules are.

Hasan worked in Ramallah, and I would see him there and in his home in Jerusalem. Now that his permit had expired, his days were a logistical nightmare; he was uncertain from one day to the next whether or not he would be able to go home to his family that evening. To mount an appeal, a long, drawn-out process, he and Fatima had assembled a mountain of documents. Fatima gestured to a stack of papers about two feet high: water and electricity bills, proof of payment of property taxes, and the like. "They request these documents, often going back ten years," she explained, "even nursery school papers for the children—as proof of continuous residency. If you were gone for a year or two, to study for example, you can often lose your residency."

In rural areas, the wall's impact was similarly hard to avoid. Encroaching colonies, land and water expropriations, unemployment, and the immobilization of people and agricultural products, as well as colonial violence were part of everyday life. In the village of Iskaka, as the bulldozers uprooted trees to make way for the oncoming wall, a young woman shook a severed olive branch and screamed at no one in particular, "Abu Ghraib? This is a prison too." Imprisonment remains a common metaphor.

To explore the wall in rural areas, I drove with a young couple, Khaled and Leila, to Leila's village of Zawiya, south of Qalqiliya, one of three neighboring villages (the other two are Deir Ballut and Rafat) cut off by the wall. Zawiya's lands abut the newly carved-out seam zone between the Green Line and the wall. As Khaled drove, Leila stayed in constant cell phone contact with her family; they would tell her what they knew about the checkpoints that day, and she would tell them our location. We encountered our first obstacle soon after leaving Ramallah, which entailed a twenty-minute drive up a steep, narrow, unpaved path, gouged out with huge holes and littered with hefty boulders. The Israeli authorities had closed one side of the road, so traffic was backed up as cars tried to go in both directions using one lane. Farther ahead, on the rocky slopes of the hill, groups of villagers were making their way from their now blocked villages to the main road, where buses waited to pick them up. Placing large dirt mounds across the only road into a village is a common practice that obstructs vehicular traffic and necessitates walking or, as the Palestinians sometimes referred to it, "enforced walking" or "getting our exercise." At the village of Abud, we had to take a fifteen-kilometer (nine-mile) detour because the road had been closed to ensure that Palestinians would not drive near a colony. All along the way, Hebrew signs were posted on telephone poles and billboards, littering the landscape. Finally, we arrived in Zawiya. The village's old, modest, white-washed mosque sat in the shadow of the glittering new stone and glass one. As we parked in front of Leila's home, her mother rushed out to greet us and started talking about the events of yesterday. "They are taking the land for the wall," she cried. Then she began telling us about those who were wounded in the village demonstration and how the Israeli soldiers and police had used a new kind of tear gas, but had taken the canisters with them so it could not be identified. Over a lunch of *maqlubah* (rice, meat, and cauliflower), Leila's oldest brother angrily related a story that highlights the cruel (il)logics of colonial occupation: "A soldier told us he wanted to help us. So we asked him what he could do. So what does he do? He ordered the bulldozer to uproot, not destroy, our olive trees; he said we could plant them somewhere else. So we asked him, 'Are you still taking this land?' He said, 'Of course.'" Her mother was in a state of near panic about the loss of the family's olive and fruit groves, which would leave them with little source of income.

After lunch, we visited the municipality and chatted with village officials. The *baladiyya* is a fairly large and airy modern office building, built with the help of the German government and the United Nations Development Programme (UNDP). Over each office door were hung colored photos of village scenes, such as the old mosque, caves and orchards, and traditional arched stone houses. A green, red, white, and black felt map of Palestine, with names of the cities and towns embroidered in sequins, adorned a wall in the mayor's office. Above it was a mother-of-pearl replica of the Dome of the Rock. Leila remarked that these items had been made by Palestinian prisoners. As I admired the national icons,

Khaled murmured, "The mayor was shot in the leg and imprisoned by the Israelis during the first intifada."

I asked one of the village officials about yesterday's demonstrations.

> We only knew a week ago what was happening. And then, they were already surveying the area and getting ready to dig it up. An Israeli military officer gave us maps of our lands in Hebrew and then they put up signs around the fields marking the route of the wall. Ninety percent of our land is going to be taken. We have 24,000 dunums; they are taking 20,000, plus the width of the wall area. These areas are planted with olive trees.

Pouring over a village map, he pointed to a plot of empty land. "They could have put the wall on uncultivated plots," he said. "Moreover, now we have no area in which to graze the animals." When I asked about what legal measures they were taking, the villagers laughed cynically. An elderly man leaned forward on his cane and explained,

> Here is how it works—we know the procedure from other villages that have already lost their lands. Israel tells us to go to court if we don't like the situation. But we go to court and the court refuses to hear the case. The land has been declared a closed military area, and then it becomes the property of the state. Thus they legalize the expropriation of our land. If they offer money and we accept it, then they say we sold it and it is a legal sale rather than expropriated. So we know we cannot accept money for our land otherwise we have "sold" it to them.

In response to my question about the economic situation and the state of agriculture, one of the mayor's colleagues replied, "Before the 2001 intifada, most villagers worked in Israel. With employment closed in Israel, they went back to agriculture, mostly olive cultivation. Now land is being lost. So we are left with nothing." "What about the future?" I asked. "What future! There is no future! In some places the wall is only forty meters (thirteen feet) from our houses; the farthest is six hundred meters (nearly two thousand feet). "We can't even dispose of our garbage—now there is no place to take garbage. Soon they won't allow us to breathe. We are three villages in a bottleneck. We have a new school. The wall will only be forty meters from the school which limits its outside areas." As for the state of the village's public services, "They have taken seven springs that provided us with water." After a lull in the conversation, someone said flatly, "They purposely started building on cultivated land. Why not build it on the 1967 line?" Another chimed in, "This is not a security fence; it is a means to steal land. They will bring the settlers from Gaza here. Then they will bring Jews from France." The conversation ended with this sad comment from a colleague who said, "The Israeli military told me: 'This is Israeli land and you should be kicked out.'" As we walked out of the municipal building into the bright sun, the village was still except for the sound of bulldozers churning in the distance and the whirring of the buzz saws. As we approached a bluff overlooking the olive orchards, it got louder. The whirring drone in the soundscape signals the coming of colonies and the wall, and as did the yanking up of the carefully planted and tended olive trees. I later heard that the village did get back some of its land, but the trees were gone.

A young man from the municipality who was walking with us around the village spat out, "If the Israelis were really attached to this land, they would not uproot all these trees." The olive tree is a paramount symbol in Palestinian culture, signifying rootedness and sustenance. Paradoxically, the Israelis both uproot and plant. By planting trees, which they do feverishly when staking out new colonies, they seek to claim rootedness and a territorial-based identity. It is part and parcel of a conscious project to craft a connection to place by literally sending down roots into the soil. In 2010, when Prime Minister Netanyahu planted a tree in the Maale Adumim colony and proclaimed that Israel would never give up the colonies, he was literally and symbolically sinking roots, staking a claim of ownership.[7] Planting and uprooting operate in tandem: to claim space for the Zionist project, Palestinian traces must be effaced and their material and symbolic links to place severed.

Qalqiliya (pop. 45,000), a medium-sized town on the Green Line, resembles a bottleneck. A funnel-like checkpoint forms the top of the bottleneck and a series of tunnels from the south that opened in 2005 are the only way in and out of this town surrounded by the wall and by "closed areas" accessible only to those with permits. The tunnels made it possible for Israelis from the nearby Alfe Menashe colony to travel on their bypass roads without being inconvenienced by the sight of Palestinians on the roads. As we drove through the tunnel, my host, a young man from the nearby village of Jayyous, commented, "We are becoming like rats." Once a relatively prosperous market town in a rich agricultural area, Qalqiliya had the earmarks of a ghost town. Many shops were shuttered because businesses had left, and about half the population was gone as well, as was evident from the eerily quiet streets. Qalqiliya has thirty-five aquifers; over half were now on the Israeli side of the wall. A close look at a map of the wall route and colony placement leaves little doubt as to the fate of Qalqiliya: with the wall on its western border with the Green Line, bypass roads to the northwest and southeast, the colonies of Zufin to the northeast and Alfe Menashe to the southeast, and a bottleneck entry or exit (plus the tunnels), strangulation was evident. The village of Habla to the southeast was no longer inhabited; with its lands in the seam zone, it was now a collection of empty dwellings. By gradually diluting Qalqiliya's population and the villages in its vicinity, already classified as Area C and thus under full Israeli control and planning, the colonies of Alfe Menashe, already positioned in a straight east-west line with the Immanuel colony, and encompassing four colonies in between, could eventually be directly linked with Ariel, the large colony to the south. The route of the wall, colony building activity, bypass roads, and the multitude of barriers to mobility in the area indicated a vision of a knitted together Jewish landscape.

Walaja, a village southeast of Jerusalem on the Green Line, was another example of near complete enclavization similar to Qalqiliya. The wall blocked the sun and there was one checkpoint and gate to enter and exit. While touring the village, my host, Bahij, born and raised in Walaja and a participant in its frequent demonstrations against the wall, described what was happening:

> Actually, our village should be inside [the Green Line] but they don't want the people, they want the land—we are supposed to dream about somewhere else because they want us out. We are surrounded and they see everything in the village—they see when you shop—what shops you enter and who you visit. We are under surveillance all the time. We have soldiers in the village all the time. There are cameras going all the time. So imagine, the Jews want you out! We are near the Green line—you can't see it but you know this is the line and you are always thinking they are going to take it [the village]. It is very stressful.

Bahij and his small cohort rarely ventured beyond the village. Unemployed, they passed the days drinking coffee, chatting, and idling away the time. Yet they also actively participated in Walaja's frequent demonstrations with the attendant tear-gassings and beatings.

The wall carves out a "seam zone," an enclave of sorts, wedged between the wall and the 1949 Armistice Line, commonly referred to as the Green Line. Figures vary, but it was generally acknowledged that around sixty-five thousand Palestinians lived in the seam zone in 2005 (Morris 2006, 30). Military Order 378 (October 2003) declared the seam a "closed military area." This designation forbade Palestinian entry or exit without permission. The wall's original planned path would have included on the Israeli side around two hundred thousand Palestinians living in the seam zone. Revision of the wall's route reduced the number to between fifty thousand and sixty-five thousand. Farmers in the seam zone must have a permit to pass through any of the over fifty military-run gates that dot the length of barrier. Gates can only be opened by soldiers, who are supposed to open them in the morning and close them at four o'clock in the afternoon. Sometimes they do not open them for days. Seam residents need one permit to live in their homes and another to farm their lands. Since few permits were being issued in the 2000s, thousands of olive trees remained unharvested. In addition, it was difficult for farmers to sell their produce because the gates were not always opened in a timely fashion. Only Israeli citizens or those eligible for citizenship could travel freely through this closed zone. The pressure on Palestinians didn't end there. Farmers had to show proof of ownership to obtain a permit to enter their lands; often, land is registered in the father's name and the sons work the fields. Each son must then obtain a deed of ownership to get a permit to enter the land to cultivate it. The difficulty of obtaining permits and the irregularity of the gates opening mean that more land will go uncultivated. It can then be "legally" declared uncultivated and expropriated. Here, too, the goal seems to be to winnow out the population by imposing an economically unviable situation.

With a small group of Palestinians and foreigners, I traveled to the seam zone just south of the town of Qalqiliya, in 2008. It was truly a space of desolation. We approached a gate in the village of Ras 'Atiya, which at first seemed unmanned. We spotted a square, white house isolated behind the coils of barbed-wire fencing. As we neared the gate, an elderly man came out and opened it so we could enter. Within minutes, four soldiers pulled up in a jeep. Guns drawn, they ordered us to get out and threatened to arrest the elderly man for letting us in. In response to a radio call for reinforcements, another jeep-load of young soldiers soon followed. Members of our small group were yelling at the soldiers: "Shame on you," "He is your father's age," and "Think of the future." Some of the soldiers looked sheepish, but finally they seemed to have had enough and herded us back through the gate with their guns. As we stood watching, they gave the old man a fine for opening the gate. In the background I could see a row of trailers, the telltale signs of a coming colony and the illegal transfer of land.

Several days later, I visited 'Azzun 'Atma, a village cut off from its agricultural fields and school by the wall. Its population of 1,500 had to get permission to enter or exit. At the checkpoint at the entrance to the village, one that the OCHA (the UN Office for the Coordination of Humanitarian Affairs) labels a "fully-staffed internal checkpoint," villagers had to pass through a body-scanning machine located in a one-room cinderblock structure—the villagers described it as an "x-ray machine" and said it was "dangerous—it causes headaches." Permits to live in the village had to be acquired from the Israeli Civilian Administration office in a nearby colony and were subject to renewal every six months. From the checkpoint that governed entry and exit, with its coils of barbed wire and looming watchtower, one could see the colony on the higher ground, overlooking the village school. 'Azzun 'Atma residents complained of difficulty in accessing medical care; the closest town is Qalqiliya, but with the checkpoint closing at night and reopening in the morning, and with the long waits to exit, getting emergency medical care was nearly impossible. These isolated and shrinking places may become unlivable.

Thus enclaves and the physical and bureaucratic apparatuses that structure them are a new means of containing those excluded from the colonial Israeli state. I have argued elsewhere that in these gray zones "inhabitants are neither refugees nor IDPS and thus highlight the limitations of current concepts" (Peteet 2016, 2).

Wall Aesthetics

Two graffiti on the wall near Jerusalem catch the eye and the imagination: "From Warsaw ghetto to Abu Dis ghetto" and "Welcome to Soweto" resonate with multiple audiences—international, Palestinian, and Israeli. For Palestinians, these graffiti graphically render an historical awareness that draws on the power of comparison across time and space. The Palestinian and Israeli sides of walls are radically different in meaning and actual appearance. The Palestinian side is ugly and menacing, an imprisoning monstrosity, threatening worse things to come. This iconic symbol of separation, isolation, and subjugation also inspired artistic expression, served as a communicative tableau, and provided fodder as well as a canvas for humor. It is a large empty canvas on which both foreigners and Palestinians write graffiti, often highly colorful and woeful as well as satirical, and paint elaborate murals of protest, opinions, analysis, commentary, hopes, dreams, despair, and solidarity. Above all, this public blackboard has been a medium for polysemic political commentary, its stone slabs registering anger, defiance, and grief.

During the first intifada, graffiti was a "print weapon" (Peteet 1996, 139). In that era of simpler communication technologies, it announced strike days and issued directives. Graffiti no longer performs in this way (Peteet 2015). With enclavization, it is more directed to the world outside Palestine, and a fair amount of it is written by foreigners expressing solidarity with Palestinians, especially in urban areas. Arabic is no longer the main language, replaced now by a cacophonous polyglot. Graffiti can be seen at heavily trafficked sites, where there is fairly easy access to the wall. There was no Israeli response to this writing, no speeding jeeps full of soldiers come to blacken it out and possibly arrest the authors, as was common during the first intifada.

Some graffiti was ironic and mocking, such as "CTRL-ALT-DELETE," and could be understood by most people. Others were bald warnings: "We will return." Comparisons were common, too—"Bethlehem looks like Warsaw ghetto"—and they encapsulated Palestinian historical awareness and the power of comparison. Some graffiti bluntly stated perceptions of the wall, such as "Wall = Horror," "Jerusalem is stronger than Apartheid," and "Wall =/Peace," which draw on comparison and ethics. The following little gem draws upon historical memory of particular instances of violence and displacement, locating the wall on a trajectory of moments in Palestinian history:

Deir Yassin 1948
Sabra and Shatila 1982
Hebron 1994
Jenin 2000
Wall 2003

"Scotland Supports Palestine," "Seattle Supports Palestine," "Ireland Supports Palestine," or "Together in Stopping the Wall" were messages of solidarity from visiting delegations. A sense of plaintive despair is apparent in this French graffito: "Ou est le monde?" (Where is the world?). Christian visitors have also left messages: "Love God, Love People," "God leads us to peace," and "English Christians want peace." "Faisons tomber le mur d'Apartheid" (Let the apartheid wall fall) speaks with an international voice, invoking the fall of the Berlin Wall and the wall's apartheid-like separation. The hardship imposed by the wall and appeals to consciousness were voiced at Abu Dis: "Children want to go to the schools" or "Who wants to be children in a jail?" Some are messages are clearly written by Palestinians, such as "We have the same blood." "Witness the Jewish shame" and "No for another Wailing Wall" directly appeal to a Jewish consciousness. The simple grafitto "Stop the Wall" is ubiquitous. Some register a simple refusal: "No Wall."

Israelis rarely see the graffiti; it is out of their line of sight. In a few areas graffiti appeared on the wall running along a road traveled by Israeli motorists, such as the road southeast to the Allenby Bridge and the Dead Sea, its blunt commentary was evident in the single word "ghetto" neatly stenciled in large angular black script every couple of hundred feet on this otherwise blank canvas.

Palestinians found humor as well as pride in some of the now well-known and well-circulated meta-linguistic images, such as the large stencil, by the internationally acclaimed muralist Banksy, of a pig-tailed girl being lifted up to the sky by the bunch of balloons she is holding (see figure 1.3). On the wall near Qalandia checkpoint, it suggests the freedom to soar above the ugliness and repressiveness of the wall and a will to persevere. Another mural depicts a ladder rising up to the top of the wall. Some murals speak to absurdity: in one a soldier checks the identity card of a donkey. Others point to the future, such as the stencil of children riding an escalator up the wall; below it an oversized bug topples a line of dominoes that resemble the wall's concrete slabs.[8]

On the Israel side another aesthetic is at work. Near the Gilo and Modin Illit colonies, the wall is neatly landscaped; a rising horizontal dirt mound is planted with flowers, diminishing the perception of height. A pastoral tableau of green fields, colorful flowers, and tidy white houses has a sanitizing effect, masking the desolation on the other side. In late 2010, the wall in Bil'in clearly displayed this two-sided aesthetic: the Palestinian side was stark cement, while the Israeli side was painted to look like a brick terrace, in alternating shades of brown, beige, and white, ironically mimicking the terraced landscape of Palestine. Parts of the wall in Jerusalem were painted in soft pastels, depicting a viaduct-like set of painted arches framing green fields and blue skies. These aesthetic devices were conscious attempts to disguise the reality of walled separation.

Figure 1.3 Wall mural by
Banksy.

The wall has become thematic in other cultural and artistic venues as well. In a watercolor by American artist Ellen O'Grady, displayed at the exhibit "Breaching the Wall," mounted by the Jerusalem Fund in Washington, DC, in May 2011, a somber Bethlehem home and its car-repair business are surrounded on three sides by the wall; looming dark clouds allude to the devastation to come. A lone male figure, his hands jammed in his pants pockets, stands forlornly on the street. The barbed-wire topped wall is the backdrop against which the house, the lone figure, and two stray cats are positioned. Palestinian artist Najat el Khairy's painting *Wall, Return of the Soul* re-creates the floral, cross-stitch patterns of traditional Palestinian red, white, and black embroidery on the wall's cement panels. The exhibit catalogue aptly frames the panels as engraving identity on the wall built on Palestinian land.

The wall has inspired a rich body of humor and sarcasm. Jokes circulate about people being lifted over the wall with a crane. A humorous postcard with the caption "the Palestinian Daily Olympics" depicts a young man pole vaulting over the wall; on the the flip side the same young man is running furiously from Israeli soldiers in a jeep. When handyman Abu Mustafa came to fix the windows in my apartment, he started telling me how difficult life had become because he and his wife were cut off from their families in Bethlehem. My landlord shouted from the other room, "Hey, we are still allowed to breathe!"

Dystopic Spaces

As dystopic spaces, enclaves can be contradictory, fostering intimacy and creativity as well as isolation and despair. I use *dystopia* less to refer to a degenerative process and more to an exclusivist utopian project that spelled disaster for the indigenous population and transformed their terrain into dysfunctional, unsustainable places. In other words, there are multiple dialectics at work here. The contradictions of enclavization were astutely seized upon by American writer Alice Walker (2009) on her trip to Gaza:

> Rolling into Gaza I had a feeling of homecoming. There is a flavor to the ghetto. To the Bantustan. To the "rez." To the "colored section." In some ways it is surprisingly comforting . . . When I lived in segregated Eatonton, Georgia I used to breathe normally only in my own neighborhood, only in the black section of town. Everywhere else was too dangerous.

Her words also describe the intimacy of Ramallah. Once a village, it is now a cosmopolitan, socially heterogeneous, modern urban center (Taraki 2008, 7), where the PA headquarters are located. Palestinians generally recognize it as a somewhat isolated bubble. I met Nahla, an accomplished fifty-year-old artist, for coffee at one of Ramallah's new cafés. She sighed as she told me she had not been out of Ramallah for more than five years. Somewhat defensively, she continued, "Ramallah is my little world. I don't have a permit to go to Jerusalem and with so many checkpoints I can't go anywhere in the West Bank. So I have my group of friends here and we are very close. They have become like family to me." When I next see Fatima in Jerusalem she dejectedly tells me: "I have not seen my close friends from Bir Zeit University for many years now. We haven't met each other's husbands or seen each other's children. What kind of life is this?" Maneuvering through the checkpoints is too difficult with small children, so she remains in what she calls her "small world." One quickly gets a sense of physically and socially shrinking space. Nahla's friend Deema, a physiotherapist who has not left Ramallah in about four years, echoes these sentiments when she tells me somewhat cheerfully, "I am happy in my little cage. I just like to be at home and safe with my family. I refuse the humiliation and hassle of checkpoints." Fatima remarks, "When I go to Bethlehem people ask, 'How are things in Jerusalem?' They haven't been here in years now." Bethlehem is ten kilometers (six miles) from Jerusalem. Confined and quarantined, Palestinians are active subjects creating social worlds, however small and contained. Yet the unbridled joy at being in open space underscores just how profound the effect of constricted space and constrained mobility is. The writer Raja Shehadeh (2008, 138) describes his reaction to open space in the time of closure: "We felt euphoric. Being stuck in Ramallah, surrounded as it was with checkpoints at every exit, the experience of open sky, made us giddy with joy." Shehadeh writes with nostalgic poignancy of walks (*sarhat*) through the hills and valleys—"To go on a *sarha* was to roam freely, at will, without restraint" (ibid., 2).

Closure blurs the line between the ordinary and crisis; new social forms have arisen around the parameters imposed by prolonged crisis. The internal dynamic in the enclave of Gaza was evident in the mundane as well as the spectacular, from simply proceeding with daily life to the infamous tunneling under the wall that kept alive trade networks and the garnering of international support, as evidenced by attempts by flotillas to break the Israeli-imposed blockade. Thus enclaves were more than simply inert zones of incarceration where ordinary life proceeds apace. Yet, their impact on an already politically fragmented Palestinian national movement was detectible. In my interview with a former political activist, he rued: "How can we build a movement if we can't meet? Now there are the Palestinians of Nablus, the Palestinians of Gaza, the Palestinians of Ramallah, etc. Each is living in his own area, living his own life, not knowing the others."

Enclavization poses a comparative and semantic challenge. Although enclaves share some general parameters with such confining spatial and disciplinary structures as the ghetto, reservation, prison, Bantustans, or the gulag, these do not quite capture its specificity. Enclaves share family features with refugee camps as well (Peteet 2016). However, each remains a distinct spatial device, with its own forms of governance and relations with the state. Yet both work to distance and contain those deemed not to belong to the state. Refugee camps serve as warehouses of the excluded, while the enclaves immobilize their inhabitants and contain them spatially. The enclaves are hedged with ambiguity as to their spatial parameters and sovereignty over them. The literature on gated communities has some purchase here. Having the military capacity to contain regional threats and with the erection of the wall, Israel increasingly resembles a "fortified haven" (Burg 2008, 16). A description of the gated community as "an elementary system of bio-segregation . . . compatible only with thinking of oneself, to the point of self-obsession and fear of the least physical contact" (Agier 2008, 60) applies. Gated communities are flourishing globally as elites and states partition and barricade space in an attempt to exclude and lock out the anticipated violence of the have-nots, cast alternatively as criminals or terrorists. Unlike gated communities, where "the outside space is left for those who cannot afford to go in" (Calderia 1996, 319), exclusion in Palestine is based on a hierarchical and ethnic-religious-national distribution of citizenship that excludes Palestinians in the OPTs. In gated communities in Los Angeles and Brazil, for example, movement by the excluded is not hindered *outside* the gates; they are simply not allowed unauthorized and unmonitored access inside the gated enclaves. Palestinian circulation, however, not only halts at the gates of the fortressed state, it is also hindered outside the gated colonies, within and between areas in a shrinking Palestine.

The term *enclave* can seem neutral, unlike *Bantustan* and *ghetto*, which are freighted with negative connotations. Yet enclaves are socio-spatial formations that similarly arrange inequality. *Gulag* captures the arbitrariness of some of closure's mechanisms; but economic factors limit comparisons with the ghetto. The economic integration, however unequal, of Jews in pre–WWII European ghettos, of blacks in the ghettos of the United States, and of the Bantustans in South Africa, is not paralleled in Palestinian enclaves, where circulation outside and between their confines is severely circumscribed. Economic opportunities are limited by immobilization but also by the decline of demand for Palestinian labor in Israel. "Stigma, constraint, spatial confinement, and institutional containment" are defining elements of the European ghetto (Wacquant 2004, 2). Institutional containment is another aspect of enclaves that departs from comparisons with ghettos. Rather than being obliterated, as Jewish institutions in Europe were, Palestine's institutions and infrastructure are gradually being strangled by severe obstacles to mobility that prevent both personnel and goods from reaching the enclaved areas. Jews were allowed mobility outside the ghetto, albeit temporally circumscribed, for they played a critical economic role (ibid.). In addition, ghetto has been used in reference to urban concentrations of African Americans in northern US cities maintained in large part by widely observed social patterns of segregation and the potentially violent consequences of transgression, rather than by actual physical structures.

Anthropologist Loic Wacquant (2004, 3) argues that the ghetto is a "*Janus-faced institution* as it serves opposite functions for the two collectives that it binds in a relation of asymmetric dependency. For the dominant category, its rationale is to *confine and control*"; for the confined, "it is an *integrative and protective device*" that "fosters consociation and community building" (ibid.). In Gaza, Alice Walker was gripped by that visceral sense of being in familiar territory—one of confinement and marginality yet also intimacy. With sieges, questions abound: How is community building or the sense of unity that arises from confinement expressed and maintained? How severely stretched and compromised are networks of solidarity such as kin or have they been newly reinvigorated, or reconfigured? In the face of extremely punitive incarceration and continued destruction, can Gazans claim pride in community building and cultural florescence as did some pre-1960s African American urban communities and prewar European ghettos? Whereas the ghetto can serve to enhance group identity and cohesion, it remains to be seen how West Bank and Gazan identities and social cohesion are currently being contoured.

When the ghetto loses it economic function for the dominant group, the inhabitants run the risk of being warehoused or annihilated (Wacquant 2004). Native American reservations, semiautonomous zones within a sovereign state, may be a more appropriate spatial analogy with Palestinian enclaves. Their land rather than their labor were coveted by white settlers, although Natives Americans were eventually incorporated as US citizens.

In the early 2000s, comparisons with apartheid came to the fore. Organizing society and the polity and allocating rights and access to resources on the basis of race, in one case, and national, ethnic and religious factors, in the other, formed the basis of comparison. The 1973 International Convention on the Suppression and Punishment of the Crime of Apartheid (UNGA Resolution 3068) prohibits acts "designed to divide the population . . . by the creation of separate reserves and ghettos for the members of racial groups, the prohibition of mixed marriages . . . [and] the expropriation of landed property." As an institutionalized system of racial exclusion, the definition of apartheid is neither spatially nor temporally bound. Yet comparative projects can be fraught with the perils of oversimplification and historical decontextualization. Elsewhere I have critically examined the Apartheid-Israel analogy, particularly the political-economy of labor and demographics (Peteet 2009, 2016b). When Israel depended on Palestinian workers, especially in pre-Oslo Gaza, comparisons with Bantustans had resonance (see Li 2008; Locke and Stewart 1985). With the shrinking demand for their labor, Palestinians were increasingly expendable. Palestine's fragments do resemble the spatial array of the Bantustans in South Africa. However, under Apartheid, there was actually close contact between majority blacks and minority whites, in some cases intimate, as blacks cleaned white homes, tended white children, and labored in the mines. A legal edifice elaborated the parameters of interaction as well as black mobility, residency, and employment. The Bantustans segregated, contained, and controlled cheap black labor. Palestinian enclaves separate and immiserate to engender conditions favorable to voluntary migration. Without a publicly circulated plan to carve out enclaves, they constitute a gray zone, with ambiguous and shifting borders. Thus, comparisons between the enclaves and Bantustans are limited by differing political economies, primarily the organization of labor, and colonial demographics: a white minority in South Africa and a more even population ratio in Palestine/Israel. To sum up, beyond the fortressed state, Palestinians are simultaneously locked in and out, stranded in a web of immobilizing devices. In this archipelago, Palestinians occupy the indeterminate gray spaces in-between as the colonies are made contiguous with Israel and connected to each other. The spaces in-between enclaves are zones of uncertainty and risk and passage through them generates an ever-present anticipation of humiliation and violence.

Abandonment

As the bulldozers uprooted the olive trees, women in Iskaka cried mournfully: "What will we eat?" again invoking the sustenance required for life. When and under what conditions does disposability occur? Sequestered behind the wall, Palestinians were not visible to most Israelis. I struck up a conversation with Aisha, an engaging young woman with three small children, while we were waiting for a checkpoint to open. We sat on the hard ground, in the cold and wind, for several hours, as she tried to calm her restless and increasingly hungry children. With measured deliberation, she explained: "Closure is not about security. It is about numbers—of them and us. They are going to lock us in these walled prisons and then they won't care how many children we have. We will be behind walls and left to our own devices. Nobody will care what becomes of us."

The historical record is full of disposable people and spaces of abandonment, with varying degrees of distance, penetrability, and fixity, including asylums, refugee camps, leper colonies, reservations, and concentration camps, among others. In a neoliberal age with a dwindling social safety net; a demand for cheap, mobile labor; and growing inequality, surplus people proliferate. Minimal protection and vulnerability characterize life in these spaces of abandonment. Do these differ from spaces of maximum control, such as prisons or detention centers, places often associated with disciplinary regimes, in which there is the potential to reconstitute life? Abandonment is a form of excision from the social order; for those under occupation, it is unfolding in the space of home. With enclaves, the question of responsibility looms large. Oslo did not end the occupation, as Selma cynically reminded me, "The PA is a misnomer. There is only one authority here. Anything with a cost, such as education and health, was transferred to the PA." Israel has absolved itself of its responsibility by rejecting the classification of their rule as an occupation, and argues instead that the PA and the international donor community bear responsibility.

What are the early warning signs of abandonment? What policies, actions, and ideologies are its precursors? Confinement is suggestive of bare life, as are refugee rations, and talk of putting Palestinian on a diet by restricting the quantity and types of food allowed into Gaza.[9] Disposability and abandonment are observable at checkpoints when even women in labor and ambulances carrying critically ill patients are kept waiting. Soldiers often avoid eye contact with

Palestinians, speaking to them through plexiglass, taking or handing back iden-tity cards through trays, and barking commands to "get down," "wait," "sit," or "shut up." I have passed through checkpoints where soldiers or private-security guards confiscated groceries from Palestinians, telling them they aren't allowed to carry that much food. The nonrecognition of, or indifference to, their physi-cal presence, rights, and humanity combined with the hypervigilance over their movements captures the paradox of abandonment.

In anthropologist Joao Biehl's (2005, 1) poignant ethnography of Vita, a Bra-zilian site housing the mentally ill, drug addicted, and AIDs afflicted, an infor-mant describes it a "dump site of human beings." Biehl calls it "the end-station . . . where people go when they are no longer considered people" (ibid.). Such sites are not unusual in a neoliberal age—shanty towns, squatter settlements, poverty belts, and displacement centers abound. In spaces of abandonment, inhabitants lose some of their human status; Bielh writes of the "ex-human" and the "social death" that precedes "biological death" (ibid., 52):

> The concept I worked with most hesitantly was that of the ex-human. I use this term neither to posit an abstract condition nor to upset and generate a re-sponse coded in our now familiar language of human rights. One of the main problems in human rights discourse is the a priori assertion of an irreducible common humanity. . . . In the face of that assertion, the term "ex-human" helped me to make relative the claims of a generic humanness and to think about the contingency and pervasiveness of the forms of human life I found in Vita.

In the context of settler colonialism and counterinsurgency, abandonment crystallizes as a sort of collateral damage. Discipline, control, and abandonment are triangulated rather than points on a spectrum of more of one and less of the other. Humanness exists on a gradient, and some lives are highly authorized, with a full complement of rights, and others are relegated to the margins. A cable from the US embassy in Tel Aviv succinctly summarizes what I will call "cali-brated abandonment": "Israel officials have confirmed . . . on multiple occasions that they intend to keep the Gazan economy on the brink of collapse without quite pushing it over the edge" (quoted in Khalili 2013, 183). Palestinians hover at the margins of abandonment, on "a diet" but not completely "over the edge." Theirs are managed and calibrated lives of misery.

There is a history and a spatio-political logic to the abandonment of the Pal-estinians. Memories of the time before separation are narratively juxtaposed to separation, dispossession, and abandonment. A conversation with eighty-two-year-old Um Hani illuminated the connections between past, present, and pos-sibilities for the future and a refusal to self-deport. I asked about her recollections of the Mandelbaum Gate, which divided East and West Jerusalem between 1948 and 1967:

> Everything in our lives is made difficult and it is all because of Sharon.[10] He must take care—is he not afraid of God? He thinks of things to do to us while he sleeps. Then he wakes up and he does these things to us. But going back to Mandelbaum—after we came to Ramallah in 1948 from Jaffa, I had an aunt who stayed in Haifa. She used to come to see us on Christmas Day. She was only allowed to come at Christmas. When she died in Haifa, we were not allowed to go to her funeral. We used to meet her at Mandelbaum Gate. It was terrible to see all the people there crying, shouting, some of them fainting. They hadn't seen their families in a long time. It was a miserable situation. There were so many people pressing against each other that it was hard to see the gate. Only on Christmas were Christians allowed to enter Jordan [East Jerusalem] through the Gate. Muslims were not allowed. Only Christians. Christmas Day only. Once a year.
>
> I was educated in Jerusalem at St. George's School. I was a boarder. Many of my fellow boarders and friends were Jews. In this school, we had Arabs and Jews and up until now, some Israelis are my friends. Up until now. I want to tell you a story that happened a month ago. They still call and invite me to go to the sea because they know how much I love it. One of my friends died last week and she told her son David: "Make a CD"—he is a very good musician. He made a song about peace, and before she died—she told David: "I want you to go to my friend Manal [Um Hani] in Ramallah and let her hear it because we all want peace." She was on her deathbed, imagine. I like Jews very much. I lived with them. We were in boarding school—we used to sleep in the same room together and eat together.
>
> We will never leave here no matter what they do with us. We have had enough walls, closures, gates, permits, and the loss of homes. We are going to stay. Where can we go? It is finished. We don't have money. We have nowhere to go. We have to stay here whatever they do to us. So whatever Sharon does with us, we don't care anymore. We are so strong in our determination. Still, I always dream of Jaffa. I couldn't find my family's house. It had disappeared.

Palestinian abandonment clearly differs from abandonment of the marginalized, the ill, and the destitute in ghettos and shanty towns. In the enclaves, there are rich and poor, the well and unwell. What people in these zones have in common is that they live under occupation by an expansionist colonial state.

Silencing and forced invisibility have accompanied abandonment. Journalists have been hindered, press reports are censored, and when Palestinians' voices are circulated or images of violence against them do slip out they are roundly denied as exaggerations, anti-Semitic, or justified in the name of security. In elaborating on Vita, Biehl (2005, 11) writes that "one is faced with a human condition in which voice can no longer become action. No objective conditions exist for that to happen. The human being is left all by herself, knowing that no one will respond, that nothing will crack open the future." However marginalized, Palestinians do, like Biehl's interlocutor, narrate themselves and, in doing so, refuse to become ex-humans.

Conclusion

Both Israelis and Palestinians live behind walls, though the meaning for each is vastly different. As Fatima pointedly, but gently, reminded me when I casually made this comparison, "Yes, but they have the whole world—we are in a jail, in many jails." The wall starkly etches into the landscape unmistakable lines of inclusion, exclusion, difference, repression, and privilege. The wall is a signpost, conveying a lack of interest in settling grievances; it references a desire to transform the demographic landscape and undoubtedly attempts to bring about ethnically homogenous and exclusivist spaces. In giving rise to spatial enclaves and trapped bodies, the wall has made stunningly visible the inscription, organization, and management of inequality. Closure prevents Palestinian circulation and engenders a surplus and abandoned population. Ultimately, it ensures the triumph of space over population. Most significantly, in Palestinians eyes, the conditions of disorder and calibrated chaos spawned by separation and closure are intended to induce emigration or self-deportation by a people perceived as foreigners in their own homes.

Although it has been well argued that the contemporary era signals a shift from discipline to control in the OPTs (Gordon 2008), I would draw attention to their concurrency, although their relative weight has shifted. Closure both disciplines the body and heightens controls as the body reaches zones where Israeli and Palestinian space edge up against each other. With their laboring bodies less in demand in Israel, Palestinians have become superfluous requiring simultaneous discipline and control. Rather than conceptually disaggregate these categories as distinct modes of power, both ultimately enable separation and immiseration.

Enclavization is more than simply a spatial by-product of colony building or a tool of expansion; enclaves spatially demarcate an "us" and a "them," rendering the colonized legible and manageable. In addition, enclaves render daily life unlivable and stifle political opposition. Enclavization imposes another level of spatial and social disconnection much as did the occupations and legal regimes accompanying the 1948 and 1967 wars. Palestinians are literally stranded in space. With enclavization, social life contracted and a localization of politics is discernable. In effect, spatial fragmentation and immobilities can rupture the possibility of collective action and identity.

With carceral politics, Palestinians under occupation join a global coterie of those expelled from the social order. Enclaves share features with the camp, the prison, reservations, Bantustans, and ghettos in intent, effect, and experience while retaining qualitative differences. Each form is distinctive, but they do consititute, I would argue, a field of analysis bound together across time and space with discernable continuity.

The active relationality of mobilities was unambiguously apparent in the unimpeded mobility of the Jewish Israelis and the obstructed mobility of the Palestinians. The wall was a new pillar in the construction of the mobile, sovereign, and rights-bearing Israeli citizen and the immobilized, rights-deprived Palestinian. In a fortressed world, time and space become unbearably stretched as distances of a few miles can take on paramount scale and each side of the wall experiences distinct temporalities and mobilities. To maintain distance and manage inequality, the Palestinian body is heavily monitored. The next two chapters explore the way an assemblage of immobilizing devices such as the road system, permits, and checkpoints saturate the everyday fabric of life with uncertainty and anticipation.

2 Mobility

Legibility, Permits, and Roads

IN A VOICE INFLECTED with measured anger, dark-haired, vivacious twenty-four-year-old Arwa described her journey to work:

> I work across the street from our house in Beit Hanina. Once the Israelis divided the main street with cement blocks and then placed checkpoints on it, I could no longer walk across the street. It was less than five minutes away! Instead, I had to go up to the Qalandia checkpoint, and go all the way around and then back down to the other side of the street in Beit Hanina. This took well over half an hour, sometimes more, to go a distance of less than five minutes! Sometimes, the soldiers would ask me for a date. One even told me he would let me cross the checkpoint if I would just sit and talk to him in a small room. I refused to do such a thing. I preferred to take the long way around.

Arwa's narrative of mobility denied, constrained, and ultimately reconfigured serves as a point of departure to explore how Palestinians live with and variously accommodate, subvert, resist, refuse, and negotiate constraints on their mobility. In Palestine, mobility's scope and speed is unambiguously differentially allocated. This chapter and the next explore Palestinian mobility as it has been shaped by physical structures, such as the wall, the segregated road network and the numerous checkpoints that at once impede and funnel it, and administrative devices such as the permit system and identity cards.[1] These two chapters flesh out the ways in which space, mobility, and subjectivity are mutually constitutive. Although these spatial and administrative devices are deeply entangled, they are disaggregated here to explore their specificity.

When religious studies scholar Sigurd Bergmann (2008, 21) wrote, "Could one restate Descartes' 'I think therefore I am' (*cogito ergo sum*) as 'I move therefore I am' (*Moveo ergo sum*), and 'I am how I move?' he linked movement and being, opening space for exploring the geography of subjectivity and habitus in a setting of pronounced disparities in mobility. In the small space of Palestine-Israel, mobilities are actively relational—on one side constrained, managed, and decelerated, and, on the other, accelerated and spatially expansive. Categories of identity, themselves imposed by the colonial regime, have been instrumentalized as an axis around which mobility is allocated. To travel in Palestine is to be caught in a slow-moving vortex of filtering by the permit system and of funneling through the ubiquitous checkpoints, and to move among spaces with varying forms of sovereignty and power. Most significantly, this geography of mobility compels a toying with concepts of subjectivity and habitus.

From 1967 to the late 1980s, mobility in and between the OPTs was not severely limited. In the wake of the first intifada (1987–93) and the gradual weaning of the Israeli economy from Palestinian labor, and Oslo's subsequent fragmentation of territory, the stage was set for closure and separation. By the late 1980s, Israel began to issue permits to workers from Gaza, and mobility between the West Bank and Gaza came under tighter restrictions. In 1991, mobility further tightened when a series of checkpoints sprang up around the entrances to Jerusalem. By 1993, checkpoints had been set up along the Green Line and between towns on the West Bank. After Oslo, the permit system expanded and gradually tightened; permits were not only required to enter Israel but frequently also to move around the West Bank. After the second intifada, in 2000, restrictions on movement within the Palestinian areas increased dramatically. Closure's mechanisms do more than the work of inclusion and exclusion. They also serve as punitive devices. For example, following Hamas's victory in the 2005 elections, the checkpoints multiplied. Following acts of Palestinian violence against Israelis, curfews were imposed and a complete sealing of the West Bank from Jerusalem and Israel took effect.[2]

By the early 2000s, over five hundred checkpoints and the large dirt mounds or cement cubes that block roads and villages, along with trenches, roadblocks, bypass roads, fences, and the wall, had physically restricted Palestinians' mobility. Today's rapid and historically unparalleled circulation of people, goods, and ideas is an index of modern social life. To this we can add speed and velocity. In Palestine, however, mobility unfolds in a time warp. If speed is a hallmark of modernity and in the era of high-speed everything, from travel to food to weaponry and communications, Palestinians wait, suspended in webs of immobility in which they move at a tempo from another century. Like Arwa, they strive to go on with their everyday lives but must do in radically altered ways; most striking was the constant re-sequencing of movement. As we shall see, traveling has become an act of subterfuge, patience, and cunning, an obstacle course to be negotiated and mastered anew every day. Trust in the predictability of everyday life is shattered, replaced by anticipation and anxiety. The future is a black hole. After being denied a permit to go to Jerusalem to participate in a professional training workshop, Selma was visibly irritated, pacing the floor and wringing her hands as she burst out, "I don't want to be excited about anything that involves the future because you don't know if it will really happen. Our whole life is like this—not knowing if something will really happen."

It is commonplace that states seek to "monopolize the legitimate means of movement" (Torpay 1998, 241). Yet what distinguishes mobility's deep entanglement with power in the case at hand is the monopolization of a non-citizen populations' movement within a territory not officially incorporated into the state but where it is the de facto sovereign. The interlocking bureaucratic and physical obstacles to Palestinian mobility are extensive and unavoidable, penetrating deep into quotidian life. On the personnel side, gun-toting colonists, private-security operatives, border police, and military personnel operate in tandem with the occupation's Civilian Administration staff and the DCO (District Coordinating Office) that regulates the permit system. In this world of differential mobilities, Israelis are simultaneously settled or emplaced and mobile. In their eyes, Palestinians are transgressive interlopers requiring surveillance and regulation; immobilized, they are distant yet observable. Thus the control of mobilities has real material and experiential consequences that are ultimately bound up with the production of different forms of space and are produced by them as well.

Sometimes conceptualized as ushering in a world of more flexible borders, globalization instead has been accompanied by a proliferation of borders, documentary and identification technologies, physical barriers such as walls, and an ever-expanding repertoire of hi-tech surveillance systems. Fortressed and gated communities are increasingly replicated on the state level. The contradictions and the unevenness of globalization were soon apparent in the "mobility gap" as a strategy of state to deal with near but socially distant populations (Shamir 2005, 199–200).

The scholarly turn to mobility resembles the turn to space two decades ago. Early on, there were warnings of an undifferentiated concept of mobility as well as indications that people and groups are unequally positioned to move (Massey 1993, 60–61). If mobility is undifferentiated by power—that is, as a right that can be accorded, modulated, or withheld—the concept risks losing analytical specificity. While some move with unprecedented and unencumbered speed and range, the movement of others is constrained and closely monitored.[3] Most significantly, human mobility remains tethered to the demands of capital, labor, securitization practices, and national boundaries and state mechanisms of identification that determine the possibility and extent of mobility: identity cards, visas, work permits, and passports—that is, the nationally encumbered subject.

States have magnified their hold on mobility in the wake of the securitization that followed September 11 and fueled the development of technologies to increase border security and surveillance, ranging from optical and body scanning machines to biometric identity cards to hi-detection fences. As the ambit of human circulation has expanded, so has its regulation. In a securitized world, surveillance works with the rules and regulations governing mobility to determine its scope, legitimacy, and risk. "Digital systems of mobility" are central to the twenty-first century, combining "exceptional freedom (at least for some, on some occasions) and exceptional system dependence" (Urry 2007, 15–16). If "control

societies function with a third generation of machines, with information technologies and computers" (Delueze 1995, 180), then biometrics may constitute the
highest stage yet of this machinery. Palestine-Israel provides an illustrative setting to explore (im)mobility and its embedding in regimes of surveillance, risk-
assessment, and security technologies. The gamut of mechanisms used to control
Palestinian mobility ranges from the latest high-tech surveillance equipment and
biometrics to the crude but massive cement wall.

In great part, human history is a story of mobility, the capacity to overcome
distance (Sager 2006, 466) and the new technologies with which to do so. Recently, mobility has become an indicator of human rights and modernity (Cresswell 2006, 10; Sheller 2008). The regime of control over Palestinian mobility, I
contend, works to transform cartographies and the meaning of space and to
manage the collective and individual body. I frame mobility as socially produced
and, in turn, productive and reproductive of particular social orders and landscapes. The 1993 and 1995 Oslo Accords gave Israel substantial control over Palestinian mobility. Maps put into relief the way Area C resembles a sea encircling
a scattering of islands. In this archipelago, how to reach another island when the
sea is forbidden terrain is the question. To move from one area to another, Palestinians had to avoid Area C and the roads running through it. This marooning of
Palestinians facilitates the crafting of exclusivist Jewish spaces.

Colonial regimes regulate and constrain indigenous mobility to organize
and regulate the flow of labor and to maintain spaces that are free of the colonized, reduce their visibility, spatially concentrate them, and obstruct their political organizing. Israel added a new dimension to these practices. Oslo limited
the Palestinian Authority's jurisdiction over the Palestinian residents of the OPT
and maintained Israel's control over significant portions of Palestinian territory,
forging a disconnection between people and territory. By controlling the space
through which Palestinians move and claiming jurisdiction over their mobility,
Israel is able to block them at nearly every turn. By creating hundreds of checkpoints, it has extended its control over almost all movement outside towns or
villages.[4] Mobility at the borders of sovereign states is mediated by the requirement that noncitizens seeking entry have passports, identity cards, and sometimes visas in order to be legally admitted. For a stateless or occupied population,
mobility is constrained by the absence of citizenship in the state exercising sovereignty and its grip on the issuance of documents that determine the legitimacy
and scope of mobility.

By differentiating mobilities and exploring them relationally (Adey 2006,
83), we can link mobility to power and the production of space. In Palestine-
Israel, (im)mobilities are relational, contingent, and hierarchized, and transgressions are penalized. The freedom of movement of some "often depends on
the denial of others' mobility" (Sheller 2008, 28). There is a direct, observable

relationship between the scope and speed of Israeli mobility and the denial of the same to Palestinians. The tight regulation of Palestinian mobility underwrites the occupiers' speedy, unhindered movement. Thus, in dialectical fashion, Israeli mobility cannot be extracted from its tight sedimentation in Palestinian immobility. As a result of closure, Israelis are able to easily traverse space they refer to as "sterile," that is, free of Palestinians. Differentially classified people sometimes traverse the same space but on separate roads and with differential velocity. On shared roads, Palestinian cars might be stopped at checkpoints for hours, while Israeli cars whiz by. In Hebron, for example, frequent curfews, streets blocked by cement-filled barrels, and violence by Jewish colonists have severely curtailed Palestinian mobility, while the colonists move through town engaging in what they "explicitly described as a form of marking their territory" (Clarke 2009, 72).

Individual Palestinians represents an aggregate population and thus the boundaries of their corporeal bodies are expansive, a conceptualization essential to strategies of population management. Palestinians' mobility has been ordered by a regime of knowledge about them that first emerged in the 1920s with "methodologically devised strategies" and continues today (Sa'di 2014, 5), as well as a keen understanding of the potential threat to stability posed by millions of marginalized, displaced, or occupied people. Whether in the Arab host states or under occupation, they have been subject to state surveillance, enumeration, and classifications that render them visible and legible.[5] Israeli novelist David Grossman wrote of the "endless intelligence that victory [1967] brought with it; documents and people, suspects and collaborators, cities and villages to be utterly penetrated, to crack the code of relations and alliances and allegiances of the people, the leaders, the clans, a great quilt work, intense study, no holds barred—knowledge is power" (Grossman 1988, 129; see also Gordon 2008).

Native Palestinians are carriers of danger and mayhem, especially when they traverse or edge close to Jewish spaces. Israeli political and social discourse has produced two types of Palestinian bodies: the explosive body of the male terrorist, the "major inhabitant of the discourse of national security," and the female body giving birth at the checkpoint, emblematic of an oppositional Israeli discourse (Kotef and Amir 2007, 978). In both images, the Palestinian is reduced to either a suffering or an explosive body; one embodied aspect of identity overrides all other, an instance of Butler's "excessive corporeality" (ibid., 984). But why is the suffering female body denied passage? Palestinians often attribute it to demographics and the simple cruelty of occupation.

In the Israeli imagination, the Palestinian body is often perceived as having hidden and violent motives that hypervigilance (surveillance) can contain. The task of the security personnel is to discern the hidden agenda, and, rather than simply discipline it, to employ immobilizing techniques to disable it. Palestinians understand these techniques and their routinization as schemata to engender a self-disciplining body, immiserate, and quell and punish resistance. This regime of spatial interdiction and deceleration of movement does not correspond with Marcel Mauss's notion of habitus as "go[ing] without saying" or Pierre Bourdieu's (1977, 72–95) largely unconscious disposition. Indeed, these dispositions—the body seemingly on task as it goes through the requisite motions of deference and sequencing at checkpoints—rarely operate as unmediated habitus. They were constantly commented on and stridently critiqued, and perceived underlying premises and goals were articulated. Palestinians seemingly acquiesced and followed the rules because they needed to move, yet they constantly analyzed the minute changes in the practice of closure and thus objectified (made it nonroutine) rather than normalized the process. Indeed, they had a firm and consciously articulated conviction about the purpose of strangulation, "They want to drive us crazy," complained Ziad, a university student and part-time employee in a shop I frequented. He was quite late for work one day because of checkpoint delays as he traveled from his home in the north. He proceeded to analyze the situation as if explaining a mathematical equation:

> If you can't plan from one day to the next and there is never any explanation for why you are denied a permit or turned back at checkpoint, you will get so frustrated—daily life just becomes unmanageable. It takes so much time to do anything; every task becomes an ordeal and you are never certain what will happen. You add it all up and you figure they want you to go crazy with frustration. Then we will start to think about leaving.

Confining a surplus population generated effects well beyond the disciplinary. The regime of control operated most visibly at the edges, in the micro-zones of interaction. When the Palestinian body nears Israeli space, Michel Foucault's (1979, 138) description of the mechanics of power and disciplined bodies is apt: "not only so that they may do as one wishes, but so that they may operate as one wishes, with the techniques, the speed and the efficiency that one determines. Thus discipline produces the subjected and practised bodies, 'docile' bodies." Yet closure was simultaneously disciplinary and antidisciplinary, ordered yet chaotic, predictable yet unpredictable. Most significantly, it produces an analyzing and critical disposition, alert to mutations in the regime of control that enveloped them. Disciplining a disposable body operated hand-in-hand with disabling it through the imposition of uncertainty. Permits, the road system, and checkpoints discipline and disable, and the ambiguity and chaos they generate forms an antidisciplinary form of rule.

"She Is Not Allowed Entrance Although She Is Allowed"

An interview and a series of lengthy conversations with Randa, a graduate student who is originally from Gaza and a former employee of various NGOs and the PA, known for her activism, quick wit, and intelligence, imparts the constrained texture of life under closure and hints at emerging subjectivities. Our many discussions brought to the surface themes of punishment and being trapped, (il)logics, ambiguity and arbitrariness, frustration and coping, family relations, heartbreak and resilience, subterfuge and resistance, adaptability, as well as quick thinking and, above all, the will not to concede—to give up, go away, or accept invisibility. In the face of strategic arbitrariness as well as danger and risk, she plowed forward, exhibiting at times daunting patience and perseverance but, most of all, an astute, analytical knowledge of the vortex of her daily life. It is this consciousness that colored Palestinian subjectivities.

In 1991, I moved from Gaza to the West Bank to study at Bir Zeit University. At that time, the first intifada was still ongoing. But then we did not have the restriction on movement between Gaza and the West Bank. Unfortunately, with the Oslo agreement restrictions became more frequent and the Israelis started issuing permits for students to move between Gaza and the West Bank. At that time, I was active in student affairs and thus was one of the few girls on a blacklist. So, I was not given permission to travel to Gaza for two years although I had Gaza identity papers. The Quakers helped me get a permit to go to Gaza.

I remember that every time something happened in Gaza or the West Bank, the Israelis would close the Eretz checkpoint, the main crossing into Gaza. This meant I could lose a whole semester, as happened to many students from Gaza. I was afraid of losing the semester, so sometimes I would borrow a friend's identity card. She is from the West Bank and we have similar features. When I would go to Gaza I would have two identities. I would enter using my Gaza identity but when I left—if something goes wrong and they close the checkpoint—I used to pack all my things, say good-bye and go to the checkpoint and show my friend's identity card as if it is mine. This was very difficult; a few meters before the checkpoint, I could hear my heart pounding. "What shall I do if they discover I am using someone else's identity card?" Either I can pass and attend school or I could end up in prison. I used to deal with that issue as a challenge. This is my life—and the only one who can control my life is me. Not the occupation. If there was a military operation, they would announce the West Bank and Gaza as closed military zones and close Eretz checkpoint. So, quickly I would go to the checkpoint and plead, "I want to go back to the West Bank. I am from Hebron." I would continue until they let me pass. But many friends were trapped in Gaza for a long time. After the 1994 massacre in Hebron at the al-Ibrahimi Mosque, they imposed a curfew on Ramallah and it was a horrible situation.[6] They closed Bir Zeit University, so we went back to Gaza. It was Ramadan—so we are supposed to go to Gaza. Then they closed the Eretz checkpoint. I was trapped there for forty days. It was very hard for us to get out—it was completely closed. One of my friends had a good connection with a priest who was visiting a church in Gaza. He had his own car and it was parked in front of Eretz. My friend shouted at me, "Randa, just get your things." This is so we can show the soldiers our passport that was then issued by Egypt. Maybe this priest can help us get out of Gaza, I thought. It was during the first intifada—just before Oslo. After seven o'clock there was a curfew. We were supposed to meet at a gas station and then be picked up by the priest. We were waiting for him, when, all of a sudden, two Israeli jeeps drove up, opened their doors, and pointed their guns at us. Then, they discovered that we are girls and not covered [not wearing a *hijab*, the headscarf]. They started to treat us as internationals, asking us, "What are you doing here?" We started talking in English with them and they said, "Oh, we are sorry; oh, we apologize. We just wanted to make sure everything is okay." But I almost had a heart attack. Eventually, the priest came and we went with him; they are used to seeing him at the checkpoint so they didn't ask him anything. I remember when we finally passed the checkpoint we screamed, "We are out of Gaza"; it had been forty days. School had started two weeks ago. All my friends were asking, "How did you get out of Gaza?" "How?" I said, "By luck—it is according to the mood of the soldiers, you know." When I had the opportunity, I left. Another time I tried to get a permit for Gaza. After six months, I got permission. It was according to the mood of the soldiers or the policy they have. Sometimes you are a "security risk" and sometimes you are allowed. So what does that mean, "for security reasons?" Is it really for security reasons, or is it just to torture and abuse me?

In June 1997, I started working with a local NGO. At that time, they [the occupation authorities] used to give permission for staff to go between branches in Gaza and the West Bank. As I was working in training and project evaluation, the NGO did their best to get permission for me to go to Gaza, but they couldn't. In August 1997, my mother had a heart attack and passed away. I tried so hard to get a permit to attend the funeral, and it was like hell. They wouldn't give me permission. We went to the Palestinian-Israeli Coordination Committee. I went to the DCO in Beit El through my organization here. We did our best to get me a permit. This was a shock—I started to realize what it means for me, for my life, to be away from my family, to be away from my mother, my father. I am like someone living outside his country, yet I am only in Ramallah. So I started working with my friends to get a permit. One of my friends worked in the Coordination Committee. He said, "Look, we will not be able to get you a permit because you are a security risk, so let's think about how to change your identity papers from Gaza to West Bank. We will do our best to change your identity card." This will solve your problem. So I agreed. We collected evidence that I was living and working here. It took six months to change my identity card. It was very, very hard to change. Because I was friends with some members of the Coordinating Committee, they took my case as a personal case. It was very hard for me not to attend my mother's funeral. After nine months—after my mother died—I was able to go to Gaza. At this time, through my organization, I had a permit to go to Gaza, first for one week and then they extended it for one month. I didn't have any trouble going in or out. I was able to do training there and follow up our projects.

Last time I was in Gaza was fall 2004, just four days before Arafat's death. My father had cancer and was in bad shape. I was panicked because I didn't want the same experience I had with my mother. I had a very close relationship with my dad. Before 2000, he used to visit me and stay at my apartment for two or three months. By 2003, I had had not seen my father for about four years—it was hell for him. He used to call and beg, "Please come. I need to see you. I am having hard time." I would tell him it is not me, it is the occupation. I am trying my best to get a permit. This was a very difficult time for me. So I contacted an Arab parliamentarian in Israel, explained my situation, and he adopted my case. I received a permit to stay in Gaza for five days. It read, "She is allowed entrance although she is not allowed." It was so confusing. I decided to go to Gaza although they had declared it a closed military zone. So my brother and I went, and we submitted our identity papers and our permit and they asked us to wait. I remember we stayed there for ten hours! I cried the whole ten hours—to see my father meant a lot to me. Each minute means something—either my father will still be alive and I will enjoy talking to him or he will have passed away. So I kept crying—talking and debating with the soldiers there. They kept saying "Just wait and we will allow you in at the right moment." We were there at 10:00 a.m. and we passed through at 8:00 p.m. My cell-phone battery was dead so we couldn't talk to my family. They did not know we were so close. During this wait, there was no water—no food—there was nothing at the checkpoint. It is a closed military zone—there is nothing there—only soldiers. It was very scary—this pressure—I couldn't do anything. You couldn't even see any cars there.

This was the first time I had seen my family in nearly four years. So I stayed at my house for four days. I only went out for coffee at the beach with my nephew and niece, and I went to my sister's house. It meant a lot to me to spend time with my father. I took a recorder with me and I interviewed him with all the family present. I tried to document his history. I was asking questions about his entire life. He was uprooted from his village during the *nakbah* in 1948—we are refugees. At that time, we were discussing the presidential elections—who do we think will win? My father was very politically aware. That was the last time I saw my family and my father. He passed away during the January 2005 presidential elections. It was a shock for me. They did not allow me to go to Gaza for the funeral. As usual, they claimed it was for security reasons. This means nothing. What is the security reason if you allowed me to go two months ago? By the way, the most horrible thing for me was that, at that time, I could go where I wanted—I could go to London, I could go to the US but I couldn't go to Gaza, which is about one and [a] half hours, maximum. So this kind of thing makes me sick. I try to understand the logic behind it. And the only thing is that I am a Palestinian! Nothing else! Because I am a Palestinian the Israelis want to abuse and humiliate me. They want to restrict my life.

During the second intifada, I lived in Ramallah and worked with a local NGO on agricultural development. We had three training centers, and I would follow up on training projects. I remember it used to take me eight hours and seven checkpoints to go from Ramallah to Zubabdah—that's a whole day! We used to go in a group—like a team—it is more secure. If something happens to you, other people will take care of you and will be aware of what is going on. I remember that one day, we were going back to Ramallah. At about the fifth or sixth checkpoint, they stopped us and collected our papers and went inside a small building. I glanced to the side of the road and saw a group of young Palestinian guys squatting next to it. It was so hot—maybe 100 degrees. I was looking with shock at these young men. As punishment they put them under the sun. All of a sudden, a soldier comes out and asks, "Who is this Randa?" On my identity card, my place of residence is Bir Zeit. Excitedly, he kept saying, "Oh, you are my neighbor, you are my neighbor." What the hell is he talking about? He keeps talking in Hebrew. I could hardly understand a word! He assumes I can understand his language. I was asking my friend what he was saying, and he said to me, "Just stay quiet. I will translate later." I wanted to know what he was saying to me. He was telling the other soldiers at the checkpoint, "Come, come, see my friend." It was scary and I was angry about how they were treating those young men. Then he was talking about some settlement. And then, "Good-bye, good-bye." He said, "Here, this is your identity card, my neighbor." The soldiers were all looking at me and smiling. My friend didn't want to tell me what they were saying because he was afraid of my reaction. He knew if I reacted angrily that most likely they will not abuse me because I am a girl, but they will punish us all, especially the males. Finally, he told me what the soldier had been saying, "You are my neighbor, you are so beautiful." He wanted your cell phone number because you are living near him. I asked my friend, "Where?" He replied, "He lives in a settlement near Bir Zeit. He was telling his friends, "Do you know what— this is the first Palestinian girl who is beautiful—I am used to seeing all those veiled girls coming through here." I was so mad! I told my friend, "You should have told me."

When the Israelis invaded Ramallah [2002], our organization decided to move; they had occupied our office and destroyed all the files and the computers. My personal computer was there as well. They were downloading sex websites. There was a curfew, so we decided to move to Ramallah, because from there we could more easily visit our projects. In Ramallah they imposed a curfew starting at 5:00 p.m. So the office rented space in al-Ram—apartments for us—one for girls and two for the male staff. I used to go to Ramallah every weekend. I remember one day we were trying to go to al-Ram in a van [a shared taxi] and the soldiers started shooting at the van, but luckily for us, the driver was skillful enough to escape. After four months, they stopped the curfew, so I returned to live in Ramallah. But my work was still in al-Ram so I was being stopped at the checkpoint in the morning on way to the office and on my way back.

In 2002, they started building the wall in the north near Jenin and in Qalqiliya. Many of our staff was doing research on that area. So every morning I would wake up and try to think of a story to tell the soldier to convince him so he will allow me to pass through the checkpoint. Now, if you are a modern girl and not covered, they try to debate and discuss with you. They would ask,

"Where are you working? Give me your card." At that time, I was working with an NGO on rural development. But I used to hold a card that shows I am working as a psychologist in a health organization, where I was actually a volunteer. At that time, they were only allowing teachers or those working with health organizations to pass easily. So sometimes they would say, "Today we are not allowing anyone. It is a closed military zone so all teachers are not allowed." It would be 7:15 or 7:30 in the morning. They would tell students— five, six, seven, or eight years old—just kids—"Today you don't have school." Sometimes they would ask teachers, "What are you teaching?" "I am teaching English." "Okay you are allowed." And they would start speaking in English to check. Sometimes I would say, "I am teaching Arabic." "You are not allowed today. Go back!" There is no logic at all! If someone says, "I am teaching math or physics," they might ask, "Oh, do you know Pythagorian theory?" They used to check our knowledge—"What does Pythagoras say?" It was according to the mood of the soldier. And you can't imagine the mood. You are forced into this scene every morning on your way to work. Students, who are just kids, are subjected to searches by soldiers. They shout "open your bag!" to a six- or seven-year-old! Once I was pissed off. I said, "What the hell are you doing! He is a kid!" Then he turns to me. "Open your bag! What do you have? A book?" he said sarcastically. So you wake up in the morning, and you are not sure you will be able to go to work or not. And even if you get to work, imagine your mood. I need to have my coffee and my cigarette and then I can start work. It is very stressful.

Once, at a checkpoint, I was going to visit a friend in Jerusalem—I told the soldier that my aunt was sick and was in Maqasad Hospital. I told him, "She has no one to visit her. You can hold my identity card until I return." I tried to be very confident. He said, "Why don't you have a permit?" I said, "This is an emergency." He saw that I was confident, and I was a girl, so he allowed me in. My friend was shocked. She said, "What did you say?" I replied, "I depend on their stupidity. They know nothing. I play with words." We went off to Haifa for three days to enjoy the sea and the beautiful weather. For me, being in Haifa means something—it means I can go there—the 1948 areas of Palestine. I lie and use stories. In 2005, I was supposed to attend a press conference at the Ambassador Hotel in Jerusalem. I tried to enter through roundabout roads but I couldn't pass. I went to the big checkpoint and told the Druze soldier I need to pass to visit my sick aunt. "Are you going to allow me or not?" He demanded, "Open your bag." He saw a pack of cigarettes and asked, "Why do you smoke?" I replied, "Because the situation is so bad." So he said, "I will allow you." It was the second time I used the story of a sick aunt.

In 2004, after the invasion [of the West Bank], I was going to Jenin for a training program. We went with employees from the United Nations Development Program (UNDP). They said, "You are a girl. It should be okay." I had a UN card that was issued only to Gazans. It says I am a refugee; it was a magnetic card, and they were not widespread then. At the checkpoint, the UNDP fellows held up their cards, and I held up my refugee card. This was a difficult checkpoint because ten soldiers had been killed there. Confident, I handed the soldier my refugee card. This card is not a permit, but the soldier was so stupid he didn't know the difference. Again, I depend on their stupidity.

Another time, driving with colleagues, I sensed there was a curfew in a village because no one was on the streets. Then I noticed a tank on a hill. Suddenly, it begins to turn and point its guns at us. I screamed and shouted, "Look it is moving." We drove off quickly and it started shooting. Our driver was very skilled, but it was a terrible experience.

Randa's detailed narrative captures the lived reality of closure and its impact on mobility, work, family relations, and subjectivity. The ambiguity and lack of logic that inhered in closure—"she is allowed entrance although she is not allowed"—paint a vivid picture of the unpredictability of once predictable, sequenced daily routines of going to work, to school, and visiting family. Her story illustrates accommodation, subversion, and, importantly, a refusal to acquiesce to the regime of immobilization and to strive for normalcy under closure.

Legibility and Classification: The Identity Card

Zeina, a forty-five-year-old mother of three and the director of a large unit in a telecommunications company, was in a fretful mood when I arrived at her home in al-Bireh, a former village that is now physically merged with Ramallah. She had invited Selma and me for lunch. When we entered her smartly decorated flat, we could hear quarreling. Her son and husband were in the middle of a dust-up over the son's identity card (*bitaqat hawiyyah*). Seventeen-year-old Jad rarely carried his card, and his father, Ishmael, went into a rage when Jad could not find the card in his messy bedroom. Ishmael was carrying on about how, once, even though he had his card in his possession, he was beaten up at a checkpoint for not being able to recite his nine-digit number. He was furious that Jad had not only misplaced his card but hadn't memorized his number. Shrugging his shoulders, Jad explained to me, "I don't carry it because I cannot go anywhere anyway. I never leave the Ramallah area, so why should I carry it?"

At the beginning of the occupation, Israel took over the Palestinian civil registry and assigned every Palestinian a nine-digit number, which is listed in the database available to security personnel at checkpoints. Anyone residing abroad or traveling outside Palestine at the time was not counted and was thus ineligible for residency. Palestinians are classified into "no less than four general classes and over forty sub-categories each of which necessitates different regulations regarding movement" (Ben-Ari 2008, 134–135). The identity card remains the most fundamental document encoding and regulating both Palestinian entitlements and deprivations (Abu-Zahra 2008, 177). The card must be carried at all times by anyone over the age of sixteen. Besides fixing Palestinians' rights of mobility and residency, it is absolutely necessary for such activities as getting married, paying taxes, obtaining employment, registering for school, opening a bank account, and getting health care. Palestinians have been required to carry the cards since 1968. They were issued initially by the Military Administration, and since 1982 have been issued by the Israeli Civil Administration of Judea and Samaria. Under the terms of Oslo, Israel retained control of the Palestinian civil registry and thus of the allocation of identity cards. The PA serves as an intermediary, submitting requests and distributing the cards, but Israel controls their issuance and coding. In short, an occupying state has abrogated to itself the power to determine the legal identities of the populace, a task of governance usually associated with sovereignty.

Such is the significance of the identity card that children incorporate it in their imaginary worlds of make-believe. During my visit to Muna's house, her two granddaughters were quietly playing with their dolls while Muna and I chatted over refreshments. They held the dolls face-to-face, as one doll "said" to the other, "Don't marry anyone with a West Bank *hawiyyah*. It is better to marry someone with a Jerusalem *hawiyyah*. Then you can travel. Baba has a West Bank *hawiyyah*, so he can't drive with us to Jerusalem like Mama, and she is bad driver." The girls' mother had a Jerusalem identity card and her application for her husband to receive a Jerusalem residency had been repeatedly denied.

To be caught without an identity card is to risk arrest, a heavy fine, and possible deportation. In October 2009, Israel issued Military Order 1650,[7] an amendment to the Military Order 329 from 1969, "Order Regarding Prevention of Infiltration," sending chills down Palestinian spines. The amendment expanded the definition of an "infiltrator" to encompass "a person who entered the Area unlawfully following the effective date, or a person who is present in the Area and does not lawfully hold a permit." The penalty can be seven years' imprisonment or deportation. "Area" is not defined, although the title of the amendment indicates "Judea and Samaria," Israeli terms for the West Bank; nor does it specify the type of permit required. In short, one can be an infiltrator at home and deportations have been legalized.

The identity card is only one of a host of techniques used to compel an always knowable Palestinian subject. Israel has long arrogated to itself the visualization of the Palestinian. For example, the colonies are hypervisible on the landscape—but their interiors are not visible to those outside their boundaries. In contrast, Palestinian villages are surveilled both from the colonies built on higher ground and from the military installations with watchtowers that afford panoramic views. Where the state strictly determines categories of space and the legitimacy of movement based on citizenship, itself a differentially allocated good, documents become critical artefacts, and legibility becomes a paramount endeavor. Identity documents at once encode, produce legal distinctions, and inflect subjectivity by creating categories of difference where previously those lines were blurred. A hierarchical rainbow of color-coded identity-card holders, or plastic sleeves, instantly signal a Palestinian's place of residence and permissible range of mobility. Green holders were instituted by the PA and issued to all West Bank residents; prior to that Israel had issued orange holders to West Bank residents. The information is in both Arabic and Hebrew, and a number at the top (401) indicates if one is a "returnee," that is, one who returned with the PA after Oslo. East Jerusalem residents receive blue plastic holders; orange is now for Gazans. A green sleeve signals that movement outside the West Bank is prohibited. The information includes the holder's date and place of birth, which determine where he or she can and cannot "legally" reside, as well as parents' names, residency, and religion. While Ziad and I waited patiently to cross a checkpoint on the road to Jenin, on the way to visit his family, he remarked, "All these different identity cards separate us from each other. Each begins to see the other as different and resents the small privileges. Palestinians with Jerusalem identity cards begin to think they are better than us in the West Bank because they get a few benefits from the Israelis. This creates divisions among us."

The sheer number of categories and their associated differential mobilities ensure uncertainty, as determinations are discussed at each checkpoint and a back-and-forth ensues between the soldiers and their superiors. That there are multiple agents, from soldiers and police to private-security personnel, who can make decisions and an excessive number of categories that often do not correspond to the complexity of Palestinian society decisions are often ad hoc and arbitrary (Ben-Ari 2008; Havkin 2011, 11–12).

When a vehicle or a pedestrian approaches a checkpoint, a ritualized set of actions unfolds. The color-coded cards are already in hand, having been retrieved from purses or pockets, usually well before the checkpoint is reached. The color of the plastic cover immediately alerts the security personnel to the general categories of classification—whether the holder is permitted residency and his or her relation to the occupying state. To the ethnographic eye, the ritual movements quickly crystallize: the approach, the hand retrieving the card, clutching it, and then the extension of the limb. The card-in-hand resembles an appendage, an extension of the body, akin to a cell phone as used by many. Seldom is there a searching through handbags or precious seconds lost fumbling through pockets or wallets. I rarely observed a Palestinian at a checkpoint, whether as a pedestrian, as passenger in a car, or on a bus being boarded by military personnel, without the card in hand. Soldiers do not need to request it, for it is always at the ready. Nevertheless, they bark or demand, "*hawiyyah*," sometimes barely glancing at the card; other times, scrutinizing it. But the geography of habitus has been set in motion, and with passage into another space, cards are put away, people relax, and the silence is broken by chit-chat and murmured curses as the bus or taxi lumbers away.

Documentation has a history dating to 1968, when the Israeli-issued identity cards were first issued, through the permit system, to the more recent magnetic cards with their biometric encryption. In the twenty-first century, with a global economy requiring calibrated human circulation, with varying degrees of enabledness and impededness, techniques of surveillance have moved beyond the panopticon to new means of identifying and sorting people (Amoore, Marmura, and Salter 2008, 97). This is not Foucault's or Bentham's panopticon, nor is it fully synoptic; rather, this is post-panoptic. Here, half the population is watched by their near demographic equals—from the soldier manning the checkpoint to border-control personnel to the various intelligence units on alert for people who appear suspicious. In this case, synoptics and panoptics work together (see Lyon 2006). Indeed, with biometrics, physically present, direct observers are less necessary, reducing the need for the costly deployment of military forces. Rendering the Palestinian visible and legible is not just about reforming and disciplining the individual body but is also targeted to the aggregate. The shift from a "hardware based modernity" to a "light, liquid, software based modernity" (Bauman 2000, 2–3) is evident in Israel's hi-tech management of the occupation. Yet face-to-face encounters continue to verify identities. For example, asking teachers to prove that they know their subject matter, or musicians to perform at a checkpoint is another, humiliating, means of verifying identities by publicly compelling their performance.

The *hawiyyah* also operates as a weapon and form of punishment. The ever-present possibility of having one's *hawiyyah* confiscated is real. Palestinian drivers of shared taxis in Jerusalem often check the identity cards of passengers entering from the Qalandia checkpoint to make sure they are eligible to enter the city. I got into a shared taxi after crossing the Qalandia checkpoint; the driver became agitated when he found out another female passenger did not have a Jerusalem identity card. He shouted at her to get out of his taxi, railing, "I could have my taxi and identity card confiscated if I get caught with you in the car! And, I would have to pay a heavy fine—around $1,800." When she was gone, I asked him what else might happen. "Well, isn't that enough?" he replied, exasperated. "How could I work without an identity card and my taxi! Who is going to feed my family?" Thus Palestinians themselves often are compelled by force of circumstances to enforce the occupation.

Another way identity cards compel obedience and impose punishment is through withdrawal. For example, during the first intifada, when Palestinian youth were painting graffiti on buildings, military personnel would force residents to paint over it by threatening to confiscate their identity cards. Stories abound of people who have been detained and asked to collaborate and provide the names of political activists in exchange for having their identity cards returned to them. Potential collaborators are threatened with the confiscation of their identity cards if they do not cooperate and inform on others.

Biometrics have become a noticeable part of the equation governing Palestinian mobility. Taking visualization to a new and unprecedented level, with biometrics the body becomes "its own technology of verification" (Packer 2008, 275–76). As a means of verifying that a person is who he claims to be, biometrics works as a classificatory and risk-assessment technology (Magnet 2011, 125).[8] The biometrically encoded document and its holder must match, and the documents must be verifiable; biometrically encrypted cards provide additional authentication of a match. Biometrics may be the most recent incarnation of "the file," a highly mobile dossier enabling states to impose legibility, assess risk, and distinguish citizen from noncitizen.[9]

Biometrics compels a turn to questions of the play of visibility and invisibility. We live in a time of "mediated visibility" (Haggerty and Ericson 2006; Thompson 2005). In this constellation of surveillance and biometric technologies that render the Palestinian visible and knowable, watching back has become a tool of subversion. For example, when the Israeli human rights organization B'TSelem (the Israeli Information Center for Human Rights in the Occupied Territories) gave young Palestinians video cameras to record colonist and military violence, they were able to return the penetrating gaze of the occupation and document its abuses. Cell-phone cameras have also magnified the ability to look back and record.

In this new technological world of encryption and the mass processing of biometric data, ethnicity and religion, and the history of arrest and incarceration, remain the driving, if not the determinate, categories. Magnetic cards, encrypted with biometric information have gradually replaced paper documents.[10] An incipient form of biometrics, the magnetic card was initially introduced as a requirement to obtain a work permit to enter Israel. Biometric technologies are touted as circumventing a subjective understanding of the body with a surefire, objective system of verification and authentication (Magnet 2011, 122). In the security world, mobility has become a matter of risk management to be solved through an ever-expanding repertoire of surveillance and technological innovations to determine its permissibility. Because the magnetic cards contain more information, processing at checkpoints is supposed to be faster, more efficient, and less reliant on face-to-face encounters, minimizing Palestinian-Israeli interactions and allowing for a downsizing of checkpoint staff. According to an IDF (Israel Defense Forces) spokesperson, "user-friendly" electronic terminals for authenticating handprints will make the checkpoint experience "more pleasant" for the 25,000 or so Palestinians who continue to cross into Israel to work (Greenberg 2010, 2)

By 2012, all identity documents were supposed to have been biometrically encrypted. I interviewed a Palestinian computer engineer who explained that the cards are designed for two purposes. First, each resident under occupation is to have a record of their iris and fingerprints on file and encoded in the identity card. Second, biometric technologies are envisioned as a means of "reducing physical contact between us and them." Initially, he said, Palestinians were "eager to get a magnetic card because they thought, erroneously, that they needed one to apply for a permit. Thus there were long waits. The impression was given that you needed it to apply for permits but it was really to begin computerizing the records of all of us for better control."

Paper Walls: The Permit System

Mervet, a middle-aged professor at Al-Quds University and a lifelong resident of Abu Dis, was invited to give a lecture in Jerusalem. As a holder of a West Bank identity card, she needed a *tasreeh* (permit), issued by the Israeli Civilian Administration, to enter the city. She left the necessary documents at the DCO and was told to return at nine o'clock on the morning of the lecture to pick up her permit. The lecture was scheduled for eleven. Mervet arrived at the appointed time, and was kept waiting three hours, until noon, to receive her permit. Abed, a sixty-two-year-old Ramallah-based businessman, applied several weeks in advance for a permit to enter Jerusalem for a business meeting. On the morning of the meeting, he received a phone call telling him to come to pick up his permit at the DCO. Once there, he was told to wait, which he did for several hours without any explanation of what was going on. By the time clerk handed him his one-day permit, the meeting was over. Muna introduced me to her friend and her friend's twenty-five-year-old daughter, Samia. A recent graduate of Bir Zeit University, Samia had been accepted into a graduate biology program in England, with a full scholarship. She applied for a *laissez passer* (exit permit) to leave the country. She waited anxiously for it to arrive, unsure whether she should begin making preparations to depart. It came a day after the university told her they could no longer hold her spot and they had given it to someone else. Her disappointment was palpable, but her restricted ability to make decisions about a major life event came as little surprise to her. The lack of any explanation as to the reasons for delays and denials is standard practice. Such stories circulate easily, as everyone has a repertoire of them to share.

With its long waits, inexplicable denials, lack of clarity as to regulations, and petty cruelties, the permit system constituted a wall of sorts, what I call a *paper wall* of bureaucracy. A mysterious and time-consuming process, the criteria for granting permits were unstated and hard to discern. On further probing, what at first seemed arbitrary wasn't necessarily so. Indeed, it was opacity that was consistent. Mervet, who had also been denied a permit to enter Jerusalem for a doctor's visit, said, "Permits are another way to strangle us, to rule us and make life so awful we will leave permanently." The permit system also exemplified relational mobilities. For example, a permit's validity is suspended during Jewish-Israeli holidays when the West Bank becomes a closed zone, operating in shutdown mode.

A word that came up often in conversations about permits was "humiliation" (*izlaal*). Ayman, an ambulance driver with a West Bank identity card, who occasionally requested a permit to visit relatives in Jerusalem and pray at al-Aqsa Mosque, lamented, "I am so humiliated by the process of asking for a permit to go to Jerusalem." My neighbor in Ramallah, forty-five-year-old Sami, who had obtained a twelve-hour permit to pray at Jerusalem's Church of the Holy Sepulcher, said of his experience at the checkpoint, "I felt so humiliated. I hold up my permit to the plexiglass window and this eighteen-year-old bitch flicks her wrist at me to go, as if I am a fly, as if I am nothing. I waited so long for a permit that she barely glanced at."

A constitutive pillar in a byzantine bureaucracy, the permit system, initiated in the late 1980s (see Bornstein 2002), was further elaborated after Oslo, and continued to tighten following a rash of Palestinian violence, particularly suicide bombings. The Civil Administration, in conjunction with the District Civil Liaison office, issues the permits; the application process requires two or more visits to their Beit El office. Discursively, the permit system is cast under the rubric of security. The system enables or impedes, legitimizes, or delegitimizes mobility across and in and out of particular spaces. The permits have a temporal dimension as well, specifying the date and time in which it is permissible to access space that is otherwise off-limits. By 2002, West Bank Palestinians had to have a permit, not only to enter Israel or Jerusalem but, often, to reside in their own villages or towns or to gain access to their cultivated lands. West Bank Palestinians desiring to enter Jerusalem for any reason—business, education, medical care, to visit family, or because they desire to enter the city—must have a permit. To drive on some roads, they must have a "Special Movement Permit at Internal Checkpoints."

With a diminished demand for Palestinian labor, those seeking permits to work in Israel were increasingly seen as potential security threats rather than just cheap labor. Yet an exploration of the labor permit system provides a critical perspective on assumptions about the binaries closure reaffirms. French anthropologist Cedric Parizot's (2015) ethnographic work on permits demonstrates the presence of "chains of mediation" between the permit applicant and the actual issuing of the permit, calling into question facile attributions of a binary. These chains still position Palestinians in "relations of dependence" but mediating sponsors, from lawyers to Palestinian citizens of Israel to Israeli employers, suggest a complex, highly mediated typology of permit acquisition and multiple actors.

In the Jordan Valley (Area C), dotted with colonies, the remaining Palestinian residents must have a permit to live in their villages. Farmers in the seam zone require a Permanent Resident Permit as well to live in their villages and another permit to enter their agricultural fields, which are now on the Israeli side of the wall. Over sixty gates on the seam zone, which open and close somewhat arbitrarily, filter passage by checking for permits. During the fall harvest season, when timely access to farmland is crucial, farmers sometimes wait for hours or days to reach their land. The enmeshment of rules governing Palestinian mobility is intimately bound up with gaining ownership of Palestinian property. Under Israeli law, land left uncultivated for a year can be confiscated.

The process of obtaining a permit requires interaction with Israeli security and intelligence forces. A lack of clarity governs the process—how long it will take, the criteria for obtaining a permit, and the reasons for denials. One may wait for days or weeks before being called to pick up the permit or be informed of its denial. The *tasreeh*, like the *hawiyyah*, is a means to compel compliance and gather information, a currency of exchange, so to speak, that then undermines communal trust. Palestinians are frequently told they can have a permit if they provide information about their neighbors, friends, or colleagues—in short, if they become collaborators. By this token, suspicions of collaboration can be aroused when someone receives a work permit or permits to enter Jerusalem multiple times.

The permit system infantilizes and humiliates those who must, in effect, ask for permission to move. There is also a gendered component. The traditionally less monitored and wider scope of mobility enjoyed by men is an index of masculinity compared to women's more monitored and restricted mobilities. Wandering around the Old City of Jerusalem one afternoon, I stopped for a *kunafeh* at Jabri's, a well-known sweet shop.[11] A few minutes later, my neighbor Sami walked in. He had managed to obtain a half-day permit to enter the city on religious grounds, to visit the Christian holy sites. As we ate our *kunafeh*, Sami animatedly described his day in the Old City. Then, glancing at this watch, he suddenly began gathering up his things. It was a few minutes before five o'clock; he still had to run to buy his mother her favorite bread from a shop in Musrara, the Jerusalem neighborhood she had been born and raised in but could no longer visit without a permit.[12] "My permit expires at six o'clock so I have to hurry to get to Qalandia," Sami explained sheepishly, like a child with a curfew.

The petty indignities I observed while moving from place to place were the routine texture of occupation. Once, when I was returning to Ramallah from Jerusalem on bus number 18, we were stopped at Qalandia checkpoint. Often, the buses entering the West Bank are not stopped, but this time ours was. A burly young soldier and a slender, muscular private-security guard accompanying him boarded the bus. They stood at the front of the bus and barked "*hawiyyah*." The soldier proceeded to cursorily inspect the documents of the first four people in the bus. Examining the permit of a well-dressed elderly man, the soldier glanced at his wristwatch and grinning sarcastically said, as if chastising a naughty child, "You are almost late. Your permit to enter Jerusalem ends at 6:00 p.m. and it is now 5:55." In the small, intimate space of the bus, the old man is silent as everyone observes the humiliating encounter.

The permit system indelibly imprints itself on family relations. We saw in chapter 1 how Hasan Fayyad's lack of a permit to live in Jerusalem suffused his family life with uncertainty. Another glimpse into life for those without legal residency in Jerusalem is provided by Nasreen, who has a West Bank identity card and is married to a man with a Jerusalem identity card; they live in Beit Hanina, a Palestinian neighborhood annexed to Israel's greater Jerusalem. Palestinians without an Israeli-issued Jerusalem identity card, easily identified by their blue plastic sleeves, are not allowed in the city without a permit even if they are married to a Jerusalem resident with an Israeli-issued residency card. Nasreen describes what this discriminatory restriction means for her daily life, mobility, family relations, and her marriage. Her narrative encapsulates how the entangled policy of closure, identity cards, and permits permeates the most intimate realms of social life and generates profound anxiety.

> If I had known it would be like this, I wouldn't have married him! I have a baby girl. We are living in Beit Hanina, very close to Ramallah where I work. We live on the Jerusalem side of the wall, so I have to pass checkpoints to go home. My daughter is registered with her father. She cannot travel with me because she is registered with him. If I try to give her a Palestinian identity card, she will lose the Jerusalem identity.
>
> When I gave birth, my husband managed to bring my mother to the hospital. The closure wasn't as bad then. To avoid the checkpoints, they drove her among the houses, and then another car came and took her. I remember once she was supposed to come to the hospital but no taxi would take her—they asked her, "Do you have a Jerusalem identity?" She told them, "No I have a West Bank identity." And they said, "Sorry, we can't." So no taxi would take her—they don't want to be imprisoned for driving someone without a Jerusalem identity card. So I spent the day alone.
>
> Our families have not gotten together since we married. My father doesn't know where my husband's house is. We were hoping I could have a permit to stay in Jerusalem as I am married to a Jerusalemite. But now I have heard this has been canceled. I can't live here anymore! Before, it wasn't that bad if they stopped us at a checkpoint and said, "Go back." I could go to my parents, or to another checkpoint. I could try other ways. It is too hard with the baby, to get in and out of taxis and buses. It is not safe. I don't want to live in an unclear situation.
>
> When I go through checkpoints, I always carry my marriage contract, but now they just tell me to go away. Now, if I am in Jerusalem with my husband and we get caught by the Israelis, we will have to pay around $1,000; they will take his identity card for one month, and then he has to sign a paper that he

is not supposed to be in Jerusalem with me. It is forbidden for me to be in Jerusalem with my husband. It is illegal; he could be put in prison. It depends on the soldiers, their mood, you see. I just go to my house and I stay there. I can't move. And I don't want anyone to come and take me because it is not safe for them. So I can't go to my in-laws. I can't join in the social activities of the family. They live exactly where the wall is in Abu Dis, on the Jerusalem side.

The future—it is so dark. It is hard for us to think about the end of the day. I don't know if I will go home to sleep in my bed. It's like being captured and locked in a tower and waiting for my husband to come and take me because I can't move. It is so hard! You know, last month we had so many problems. Two-three weeks ago I went to my family and said *"Helas!* [enough] I want a divorce." My husband is always worried because of the situation, and thus he is always so upset and angry. And me, I am the same way.

Closure reaches deep into the realm of the intimate, disrupting marital and family relationships and intruding on major life decisions. The future is unimaginable; time is suspended in the immediate present. The poignant desire for normality, to live a life with clarity and predictability, points to a subjectivity inseparable from closure's penetrating techniques.

It is possible to make comparisons between Apartheid South Africa's notorious use of passbooks to limit the movement of its populace and the draconian controls implemented over Palestinian mobility. Apartheid legislation mandated that blacks carry on their persons at all times a passbook containing a photograph, fingerprints, and employment history. The passbook made it easy to classify blacks and regulate their mobility. Israeli controls on Palestinian mobility through the permit system are arguably worse than the passbook system because they are capricious and random. A trucker headed from Ramallah to Hebron never knows which checkpoint along the way will be backed up for hours or where a "flying checkpoint"—one or two army jeeps and a cement block—will appear. The constant and arbitrary changing of the rules renders daily life unpredictable. In comparison, Apartheid in South Africa was highly regulated and predictable.

Roads

In midsummer, 2009, four friends and I decided to attend a conference at al-Quds University in Abu Dis. We met on a street corner in Ramallah at the appointed hour, and then realized that no one had seriously plotted out how to get there. The men own cars but are not sure how to get to Abu Dis. Sheepishly, each admitted that they no longer know which roads now go there. Indeed, these four middle-aged men rarely left Ramallah anymore. They certainly hadn't driven to Abu Dis during the time of closure, a place all of them once easily visited. After some confused discussion, we decide to take the bus. This decision-making process provided a good example of how in Palestine, mental maps, or the geo-graphic imagination, those socially and experientially configured understand-ings of space and terrain and the ability to determine routes to a destination, are no longer constitutive of geographical knowledge (see Laurier and Philo 2003). Such knowledge once flowed from repetitive, embodied engagements with roads, with their twists and turns, ups and downs, side roads, intersections, locales passed and experienced through the sensation of moving to, through, and from these spaces as a driver or a passenger in a vehicle. The geographic imaginar-ies of a lifetime of presence and movement were being undone by the colonial reconfiguration of the road system. Local, experiential geographical knowledge has diminished, as mobility is constricted except for bus, truck, and taxi drivers, whose livelihoods depend on its constant updating.

Far in the future, archaeologists will perhaps excavate the West Bank road system uncovering the ruins of what may well then be coined the "occupation era." Topographically etched into the road system, inequality and privilege will be read by the trained eye in the excavated strata. The smoothly paved bypass roads with their ubiquitous surveillance devices will be juxtaposed to the circuitous, often old, heavily rutted roads consigned to Palestinians. Rusty, tangled, barbed wire and crumbling watchtowers will indicate the presence of a checkpoint; tell-like mounds will mark the once blocked villages; perhaps archaeologists will also uncover the crumbling, yellowed, and frayed remnants of the permits.

Archaeologists have begun to research mobility, roads, and routes, as have some cultural anthropologists.[13] Coterminous with the domestication of plants and animals, developments in metallurgy, the rise of urban centers, and thus of long-distance trade in the Middle East, roads began to appear as permanent fix-tures on the landscape, whose traces can still be discerned. Roads "weave together the disparate elements of daily lives, bridging distance and obstacles to connect us to each other" (Snead, Erickson, and Darling 2009, 1) and forge connections between people and places. Thus road systems are material artefacts designating patterns of circulation of people and things as well as symbolic markers of social-ity. When mobility is obstructed, it is precisely these relationships and connec-tions which suffer disruption.

From the rudimentary, unpaved rural tract, trodden over the centuries by humans and animals, to stone-paved Roman roads linking far-flung places in the empire, to contemporary superhighways, roads are artifacts, part of the mate-rial and analytical framework for understanding and conceptualizing a society's circulation, movement, and world view as well as its economy and trade rela-tions, and level of integration and relations with the exterior. These "landscapes of movement" (ibid), the pathways and the built environment devised to con-nect people with one another, embody meaning, whether a paved superhighway, bramble-edged dirt path linking one village to another, or a paved single-lane road to the local school.

Roads have been critical to expansionist political formations and occupying powers from the Roman Empire to modern-day Afghanistan and Iraq, where the US government has spent millions of dollars to refurbish roads. The seemingly mundane, taken-for-granted road remains essential for foreign invasions, occupations, and trade, as well as territorial expansion and military-political dominance. In these contemporary endeavors, roads further the movement of militaries, incorporate territories into the state, and facilitate the management of occupied populations. Israel's occupation is no exception to this dependence on paths, trails, or roads to forge connections among colonists, enhance the movement of occupying forces, and in the case of Palestine, exclude the ruled. In Palestine, the road system embodies and displays a specific intent and a set of privileges; it encodes hierarchy, asymmetrical rights, and zones of safety and danger. A road system in which a particular group is authorized to traverse designated roads, and others are expressly forbidden from these same roads, is a hallmark of inequality.[14] In linking colonies to Israel and each other, the segregated bypass roads compress time and space for colonists while stretching them out for Palestinians.

The West Bank road system has been described as an "octopus . . . which holds a grip on Palestinian population centers" (Efrat 2006, 85). Recalling the maxim "build it and they will come," the Settlement Master Plan for 1983–86 states, "The road is the factor that motivates settlement in areas where settlement is important." Roads were an inducement to take up residence in colonies, guaranteeing direct access to Israel since most colonists commute to Israel for work. The road system connecting the colonies directly to Israel and knitting them to each other gives material reality to their cohesion and integration into Israel. As part of crafting contiguous territory, colonies are integrated with and thus physically linked to the political center. Bypass roads craft zones of seeming safety, distant from the dangers of traveling through Palestinian areas, giving colonists confidence that they can move not just securely but at a modern tempo as well.

With their medical lexicon and imagery, "bypass roads" are so called because they literally bypass Palestinian areas, allowing Israelis to move without coming into contact with Palestinians. Three designations govern Palestinians' road access: prohibited, partially prohibited, and restricted usage (B'Tselem 2004, 12). *Prohibited* bypass roads are reserved for colonists. The *partially prohibited* roads are for Palestinians, although their movement can still be restricted by checkpoints. Last, the *restricted* roads, or portions of them, can be traversed by both Israelis and Palestinians, although Palestinians are subject to inspection at checkpoints before being allowed access. Denied passage on the majority of the West Bank's roads, Palestinians have little recourse but to use alternative, sometimes unpaved, often rocky, old roads.

Roads can be a diagnostic of the state's view of its borders but also, given Israel's de facto sovereignty over the West Bank, as marking what is excluded from the state. With Oslo, Jewish colonialists retained de facto rights to unhindered mobility in Areas B and C, but not Area A; prior to Oslo and the second intifada, they freely traversed the whole area. Their bypass roads have been constructed largely by the government as well as by colonists themselves.[15] Aside from connecting colonies directly to Israel and each other, a corollary stated objective of the bypass roads was to limit the growth or expansion of nearby Palestinian villages (B'Tselem 2004, 6). For example, the bypass roads connecting colonies east of Bethlehem have obstructed its expansion eastward.

In the A, B, and C Oslo scheme, Israelis could move freely through Area C, which was contiguous, while their entry into Area A was discouraged. The challenge for a Palestinian in this archipelago becomes, how to reach the islands, Areas A and B, when passage on the sea, Area C, is forbidden. For the bypass roads carve up the West Bank into a series of noncontiguous areas for Palestinians and create a contiguous landscape for colonists.

The Israeli map "Judea, Samaria and the Gaza Strip. Major Routes, Settlement and Civilian Outposts," is a blueprint of threat, danger, and safety. Each colony is pinpointed and all roads are well-detailed. In block letters at the bottom of the map's glossy cover, next to the logo of its publisher, Carta Jerusalem, is printed "SAFETY." Areas A and B are denoted by color and in the legend, but the map does not label the white Area C, which is under full Israeli control. Area C is the unmarked category. Erasing the Green Line is an unavoidable statement about conceptualizations and enactments of sovereignty. The bypass roads indicate the direct route from a colony to Israel, and from a colony and to other colonies, enabling through unhindered mobility the sociopolitical and kinship networks that link colonies to each other. The map's colors signal vital information: red for roads that are "no entry—danger ahead"; green signaling "road open to regular traffic (always check in advance)." "Regular traffic" means Israeli-only; red indicates the Palestinian roads. Jewish colonies are indicated by either a blue circle or square. The map's icon for the wall is "security fence." Small yellow rectangles stating "Emergency Hot Lines" and their phone numbers are located in large colonies, such as Ariel and Maale Adumim. The small, rectangular, plexiglass bus stops in the colonies have emergency phones. The map also locates fifteen IDF "medical clinics." A yellow triangle with an exclamation point indicates "warning sign at crossroads leading to dangerous areas." There is no icon for Palestinian villages, though they are shown on the map. The "rescue services" indicator heightens the sense of danger. "Military roadblocks" are designated on the map, particularly at entrances to population centers in Area A, such as Jericho; small dots on the map correspond to checkpoints on the UN Office for the Coordination of Humanitarian Affairs (OCHA) map, but there is no corresponding icon in the map's legend. Accordingly, the major checkpoints like Qalandia and Bethlehem are marked by icons, but not so the other five hundred or so checkpoints, except those situated at the intersection of a Palestinian road and Israeli road, as indicated by a small dot. Comparing the Israeli map with that of OCHA, which indicates over five hundred obstacles, is like looking at two different, if not indeed opposed, cartographies of the same space. Geared to the mobile colonist, the Israeli map omits obstacles to Palestinian mobility including the gates in the wall which the former speed through and which separate Palestinian farmers from their land in the seam zone. A navigational tool for colonists, it signals the presence and danger of the native but it is also a roadmap of conquest, ownership, and sovereignty.

Forged across Palestinian land, the bypass roads slice up and dis-aggregate the landscape with little regard for the environment or topography.[16] Aesthetically unpleasing gashes on the landscape, these quiet, well-paved bypass roads are often flanked by barbed-wire fencing and dotted with sensors and security cameras to monitor traffic. Palestinians are not allowed to drive on these roads or on portions of some of the roads that existed before occupation. Where they intersect with Palestinian roads, bypass roads are well-secured by checkpoints.

Israelis refer to spaces emptied of Palestinians as "sterile" (B'Tselem 2004, 13), a racially charged, biomedical metaphor; "sterile" also suggests quarantine, of non-Jews whose cordoning off renders an area "safe." Evoking cardiac bypass surgery, what the roads "bypass" is the indigenous population. The roads and the wall obstruct line-of-sight, minimizing Israelis' proximity to and sight of the indigenous population. The violence of the road system extends even deeper. Much of the land on which the Israeli bypass roads were built had belonged to Palestinians but was expropriated using two standard legal arguments: military need and public use. Neither legal argument was met by the roads, which then served the colonies rather than the public and limited Palestinian growth.

Bypass roads are often built on higher ground than the roads used by Palestinians. Tunnels and underpasses contrast with newly paved, multilane bypass roads. This distinction between high and low ground corresponds to "verticality," or the taking of high ground for settlements (Weizman 2007). Entering the town of Qalqiliya, one drives through a tunnel under a bypass road. Tunnels allow Israel to claim it does not obstruct Palestinian geographic contiguity even as it segregates and fragments Palestinian lands. In some areas, tunnels are for the Israelis so that they can avoid driving close to densely populated Palestinian areas, such as Beit Jala, on the way to colonies in the Hebron area. Fatima lamented that for Palestinians, the tunnels force them underground, where they traverse space like "moles or rats."

In the pre-occupation era, two main roads connected major population centers along a north-south axis: the Nablus-al-Quds Road, known as Route 60 in Israel, running from Jenin in the north to Hebron in the south via al Quds (Jerusalem), and Route 90, running north-south through the Jordan Valley. A multitude of small lateral roads, many of which were centuries old, connected villages to urban centers via the Nablus-al-Quds Road. The hilly towns and villages, the ancient spine of the West Bank, were connected, forming an economic lifeline along the main north-south route. Only in 2000 were parts of the road closed to all but Israelis. In fall 2010, Hani, an archaeologist, and I drove the road to Nablus. We had to detour twenty kilometers (twelve miles) to the northwest, passing through Bir Zeit and Abu Qash, because Palestinians were forbidden to drive on a three-kilometer (one mile) stretch of Route 60 that passed close to a colony. After detouring through Surda and Atara (once sites of infamous checkpoints), we reconnected with the Al-Quds-Nablus Road near the village of Ein Sinjil. A quick glance to the right brought the old road, now blocked by cement barriers, into focus. Significant parts of this five-thousand-year-old road, an artery connecting Palestine's north and south, have been closed to allow Israeli motorists to bypass indigenous areas and to prevent Palestinians nearing the colonies.

Back on the al-Quds-Nablus Road, we drove on a shared portion of it. On this and others main roads on the West Bank, the eye is drawn to numerous earthen mounds, trenches, and cement blocks on the side roads that hinder access to and from the villages. Villagers are obliged to walk to the main road to catch a bus and to haul goods in and out by unloading them from cars, taxis, or buses, carrying them across the main road, and then picking up another such vehicle on the other side. If they own a car, they must often use a circuitous series of rough back roads to reach the main road.

The Qalandia checkpoint is a funnel-like structure that processes Palestinians moving north to south. Since Jerusalem is off-limits to West Bank Palestinians, to travel to Abu Dis, for example, they must go around Qalandia and the Maaleh Adumim colony, which sits just above the Jericho-Jerusalem road. To travel farther south, Palestinians must detour around the colonies down the curving road to Wadi al-Nar (Valley of Fire) to the east and then drive back up to the road to Hebron.

In 2005, I spent a couple of nights in Haris, a small village southwest of Nablus, with an international women's peace and solidarity organization. When several of us wanted to take a shared taxi to the nearly village of Iskaka, and later to the group's regional center in Salfit, we were obliged to take a twenty-kilometer detour (twelve miles) to avoid the Ariel colony and the winding path next to the wall that cut off these villages from one another. A trip that once averaged five minutes now took well over half an hour and entailed a stops at three or four checkpoints along the way. At one checkpoint, we had to disembark, walk through, and pick up another taxi on the other side.

B'Tselem (2004, 26) has labeled the restrictions on Palestinian mobility the "forbidden roads regime" and duly noted one of its outstanding features, the lack of "written orders." "The forbidden roads regime is a collection of undeclared measures that together form a single, undeclared policy. This policy has never been enshrined in legislation, nor stated in official declarations, nor even indicated by road signs on the relevant roads. The policy is entirely based on verbal orders given to soldiers in the field" (ibid., 36). Reliance on verbal orders opens the way for opacity and inconsistent practices and stymies accountability. In both Apartheid South Africa and under Jim Crow in the United States there were written laws and signage, as well as an embodied habitus, to govern the subjugated and compel compliance. In both, the official and popular discourse and the laws were explicit about goals and policies. Israel engages in strategic ambiguity so that the intent and effects of their policies must be observed on the ground, and daily, to be fully comprehended. Former Israeli education minister Shulamit Aloni, brought to the fore the absence of written orders and legislation in an episode she witnessed at a bypass road:

> On one occasion I witnessed an encounter between a driver and a soldier who was taking down the details before confiscating the vehicle and sending its owner away. "Why?" I asked the soldier. "It's an order—this is a Jews-only road," he replied. I inquired as to where was the sign indicating this fact and instructing drivers not to use it. His answer was nothing short of amazing. "It is his responsibility to know it, and besides, what do you want us to do, put up a sign here and let some anti-Semitic reporter or journalist take a photo so that they can show the world Apartheid exists here?" (Aloni 2007, 45).

The lack of clear and consistent signage means that opacity is a modus operandi, yet this can be plausibly denied. Aloni's encounter exemplifies the expectations of habitus—that the indigenous will simply know, without giving it much thought, which spaces are off-limits. Entrances to Jewish-only roads do not proclaim them as such, nor do the settler maps. "Regular road" on an Israeli map signals Jewish, and a red road warns them of the "danger ahead." Large, hard-to-miss signs at the Qalandia and Huwwarah checkpoints inform Israelis they cannot enter Area A; no such signs inform Palestinians of the "danger" of an Israeli road. The unwritten and the ambiguity it engenders is integral to the daily operation of domination and denial and assumes habitus, that the indigenous read the changes on the landscape and know their place.

If there are no signs indicating a forbidden road, how do Palestinians know which roads to avoid? In the familiar environment of home, Palestinians don't use maps. The only time I ever saw a someone with a map was an ambulance driver who was poring over a book of OCHA maps that showed the location of roadblocks, checkpoints, and barriers. He said he knew the West Bank fairly well but carried the map to stay up-to-date with road changes and to ensure he could reach destinations as quickly as possible. Few taxi or bus drivers set out each day without some knowledge of which roads are open and closed to them. Knowledge circulates by word of mouth and via cell phones, especially among taxi and bus drivers, who serve as up-to-date, mobile road maps, since their livelihood depends on knowledge of a constantly shifting set of rules. They can be counted on to know about flying checkpoints and new roadblocks. At the bustling bus depots and the open areas where taxis and buses gathered near Qalandia, drivers engaged in lively exchanges about the best routes to take and those to avoid. On the roads, drivers will use a hand signal or flash their lights to let vehicles coming from the other direction know that a flying checkpoint is ahead.

In this complex road system, the ability to quickly and accurately ascertain the identity of a car's occupants is critical. Color-coded license plates distinguish Palestinian and Israeli cars: Israelis' cars, including those of East Jerusalem Palestinian residents, have yellow plates, whereas West Bank Palestinians' plates are blue, signaling that they are forbidden entry to bypass roads. In any case, few Palestinians would drive on a bypass road forbidden to non-Jews. The potential consequences are simply too harsh—a possible beating, arrest, and confiscation of the identity card and sometimes the car. In spite of the absence of signage indicating separate roads, knowledge of their proper place, of zones of danger and safety, is well-understood by all Palestinians. They are aware of their performance of deference, and that is why it can be referred to as "surface habitus," a conscious recognition of the structures of power and the requisite behavior. A response to or clear deviation from the play of domination and privilege is punished, often publicly and swiftly, displaying and reaffirming the social order.

The coupling of ordering and disciplinary measures with ambiguous rules is evident in the road system and at checkpoints. On the partially prohibited and restricted roads, where Palestinians are not absolutely forbidden, several tactics nonetheless discourage their use. Long waits at checkpoints, ostensibly to check cars for explosives and the identities of each passenger, force the Palestinian body to move at a tempo, speed, and direction set by the occupation. The unwritten rules, constantly changing orders, and the personal idiosyncrasies of a multiplicity of unaccountable agents, impose both predictability and unpredictability. Operating in tandem, they imprison Palestinians in a suspended state of waiting, uncertainty, and anxious anticipation. Israeli security forces patrol the shared roads, and Palestinians drive them with trepidation. On a warm autumn day, I and a group of four young women went to the Dead Sea for a picnic, a relaxing float in the salty water, and to slather ourselves with its mineral-rich mud. Our excursion ended poorly when driving back to Ramallah at dusk, we were pulled over by an Israeli policewoman, for no apparent reason. As she walked slowly around the car several times with a scowl on her face, no one said a word. Peering into the backseat, she spotted an unbuckled seatbelt, a contravention of Israeli traffic regulations. This could not have been detected from outside a moving vehicle at dusk. It was clear that she was looking for an infraction and a pretext to slap us with a large fine. It was costly (around $100), and the rest of the way home the driver berated her friend for not buckling her seat belt, saying she was partially to blame for the incident. Ethnographic observations of seat-belt usage shed light on the unsettled and shifting geography of habitus. When Palestinian taxi drivers drive on shared roads, or know that a checkpoint is ahead, they are assiduous about fastening their seat belts. As soon as they are out of space controlled by Israeli forces, they unbuckle them with hardly a second thought.

Another friend driving the same road as my friends and I that day was also stopped, and when the police couldn't find anything amiss with his documents, they asked him to turn on the windshield wipers and spray the wiper fluid to clean the windows. When the fluid would not come out, he was fined for not having a straight pin in the car to unplug the clogged wipers. Again, it was a costly venture to drive on a road patrolled by the occupation forces, a sort of local version of the American DWB, in this case DWP, driving while Palestinian.

Conclusion

As the workday draws to a close, Selma tells everyone in the office where she works to take their laptops home because "none of us really knows if we will arrive here tomorrow." Daily life lurches forward in crisis mode; its sequencing enveloped in uncertainty. Selma's comment underscores the way the pragmatics of daily life—ordinary comings and goings—are unknowable and contingent on the actions of others. The entanglement of subjectivity and mobility is stark: "I move therefore I am" (*Moveo ergo sum*) and "I am how I move" (Bergmann 2008, 21). Mobility occupies center stage in human subjectivity. It is essential to being human and to having a sense of self—the *I*, and the quality of that being is contingent on how one moves, or doesn't.

A geographically honed approach to habitus captures the spatial and temporal dimensions of this concept. Recognizing the reality of the actual and the potential for rapid and conscious changes in disposition called forth by spatialized arrangements of power compels us to think of habitus in the plural and endows the concept with new applicability.

Mobility is also central to the production of space and of meaningful places. Place is dynamically produced and reproduced through the activities that unfold in it and the social relationship formed and performed in it. In the West Bank, the asymmetrical contest over producing place is enacted daily through the regulation of mobility. Israel expands the territory of the state, which, in effect, shrinks the territory vital to a contiguous Palestinian state. Yet Palestinians still produce place even in these confined spaces. Denied access to local roadways and forced to traverse the same route with others, whether a trail, path, or rutted road, is to participate in a shared, collective relationship to place and the emotional life of occupied, disposable subjects.

The segregated road system is an integral component of closure. Whether it is tunnels or bypass roads, Palestinians are acutely aware of the segregated road system in which they occupy the bottom rungs, literally, whatever design it takes. The segregated road system has given rise to "partition of three dimensions," where tunnels, overpasses, bypasses, and road systems do not converge but instead curtail interaction and visibility (Weizman 2007, 180). Mobility has become a scarce good, unevenly distributed. The maze of bypass roads fractures the Palestinian landscape while stitching together colonies and Israel and carving out ethnicized space.

In the time of closure, the permit system and a segregated road network smooth the connectivity of colonists with Israel. The spatial contiguity of colonies with Israel and the speed of connection with other colonies and the state ensure Israeli participation in state and society and facilitate the production of an expanding Israeli-Jewish space. Although it is sharply asymmetrical, relationality, the interdependency between Israeli and Palestinian mobilities, plays out in visible and tangible ways as part of quotidian life. The scope and speed of Jewish-Israeli mobility depends on the constriction of Palestinian mobility.

While the wall now serves as a border of sorts between Israel and Palestine, the checkpoints, to which we now turn, are central fixtures separating Palestinians from Jerusalem and Israel, and most tellingly, they impose an internal closure or separation by filtering and funneling mobility within the West Bank. Shrouded in the potential for violence, the checkpoints catch Palestinians, individually and in the aggregate, in funnel traps. Through bodily repetition at checkpoints, Israeli security is continuously and routinely performed and reified, and relations of dominance and subordination are enacted. While disordering tactics may initially appear to generate chaos and uncertainty, the pattern underlying them is readily apparent—entrapment, subjugation, and immiseration. Chapter 3 takes up checkpoints and the colonizer's attempts to produce space through a mobility regime that miniaturizes space and accelerates the mobility of some and ensures a slowdown and gridlock for others.

3 Geography of Anticipation and Risk
Checkpoints, Filters, and Funnels

As our ford van rounded a curve, the easy chattering abruptly ceased. A young man who was en route to his parents' home had just mumbled *"al-jaysh"* (the army). Everyone stiffened, on alert for what awaited them at the flying checkpoint. Palestinians have several words for a checkpoint: *ma'bara*, which means a crossing between two states; *hajiz*, standard Arabic for checkpoint; or the Hebrew *machsom*. (Years of crossing the Green Line to work in Israel has familiarized them with rudimentary Hebrew.) But for the most part, Palestinians refer to checkpoints by their place names—Qalandia, Surda, Hamra, Huwwarah, etc.—each evoking particular sets of experiences and encounters. As pivotal mechanisms of closure, checkpoints are a constant presence in everyday life, collective consciousness, and subjectivity. They are spaces where the anticipation of violence and humiliation (*izlaal*) are ever present. Checkpoints are transit zones where colonial dominion is inscribed and exercised; they involve embodied, habitual, although not normative, practices. Palestinian experiences of being funneled and filtered through the checkpoints provided an opportunity to explore the spatiality and temporality of habitus(s). A geography of habitus in the plural suggests its multiplicity of forms given the shifting and contingent nature of daily life. As Palestinians moved from one place to another differing habitus were called forth, as were subjectivities. The randomness and capriciousness of checkpoint experiences reconfigured subjectivity and habitus.

This chapter explores checkpoints as movement spaces and encounter spaces, the spatiotemporal meaning of these, how Palestinians experience them, and what they can tell us about habitus and subjectivity. In these encounter spaces, bodily discipline is self-conscious, situated, and calculated. Palestinians have cultivated silence and a stoic demeanor that alternates with anxiety and anger. When the body moves from Israeli to Palestinian space, it relaxes, loosens up, and relief ensues. The bitter taste of humiliation subsides in the move from one space to another.

In this geography of risk, humiliation, and anticipation, the checkpoint occupies a critical position in shared narratives of moving through space as a Palestinian. Checkpoints obstruct mobility and, in doing so, violate the human right to mobility, on which hinges rights to education, employment, health care, and family life.[1] Mobility and space are mutually constitutive and relational: checkpoints facilitate Jewish-Israeli mobility and constitution of space and curtail that of Palestinians. Mobility implies a meaningful act that occurs through, and is constitutive of, space and time. The checkpoint is the linchpin in the matrix of control—of the direction, speed, and destination of Palestinian mobility.

Checkpoints give daily materiality to Israel's heterophobia and impulse to separate. To Israelis they are security measures that deter violence. As microcosms of the colonial constellation of power, these ritualized encounter spaces are the principal sites of Palestinian-Israeli interaction, where the Palestinian body is ordered, surveyed, interrogated, tracked, and disciplined, where lessons in subordination are practiced and subjectivity takes shape, and, most significantly, the boundaries of the body are violated as the Palestinian is subjected to scrutiny and visualization and can at any moment be stripped, exposed, and man-handled, making these intimate encounters. Each reads the other for signs: one to detect what the day's orders and what the mood of the checkpoint personnel might be; the other, to detect danger and risk. Israeli soldiers' attribution to Palestinians of an inner state of a potential violence animates their constant search for its signs; the very performance of security and domination may produce the violence it seeks to discover and impede.

Overall, the checkpoints do two things: they organize and display the spectacular nature of separation, and they monitor and manage the scope and speed of Palestinian mobility. Checkpoints are not liminal spaces between two contending parties. Although they are shared time/spaces, ultimately, they are Israeli spaces within occupied territory, spatializing the idea of two distinct sides and the ostensible homogeneity of space. For the Palestinian, space is constricted and time is suspended. In this small, intimate space, a colonial arrangement of power is repetitively enacted, embodied, and performed.

As physical structures, checkpoints are "movement-spaces," filtering and funneling nodes, where the built environment connects spaces (Thrift 2004). They are also encounter spaces that are emblematic of a cartography of privilege. Space is the "site of control" rather than actual mobility, for if mobility were the site of control, space would be a "perpetual checkpoint" (Packer 2008, 276). Yet this may be the case when over five hundred checkpoints operate on any one day. As I drove with Bassam from one checkpoint to another, we decelerated and then inched forward and then stopped, waited to be given permission to pass, and only then accelerated again. He joked, "We Palestinians do not need cars with fourth or fifth gears. There is not enough distance between checkpoints to gain any speed!"

The large terminals at Qalandia and Bethlehem resemble funnel traps: they channel a human mass from a wider, somewhat disordered space, through a narrow, covered, box-like passageway, and then out into an open space. Checkpoints trigger a feeling of entrapment *(masiniyya)*, for once one is inside, there is little chance of reversing the sequence.

Since the occupation, checkpoints have been a feature of daily life. The "open border" between Israel, the West Bank, and Gaza ended with the beginning of separation in 1993; additional permanent checkpoints appeared on the Green Line, and permits became more difficult to obtain. This sudden sprouting of checkpoints coincided with the dramatic proliferation of colonies in the post-Oslo period. The rationale behind the placement of the five-hundred-plus checkpoints on the West Bank is multifaceted: to protect Israelis living in the colonies from Palestinian violence and allow them speedy mobility; to limit Palestinians' travel to certain areas and roads; to fragment the West Bank; and to discipline, punish, and immiserate. At the checkpoint, various identities are performed and reaffirmed. These performances unfold before an audience and have an effect on them (Goffman 1959), and through purposeful, ritualized action, they convey a message of domination and subjugation (Bauman and Briggs 1990; Goffman 1959; V. Turner 1986). Palestinians are compelled to perform publicly visible rituals of obedience and submission. Checkpoints assert and make visible, as well as embody, the occupier's assumption of sovereignty but also its fragility. In this, they resemble stage sets in a performance of security, threat, and control.

Allenby Bridge: The Modular Funnel

Long before I began doing ethnographic research in Palestine, I had heard tales of crossing the Allenby Bridge between Jordan and the occupied West Bank. Stories of chaos *(fowda)*, crushing crowds, stifling heat, endless waits, uncertainty, and humiliation were common. At Allenby, I came face-to-face with the Israeli performance of sovereignty. The Palestinian poet Fadwa Tuqan vividly depicts the dehumanizing cruelty and humiliation of this passage, and the smoldering emotions it inspires, in her poem "At the Allenby Bridge":

> I stand at the bridge, begging
> Yes, begging to pass. I choke,
> My halting breath hangs
> Over the heat of high noon
> Seven hours, waiting . . .
> The heat whips my forehead
> Sweat drops salt into my eyelids . . .
> Oh yes, we beg to cross
> The sound of a soldier
> Roars, like a blow to the
> Face of the crowds:
> "You Arabs of chaos

You dogs, step back
Do not approach the roadblock
Go back, you dogs" . . .
A hand closes the permit window
Shut, blocks the way
My humanity bleeds, my blood oozes, bitterness, poison and fire.[2]

Each time I cross the Allenby Bridge, the procedures are different enough that I can never be quite sure what comes next. Understanding requires a historical approach, so I start with eighty-year-old Um Fuad, who has been crossing the bridge since 1972. I asked her if she remembered the first time she crossed.

We used to come every year, my husband and me, and stay in his village for a couple of weeks. We visited relatives and took trips to Haifa, Yaffa, Tiberias—all the places that we knew. The first time, in 1972, the search was fairly easy. The bridge was like any place where there are many people. You had to wait your turn. Later, it got worse. In the summer it is very hot; it is like death. One time the female soldier made me take off my clothes, even my underwear—all of it. I had a sanitary napkin. She took it, threw it in the trash and gave me a clean one. She thought there was something inside the napkin—imagine! What can we do!? The first thing, when we entered, they made us take off our shoes. They took the shoes to examine them. All the shoes! And then they threw them in a heap like this [gestures a big pile] and then you had to look through it for your shoes. There was so much chaos. They used to search our suitcases piece by piece, and they will do like this, put them like this [gestures holding up clothing] and anything that fell was lost to us. If it fell to the ground, it went behind the big barrier. Sometimes they put things in a big basket, and then we had to put them back in our suitcases. Imagine! Everything was like this [gestures piles and a mess]. It was very bad!

Of course I was angry, but what can we do? We can't talk. We can't do anything. If we shouted or said something, they would make us stay the night. Everything was in their hands. We couldn't do a thing. Every time we crossed, it was different. Only once they made me take my clothes off. Only that time. Afterwards nobody did that. But they would feel us to see if we were carrying anything.

I have had to sleep at the bridge. One year, it was the end of Ramadan, and people were coming from the *hajj* and the bridge was full of people. We wanted to cross to the Jordanian side, and the Jordanians said no. So we went back, and there was a place—a roof of wood and some columns and only a thin ledge on which to lean. I sat there all night hugging the pillar that was holding the roof. There were many people. People were lying on the ground—all these pilgrims. They put a stone under their heads! We tried to cross at 7:00 p.m. and they sent us back at 10:00 p.m.—for three hours we stood on the border. They told us they were finished for the day. We had been waiting there all day. We only reached the Jordanian side at 7:00 p.m. Israel and Jordan treat us the same. The Jordanians are not better than the Israelis. There was no place to buy food or water. At 7:00 a.m. we were the first to board the bus because they knew we were the ones who had to return the evening before. So they told us to go back. I carried my suitcase. I paid a porter to get my suitcase—it was under piles of other suitcases. I had put a colored ribbon on it and I saw the ribbon under all the other suitcases.

I don't get too anxious the night before, like most people—we have some idea of what will happen, of the chaos. The last time I crossed, it was Christmas. It is always crowded then. It is terrible, the worst travel I have had. I have been to America, London, Paris, Italy, Egypt, and Iraq. The worst travel is between Palestine and Jordan. The worst! It is like punishment. That's why I am not so keen to go to Jordan. But if my son goes, I will go. I don't like to go alone. The worst thing is every time we travel something is different from the time before! It is not the same way. Every time there is something different, something you didn't know about! All this trouble . . . it is not pleasant. We have to bear it. What can we do? I used to have to come every year for a month just to keep the residency.

After that body search, I felt dirty—I don't know . . . it was very hard. Something like that had never happened to me before—never. Once there was a little girl and the Israeli soldier wanted her to take her clothes off—she was a little girl—about five or six years old. She wouldn't take them off. She started crying and screaming. She [the soldier] made her take off her clothes and stay waiting until all the people after her in the line finished, and then she told her to go. It was like a punishment for the little girl. She made her stand naked while she examined all the other people. Everyone saw the little girl, but they couldn't say anything. They do what they want to do. Nobody tells them not to. You see, there is nobody to stop them. They are without any feelings, any feelings for other people.

Randa, now a student in the United States, described crossing the bridge in 2010. Her experience echoed that of Um Fuad.

Our bus was kept waiting for three hours to cross to the Israeli side, with no explanation and no line of cars ahead of us. Finally, after three hours, the bus was allowed to proceed. I went through the Israeli checks easily until the very end, and then one of them said to me, "You are coming from the States and you have a computer." They took it, and then said, "You have to pay a tax on it." They gave me the forms to fill out and said it would cost 400 NIS [more than $100]. I asked, "For whom and why am I paying this tax?" They said, "You are a citizen." I said, "I am not a citizen." They said, "You are a citizen of the PA. We will give your money to the PA." The staff all discussed it. There was an Ethiopian there. I said to him, "Now you are a first-class citizen?" He looked sort of ashamed. I told them I had already paid tax on the computer in the US and showed them the receipt. It meant nothing to them. I almost cried, but I tried to be strong. Why did we sign Oslo? This is the impact. What is the PA without the "authority"? This was very painful. Under the PA, we have no authority, not even to enter our country!

Widad, a university student, remembers crossing in 1995, when she was twelve years old, "I was crying the whole time because I was so upset about the treatment. They treated us like rubbish, as though we were nothing. The searches, going through all our things, so many questions, their attitudes toward us—that we were just nothing." Recently, her older brother attempted to return home for the funeral of his grandmother; he had an American passport. After waiting for twelve hours without being told why, he burst out, "Arrest me or send me back!" They sent him back, and he missed the funeral. I spoke with an African American Muslim traveling to Jerusalem who was asked to recite the fatiha, the opening sura of the Quran, before being allowed entry. Her encounter moment entailed a low-tech, embodied verification of identity through this performance.

Um Fuad's, Widad's, and Randa's stories have common threads: physical discomfort, violations of bodily integrity, fear, trepidation, and most markedly, ambiguity and humiliation. Palestinians are both audience and performer in this public enactment of domination and subjugation. Young men in particular anticipate interrogation and physical abuse. Muna travels a couple of times a year to visit family abroad. At dinner before her departure, she expressed a profound sense of anxiety. "I can't sleep for several nights in anticipation of the bridge." Likewise, Widad, who occasionally visits family in Amman, reported intense trepidation, a feeling of anxious anticipation, which starts about ten days before she crosses. In sum, crossing resembles an ordeal.

The Allenby Bridge crossing soon revealed two key features of Israeli checkpoints: willful inefficiency, or calibrated chaos, and the funnel-like structure. On each trip slightly different procedures were followed, but the basic sequencing remained. Buses are stopped midway across the bridge; the passengers are made to disembark and must wait while the bus is searched and their documents are inspected. Upon arriving at the border post, they pour out of the buses as their luggage is whisked away by plainclothes security employees, who disappear into a cavernous building, saying that they will return. In the meantime, a crush of people strains against the neck-high metal barriers for the first perfunctory passport inspection. On entering the main building, everyone must walk through a body-scanning machine that sprays them with a mist, assumed to be chemical, designed to detect any residue of explosives. Then they are funneled single-file through two or three inspection stations. A square room before the inspection stations is so small that a queue cannot form, but, gradually, everyone passes through and then must push through a metal turnstile to see the luggage coming down an overhead conveyer belt and being dumped into a large pile. Like Um Fuad, I had to wade through the pile to locate my bag. Before the Israeli visa is issued at the final inspection station, everyone must answer questions about the purpose of their visit: whom they plan to see, including their occupation, phone number, and address; or, they must say why they want to see them, and to what places they plan to travel. This can take five minutes or can continue for hours in a small, barren office in which there is a single computer and one official. Improvements, such as air-conditioning, have been made over the years; nonetheless, the funneling process is the same as is the interrogation process. In this long, drawn-out encounter space, Israelis scanned Palestinian bodies for signs of risk and foreigners for any indication of relationship to Palestinians. Palestinians searched Israelis for signs of humanity.

Checkpoints and Funnel Traps

Because it is a pervasive feature of daily life in zones of conflict and counterinsurgency, the checkpoint has become a subject of ethnographic inquiry.[3] The Israeli checkpoint is an encounter space and a movement space between hypermobile, rights-bearing Israeli Jews and hypomobile and rightsless Palestinians. Munira's description of passing through Gaza's Eretz checkpoint sheds light on the incarceratory and nonhuman quality of a hi-tech checkpoint. Significantly, her critical narrative suggests less-standard understandings of habitus and a keen analytical consciousness about structures of control:

> To go through Eretz is like being part of an experiment on human beings. It is so complicated that the first time I started to go through I had to ask people four times to get instructions on how to proceed. There are no directions. It is a maze—like a Kafka story—no one is there—it is a faceless place. There is no one there that you can see. You face four doors with no directions as to which one to open. You just wait, and then one of them opens. The exit from Gaza is designed to manage hundreds of Palestinian workers. You go through another corridor and there are eight doors and a wall to the right—you are always confined in small spaces. You don't know which way to go. You press a button and wait for a green light over one of the doors. Then it opens and you exit. There is a Palestinian waiting there to help you with your bags. Then you go through the scanning machine—everything is glassed-in around you, but above you is a sort of mezzanine or loft—in it are Israeli forces with computers. You go into the scanning machine, and they shout at you from up above. You are always surrounded by glass and observable, but you can't see them. It is like a prison—if someone was designing the ultimate prison, they should come and look at this. They can see you at all times but you cannot see them. To pass Eretz is to participate in a marketing experiment in the latest security technology!

"Almost all mobilities presuppose large scale immobile infrastructures that make possible the sociality of life" (Urry 2007, 19); airports and train stations are prime examples.[4] Yet these same infrastructures can impede mobility and minimize social interaction. The checkpoints are an apt illustration of the highly mediated and relational nature of mobilities: the mediation of one facilitates the unmediated possibility of the other. Asymmetry is starkly evident when Palestinians endure long waits, while Israeli-plated cars whiz through the very same infrastructures.

In Palestine, immobile infrastructures range from a couple of cement blocks and a guard booth manned by two or three soldiers to large sites, such as Eretz, Qalandia, and Bethlehem, which gradually have been transformed into terminals resembling international border zones. There are also permanent checkpoints that have not developed into terminal-like structures. For example, the checkpoint in front of the Shavei Shomron colony was a simple affair, just some cinderblocks and a guardhouse. Some checkpoints can be driven through; at others, one must leave public transportation, walk across the checkpoint, and then pick up another bus or taxi on the other side. Palestinians bitterly complain that this adds time and extra fares to a daily commute. Not all are immobile infrastructures; there are "flying," or temporary, checkpoints that appear with little warning. But they all share several characteristics: involuntary waiting and scrutiny and the unpredictability of regulations and behavior, succinctly summed up in the frequently heard refrain, "It all depends on their [soldiers'] mood (*hasab mizajhum*)."

The potential for violence at checkpoints is palpable—a small group of well-armed personnel can open fire on unarmed civilians or detain them at will. Hundreds of Palestinians crowd the checkpoint, worried about getting through, angry, and frustrated. Those who ask questions can be swiftly sanctioned: a forced wait in a cell or by the side of the road, confiscation of the identity card and holding it for a long time or threatening to keep it, a beating, or an arrest. As Munira noted, Palestinians at checkpoints are hypervisible through observation and regulation, even as they are invisible to most Israelis because of the wall.

Some checkpoints are notorious for cruel treatment, harassment, and denying passage, for example, the Huwwarah checkpoint, near Nablus, and the "Container" at the entrance to Jerusalem (on the Wadi al-Nar Road).[5] When checkpoints were built to restrict Palestinian access to Jerusalem in 1991, the Wadi al-Nar Road was frequented as a route from Bethlehem and Hebron to central and northern Palestine. The "Container" literally corrals people, propelling them through a progressively narrowing funnel where identities are ascertained and, in a filtering process, are either allowed to pass or turned back.

Named after a nearby village, Huwwarah checkpoint sits imposingly on the main road into Nablus from the south. Outlying villages with deep, historical, commercial, and kinship ties to Nablus used this road to reach the town and points south as well. Set up in late 2000, the checkpoint splits the West Bank and cuts off Nablus from its hinterland. The Israelis closed and opened the checkpoint without warning, and the Palestinians complained vociferously about the lengthy delays, large crowds, and constantly changing orders.

Tariq, a development worker and father of two, showed his resourcefulness in the face of adversity:

> I try to visit my parents every two months, but I don't take my two children. It is too difficult at the checkpoints, even though our village is only thirty-eight kilometers from Ramallah. This is the ugly face of the occupation. But this is the reality of our lives. I will tell you a story. I was working in a village near Jenin on a project. I finished work one day at 12:30, so I decided to visit my family. I arrived at Hawwarah checkpoint, and it was closed because, they said, they had found a woman with a suicide bomb. I had only twenty shekels. I couldn't sleep in Nablus, and I didn't have enough money to go to Jenin. Eventually, there were two workers and me left at this checkpoint. The soldiers would point their guns at me if I tried to talk, whether in Hebrew or English. Finally, one soldier speaks, "Stay here, and we'll talk later." After two hours, when it was 11:30 p.m., he allowed me to go through the checkpoint. It was winter. I saw a taxi. He stopped and I told him, "I have no money but if you drive me to Ramallah I will pay you there." So I paid him ninety shekels when we arrived in Ramallah in the middle of the night. The experience of facing them has encouraged me to challenge them.

Later, after another long and unexpected delay at Huwwarah, Tariq exclaimed in frustration, "What is the message of the checkpoint? Leave! Life is not going to be easy."

In fall 2010, Huwwarah was unmanned, but the physical structure, the looming watchtower from which soldiers continued to monitor the road, and the cement blocks were still standing, ready to be reactivated at any time. A couple of soldiers slouched against the cement blocks adjacent to the large, red sign in Hebrew that forbids Israelis from entering Area A; they barely looked up as we drove through. My traveling companion said, "With [President] Obama and some pressure on Israel, they eased the checkpoints, and now we can move a bit more freely. We have suffered with this checkpoint for nearly nine years." With Nablus economically strangled by the checkpoint, Huwwarah had become an active and bustling commercial center, as Nabulsi businesses moved shops there and to Ramallah. The former village now teems with auto repair and sweet shops, among others.

At large checkpoints like Bethlehem and Qalandia, the crowds can be frightening as people push and shove to reach the metal turnstile. Age is often made a criterion for passage. On some days, soldiers have orders not to admit anyone under the age of forty, or thirty-four; on others, it might be anyone under twenty-five. Bus and taxi drivers learn about these restrictions and alert their passengers.

A discernible logic governs the organization of space and the sequencing of passage: unidirectional movement through well-delimited spaces. Israeli personnel roam the checkpoint, moving from air-conditioned offices to the inspection spots, or walking up and down the long lines of waiting Palestinians, guns at the ready. A striking characteristic of checkpoints is the age of young men and women running them. They are typically between eighteen and twenty-two years old, drawn from the regular army, the border police, and reservists. Since 2006, when border checkpoints and the checkpoints Israel considers de facto border terminals, such as Qalandia, were reorganized and some of the security was outsourced, private-security employees have been present (Havkin 2011). Determinations as to which Palestinians were allowed to pass was made by higher-ranking military officers or lower-ranking field commanders (Ben-Ari 2005; Havkin 2011). The military training of the guards, as well as of the private-security guards who have done military service, was replicated in their treatment of Palestinians when they referred to them as the "youngsters of the youngsters" or aimed to "educate" them (Ben-Ari 2005, 30) and "teach them [the Palestinian] a lesson" (Grassiani 2013, 77), thus mimicking the paternalistic hierarchy of military culture.

Israeli soldiers are, by turns, bored, rude, aggressive, alienated from their task, occasionally kind, and embarrassed, but always in control. They are posted for weeks at a time at a checkpoint, working eight-hour shifts, on and off. Trained for combat, these post-adolescent men and women must spend their days policing people who are just trying to get to work or school, see a doctor, or simply shop and visit family and friends. One of the most striking scenes at a checkpoint is the sight of three or four soldiers or police managing hundreds of unarmed Palestinians waiting to move. With their military paraphernalia, such as walkie-talkies, heavy boots, uniforms and helmets, rifles and ammunition; and police equipment, such as night sticks and handcuffs; as well as the accessories they wear, such as sunglasses, they visually convey dominance, in stark contrast to the iconic figure of the Palestinian quietly waiting for permission to move. The ubiquitous sunglasses mimic the uneven visuality at the checkpoint: Israelis see and are not seen, while the Palestinian is starkly visible. In his reflection in the sunglasses, the Palestinian witnesses his own subordination (Tawil-Souri 2011).

Some of the misbehavior by checkpoint personnel has been attributed to boredom and frustration (Ben-Ari 2008). Checkpoint duty does not easily cohere with combat training and the warrior self-image. They control thousands of people from whom they anticipate possible violence and are confronted with multiple categories of identity cards, negotiations between Palestinians and commanders, language barriers, as well as unwelcome monitoring by local human rights organizations such as Machsom Watch (Checkpoint Watch).[6] On the cusp of adulthood, these young people have the power to make decisions about a person's need for medical care and whether a woman in labor should be allowed to pass, the elderly can go through, or students can attend school.

My field notes record the obstacles to mobility and its unpredictability. In summer 2007, Françoise, a European colleague, and I were invited to the northern city of Jenin by our mutual friend Ziad. On a sweltering Friday morning, we headed to the cavernous bus terminal in Ramallah. We hopped aboard a van headed to Jenin, settled into our seats, and paid our fare. We knew that the once one-and-a-half-hour trip to Jenin, a fairly straight shot north on Route 60, was now estimated to take several hours. These delays limit the number of trips bus and taxi driver can make, and thus reduce their income. They know detours on often unpaved backroads that were rarely used until the checkpoints and bypass roads made them necessary alternatives. So, the best way to reach Jenin on this day necessitated a roundabout trip through arid terrain on a rocky mountain road, down to the flat, humid, and verdant Jordan Valley, and then due north.

As we descended through the rocky reddish-brown hills, the landscape gradually became greener. At several small checkpoints, our documents were examined, but there were no delays. After driving through the valley for more than an hour, we reached al-Hamra checkpoint, which has a well-deserved reputation for harassment and long waits in the valley's punishing heat. A red sign in Hebrew, Arabic, and English read, "Palestinian Authority Territory Area A Ahead. No Entry for Israelis. Entry Illegal by Israeli Law." As the sun rose higher, so did the heat and humidity. In the un-air-conditioned van, my sweat-drenched cotton clothing stuck to the hot vinyl seat. Cautiously, the driver pulled up to the checkpoint. It was eerily quiet, and no one appeared. Experience had taught him to never drive through a checkpoint, however deserted it might seem. To do so gives the Israelis a good pretext to shoot. Twenty feet away we saw four young soldiers perched on squat wooden stools, arrayed around an short, makeshift table, eating a morning meal. We waited about fifteen minutes in the sweltering van while they finished eating. The driver knew better than to ask questions, and we passengers knew the drill as well. Palestinians are forbidden to leave their vehicles at checkpoints, and to get out of the van was to invite arrest or, worse, a soldier opening fire. It was routine at many checkpoints, especially the smaller ones on less traveled roads, for all the guards to eat meals or take breaks at the same time, in effect, closing the checkpoint. Finally, two young soldiers sauntered over and motioned the van forward. They collected our identity cards and passports and disappeared for another ten or fifteen minutes, while we roasted inside the van. Then one of the soldiers came back and told Françoise and me to get out of the van. Handing us our passports, he snapped in English, "No foreigners allowed to enter Jenin. This is for your own protection. Get your things and go back to Ramallah." We would not be allowed to enter Jenin today. The iteration of "your own protection" evoked the discourse of security that is invoked to justify the obstruction of foreigners' mobility. Françoise argued with him, to no avail. Eventually, our driver indicated that he had to proceed. As we collected our bags, Françoise continued to argue. "Why can you [Israelis] go into Jenin?" she asked sarcastically. "Are you going to make us sit here, without food and water, in this heat? What will we do?" Becoming more agitated, she exclaimed, "We are guests—we've been invited. You are the foreigners here!" "These are our orders for today" one of them replied, somewhat sheepishly. Another suggested we hitch a ride back in one of the cars that occasionally drove by. A bypass road from a nearby colony intersected the checkpoint. A few cars came down this road over the next half hour or so, but neither of us was willing to hitch a ride with a colonist. We started walking south. Our water bottles were empty, and we had no food, and worse, the sun was at its peak. After we had gone about 100 meters, one of the soldiers came running after us and said, "Mamam, you forgot your bag at the checkpoint." I returned to the checkpoint and found my small bag sitting there, untouched. They had not even opened the bag to inspect its contents. So much for security, I thought!

The indigenous population of the Jordan Valley has been heavily diluted; those who have stayed must have a permit to be there. Because it is classified as a closed military zone, part of Area C, 94 percent of the land in the valley is unavailable to Palestinians. Eventually, a car with a Palestinian license plate appeared. We flagged it down and were delighted when the driver beckoned us to into his air-conditioned car. We explained our plight, and he kindly offered to drive us to the small town, near a colony, where he worked as a singer in a café. At the café, he offered us cold drinks and called a taxi to drive us to Jericho. There is no way in or out of Jericho that does not necessitate a stop at a checkpoint. After about a twenty-minute wait at the checkpoint, we finally drove into Jericho, where we lunched and plotted how to reach Jenin. In the late afternoon, we headed back to the Qalandia checkpoint, crossed it on foot, and caught a van to Ramallah. It had been a frustrating, hot, and miserable day, and more than eight hours after leaving, we were right back where we had started.

Determined to visit Jenin, the next day we headed to the bus terminal and found a van driver who would use roads that circumvented the al-Hamra checkpoint. Delighted, we climbed in, reaching Jenin exactly four hours and five checkpoints later. First, we passed the 'Atara checkpoint north of Bir Zeit, which sits on a rocky hilltop at the juncture of three roads. We arrived to a scene of sheer pandemonium. A jeep was parked horizontally across the road effectively narrowing it to one lane. In addition, there was vehicular cross-traffic at the top of the road. Throngs of people from the blocked-off villages were making their way down the hill to catch one of the waiting busses or vans. Drivers were stepping out of their cars to see what was going on, horns blared, and the gridlock was exacerbated by drivers trying to cut ahead in the line. Eventually, movement came to a complete stop. A few resourceful young men hopped out of cars and started directing traffic. One of the two soldiers manning the checkpoint stood back while the other aimed his rifle at the line of cars. When our van finally reached the checkpoint, the other soldier peered into the open window, pointed his rifle at the backseat, and shouted "*hawiyyah*." Holding my passport upside down, he demanded, "Where are you from?" After a superficial check of the identity cards of all of us in the van, he waved us on, and loped toward the next car in line. One of the young men in the van said bitterly: "These Russians—they can't even speak Hebrew, let alone Arabic or English." It had taken us about forty-five minutes to travel a hundred feet. Two soldiers were tasked with funnelling hundreds of people and cars though this narrow strip of road, a recipe for chaos.

The second checkpoint was rudimentary, consisting of two large cement blocks on each side of the narrow road, in a lush and well-cultivated area. The wait was short, and the lone soldier checking identities was quite pleasant. A young Palestinian boy walked along the waiting line of cars selling coffee from a thermos for a shekel (twenty to twenty-five cents). The soldier told us, "He has good coffee." Once we were out of earshot, the silence that inevitably descends when the van is being inspected was broken. I struck up a conversation with another passenger, who lamented that his wife lives in Jordan and cannot join him because the Israelis refuse to grant her a residency permit.

The third checkpoint was in the Funduq area. We were allowed to proceed without having our papers checked or the van inspected. I spotted a rare road sign in Arabic and English indicating that it was fifty-seven kilometers (thirty-five miles) to Jenin. Our fourth checkpoint was run by Druze border police. "They hate the Palestinians," says one of the young men. But they allowed us to proceed without checking our documents or the vehicle. I asked the man seated next to us why. He said, "The driver is a sheikh—a very religious man. He recites Qur'an. They know this, and so they let us go."

Checkpoint five was in front of the Shavei Shomron colony, which was surrounded by chicken-wire fencing topped with coils of barbed wire; the fence was lined with a three- to four-foot-high strip of black cloth, blocking the view of the colony. Although there are only two cars ahead of us, our driver is visibly annoyed. He tells us that if we are not allowed to pass he will have to turn around and go another route, adding an hour and a half to the trip. We waited about thirty minutes. The two cars ahead of us were blocking off a lane, turning the road into a single lane, which slowed things down even more because they were checking cars coming from both directions. When all the cars coming from the other direction had moved, we had to wait for another ten minutes while the checkpoint personnel waited for another car to come up on the other side; it was hard not to think that the delay was deliberate. Finally, after almost five hours of driving and stops at checkpoints, we reached Jenin.

Qalandia, the largest and most infamous of the checkpoint/terminals, is a colossal monument to separation. Once the site of an airport, it is an immobile infrastructural node and a physical and experiential marker of fragmentation and immobilization that epitomizes the Palestinian condition. It is situated at a busy intersection on the southern edge of Ramallah where it meets the northern edge of an expanded Jerusalem, the Qalandia refugee camp, stone quarries to the east, the al-Ram neighborhood, and the wall. Behind the scenes at large checkpoints are DCO personnel who make decisions about Palestinian movement. Qalandia severs the West Bank from Jerusalem and points south. Built in 2001 as an open-air checkpoint, it has since grown in size, requiring more and longer procedures for passage and technological accoutrements. By 2006, it had grown into what Israel dubbed a "terminal," akin to a border crossing staffed by military personnel, border police, and private-security guards as well as DCO staff. Cars had to wait in interminably long lines to be searched. At the same time, the rules governing who could cross constricted: initially, women, children under the age of fourteen, and those over sixty were all allowed to cross; now only holders of Jerusalem identity cards and those with permits or visas could cross.

In fall 2005, vans and taxis ferry people to Qalandia from Ramallah. Women, shopping bags overflowing and children in tow, struggle to board the buses. Well-dressed students traveling home from Bir Zeit University are quiet and apprehensive. As the van approaches Qalandia, the wall comes into sight, running from the west directly up to the checkpoint, where it ends at a watchtower (see figure 3.1). As happens near train stations and airports, a market had sprung up there, with vendors selling hot corn on the cob, bread, juices, and hot drinks. Peddlers sell ice cream, pots and pans, and assorted small household utensils, as well as underwear and socks, Qur'ans, birds, and fresh produce. Cars, buses, and vans pull up to designated areas and disgorge their passengers, who then head for the open-air pedestrian walkway. Sensory overload easily sets in as drivers honk their horns or rev their engines, children cry, vendors hawk their wares, people chat or grumble to no one in particular, brakes screech, and throngs of people mill about. The exhaust from the idling buses and taxis, the smell of garbage, and of sweat from bodies packed too closely together in the heat of summer or wearing wet clothes in winter, assault the olfactory sense. Inside the checkpoint, the auditory sense is shocked by the din of mechanical sounds: the clang of metal, squeaking turnstiles, and orders blaring from loudspeakers in unseen places. Calibrated chaos ensues as hundreds of people mill around and then funnel into multiple lines to start the filtering process. Noise alternates with silence as documents are checked and bodies advance one-by-one through turnstiles and body scanners.

The Qalandia checkpoint, like the Bethlehem checkpoint/terminal and Allenby Bridge, has a structure that funnels people single file into smaller, enclosed

Figure 3.1 Fire-blackened watchtower at Qalandia checkpoint. Photograph by the author.

passageways before they eventually come out into open space. At Qalandia, the outside area resembles a large funnel opening which then progressively shrinks to squeeze the crowd through its neck. While all checkpoints can be said to funnel people, Qalandia, the Bethlehem checkpoint, and the Allenby Bridge stand out for their sheer size, the number of personnel working them, and the more numerous set of stops one must pass through. Indeed, they resemble a border crossing between states. Passage through Qalandia proceeds in a fairly well-defined sequence. First, pedestrians are made to queue along a passageway delineated by chicken-wire fencing topped with barbed or razor wire. After passing through the metal turnstile, they enter an enclosed square area. Their packages and bags are loaded onto a rickety conveyor belt for screening, while their bodies pass through a metal detector. And then documents are verified and registered. There is little face-to-face contact; checkpoint personnel are stationed behind bullet-proof plexiglass windows and issue orders through a microphone. Everyone holds up a passport, identity card, or permit to the window for inspection; staff rely on the information on the identity cards all Palestinian carry, many of which now contain biometric data or fingerprint readers, to decide whether someone can pass or not. A flick of the hand indicates that passage is allowed, as the Israeli personnel continue to talk or laugh or engage with studied indifference. One is then allowed to proceed or detained for a body search or interrogation or to simply stand and wait at the checkpoint. Sometimes, people are denied entry for no apparent reason. In this unidirectional space, a sense of entrapment sets in—hence the funnel-trap or cattle-chute analogy. The two sets of turnstiles at Qalandia resemble a double funnel—one through which to enter; the other for exiting. The severely constricted space in-between, the neck of the funnel, is where the determination of passage is made. A final turnstile and then a narrow lane lead to the exit. In other words, there is a progression from anticipation and waiting to validation, passage or denial, and finally, exit. The body has been pushed and shoved, prodded, scanned, and often manhandled, although the haptic aspect of checkpoints has changed. Hot and dusty in summer, cold and wet during winter, they can be exhausting places.

When I began this field project in 2004, it took well over an hour to travel between Ramallah and Jerusalem, compared to about twenty minutes in the pre-closure era. I often rode buses to get a feel for the temporal rhythm of mobility as well as to observe encounters at checkpoints. One day in 2005, when I waited in line with a large group of men at Qalandia, they kindly advised me to go to the women's line. After more than an hour of waiting in the heat and dust, my legs aching from standing, I finally reached the inspection station and handed my passport to a young soldier, who cheerily told me, in American English to "have a nice day." Once out of the checkpoint, I began inquiring about the *services* (shared taxis) to Jerusalem, when a high school girl on her way to Shofat, on the outskirts of Jerusalem, said, "Come with me. You can get a service from Shofat." We finally found one going toward Jerusalem. With his radio blasting the Qur'an, the young driver drove about half a mile on a rough, pot-hole-filled road and stopped suddenly in front of three square cement cubes blocking the road. He said we should walk through them and find another car. When we tried to pay our fare, he repeatedly refused to take money from us saying, "You have not reached your final destination." We walked for a few minutes and found a bus filled with young men, women with children, and a few elderly going to Shofat and Jerusalem. We quickly boarded and took two seats together. This young girl insisted on paying my bus fare—I had a large bill but not the required small change. Although I was concerned because she was a young student with what I assumed were limited funds, it quickly dawned on me that she was offering hospitality, a gesture that said, "I belong here and this is my home."

Soon a soldier from the checkpoint just in front of the bus climbed on board. Chatter abruptly ceased. Two women were seated in the row across from us. The minute the soldier had mounted the steps into the bus, the elder of the two, wearing the colorful embroidered Palestinian dress, quickly rose from her aisle seat and sat down in an empty seat next to a young man, in his late teens or early twenties, sitting in the seat in front of us. They didn't exchange a word—it seemed to me that she had moved next to him to to protect him if the soldier bothered him. I could imagine no other reason for her to change seats. There is a kind of maternalism writ large among Palestinian women that emerged as an iconic form of resistance to occupation. During the first intifada, middle-aged and elderly women, singly or in groups, would surround a young boy to shield him from a soldier's blow or arrest (Peteet 1997). The soldier growled *hawiyyah*; blue plastic identity cards indicating Jerusalem residency were at the ready as he walked down the aisle collecting cards from several people, but mainly from young men, whose age and gender assigned them to the potential risk category. Then he left the bus and showed them to another soldier. A good fifteen minutes later, he returned the identity cards. In an act of petty resistance, and relying on age and gender norms that sometimes excluded women, particularly elder women, from security checks, some of these women had their cards ready but did not actually hold them up for inspection. The young girl sitting next to me did nothing, perhaps banking on her young age. When he left, the woman who had changed her seat quietly returned to her original seat. The silence lifted. The young girl told me that she went through Qalandia every day going to and from school in Ramallah, adding hours of uncertainty to her day. Finally, we reached East Jerusalem. It had taken two-and-a-half hours. The shifting of habitus, its multiplicity of spatially and gender-contingent forms, could be read in the silence inside the bus when soldiers entered and ID cards were quickly proffered. Yet, as we have seen, women and sometimes younger girls exempt themselves from the routine of subjugation.

Traveling from Jerusalem to Ramallah, I quickly learned, was less laborious and involved less compulsory legibility. Bus 18 departs from the bus terminal near the Old City.[7] The full mid-morning bus was unusually quiet except for the rhythmic chanting of the Qur'anic verses on the radio. Typically, the bus loads passengers heading for Qalandia or for Jerusalem neighborhoods, such as Shofat or Beit Hanina. Walking through the checkpoint to enter Ramallah was a breeze compared to crossing the other way. Israel was a bit less interested in who was leaving than who was entering. When the security guards do check the identity cards of those leaving, it is often to search for Palestinians who have been in Jerusalem "illegally" or are wanted by the authorities.

By 2010, the Qalandia "terminal" resembled an international border. In a redesigned layout, entry was through a cavernous, smelly, garbage-littered, metal-roofed building. The terminal gave way to a series of numbered lanes about fifteen feet in length, which get backed up quickly, making queuing difficult. A maze of metal barriers funnels people into five lines for single-file passage through the numbered turnstiles. On this particular fall morning, only about a hundred people are at the checkpoint. People are lined up to go through the remotely controlled turnstiles. When the light above the turnstile turns green, two or three people push through, and then, without any intermediate warning light, the light turns red and the turnstile locks. A female voice comes over the sound system to say, "Line three is open." Everyone moves quickly to line three, and, after five to ten minutes, the green light begins to allow people through. Then the disembodied voice announces, "Lines four and five are open." Again, people hustle over to these lines—two or three pass through the turnstile, and then nothing for five to ten minutes. After about half an hour of this inane stop-and-go game, the voice instructs, "Lines one, two, three, and four are now open." We push through the rattling turnstiles as quickly as possible. Now we are in the heart of the checkpoint. There is a sign in English and Arabic saying, "Please put your things on the conveyor belt and wait for further instruction." Next to it is another sign: "Put your documents in the slot and wait for further instructions." We place our bags on the conveyor belt and walk through the metal detector. On our immediate left is a small office with a plexiglass window and three soldiers inside. A small electronic device scans our documents. A sign posted on the corridor leading to the exit says, "Have a pleasant and safe stay."

According to Machsom Watch's posting about the lexicon surrounding checkpoints, Israelis use the Hebrew word for carousel, the kind seen at children's amusement parks, to refer to the turnstiles, conveying an image of an innocuous children's ride at an amusement park. At checkpoints Palestinians are sometimes referred to as the "animals," and Palestinians sometimes refer to going through them as "de-feathering." The width of a checkpoint turnstile is about fifty-five centimeters (twenty-one inches), narrower than the standard width of seventy-five to ninety centimeters (twenty-nine to thirty-five inches).[8] For anyone slightly overweight, women with infants or small children, or people carrying bags, the turnstile poses a challenge. Ordinary turnstiles are controlled by pushing. Here, there is no such control. You can only enter the turnstile when the light turns green, and it is not uncommon for the turnstile to be stopped abruptly with someone still between the bars. This happened to me once, and I was stuck in this claustrophobic metal space for about ten minutes; the same thing happened to an elderly man behind me. The staff do this without warning and for no apparent reason, sometimes not reactivating the turnstile for as long as twenty minutes.

Passing through checkpoints is a traumatic, repetitive engagement with risk, deceleration of mobility, and subjection. The anxiety is palpable when the *hawiyyah* is handed to the guard. When deference is not forthcoming or questions are asked, the response may be punishment or being made an "example." A public beating, arrest, prolonged waiting, being forced to sit at the side of the road or in a ditch in the hot sun or in the cold for long stretches, and confiscation of car keys and identity cards constitute familiar forms of punishment. Exactly at what point to stop the car is not always clear. Those running the checkpoints speak in commands: "sit," "get down," "*hawiyyah*," "shut up," "stop," "go," and so on. Drivers wait until commanded to "come forward" or "stop." An ethnography of Israeli soldiers reaffirms conceptualizations of checkpoints as punitive and didactic mechanisms where they mete out "corrective punishment" to make sure the Palestinians know "who is in charge" and where they are "taught a lesson" (Grassiani 2013, 126).

That questioning can be costly was evident when Arwa's brother argued with a soldier at a checkpoint. He was then pulled from a bus and made to stand for hours, and then taken to the Moscowbiyya prison complex in West Jerusalem. His father, who was called and told to pick him up, admonished him, "Choose your battles. You can't fight with them this way. They will shoot you without a thought." Masculinity was at play here, on the part of both the brother and the father. The father wielded the caution and wisdom of the elder male, while his son had argued with the soldiers out of his feelings of humiliation and anger at being ordered about and insulted by young men his own age.

Women sometimes do argue at checkpoints, gauging that they will not be treated as harshly as men. At Qalandia, I observed a young mother carrying a sick child. She had a permit to take him to a hospital in Jerusalem. Without warning, the checkpoint closed. She waited a while and then approached a soldier, thrust the permit in his face, and pleaded with him to allow her to cross. He kept repeating, "It is an order, it is an order." She would alternately shove the permit and the baby in his face, crying that the child needed medical care. Sweating profusely in the August heat and annoyed by her badgering, he nudged her back into the crowd with his rifle.

Body movements communicate information; the automatic readying of identity cards is of the first magnitude. But Palestinian deference usually goes no further. Palestinians rarely defer by trying to please, neither smiling nor even nodding. There may be a few obsequious smiles, but usually just silence and restrained anger. The meta-language of silence crafts a personal space of dignity and but also references the knowledge that to question is risky; it can be interpreted as uppityness and invoke the wrath of bored young men, indifferent to the suffering of others, and frustrated by the mundane job of policing rather than the excitement of combat. In this highly asymmetrical encounter, silence is part of a strategic set of behaviors and a refusal to actively participate in their own subjugation.[9]

Language use at checkpoints is telling in several respects. In a shared taxi from Ramallah to Bethlehem, the driver and I were complaining about the length of the trip. When I asked him why he spoke English at the checkpoints, he replied, "I don't speak to them in Hebrew. They want us to accept them and their presence—this is an occupation! I speak to them in English—it bothers them that an Arab can speak a second language." Refusing to speak the occupier's language is a refusal to recognize. Three languages are spoken at checkpoints: Arabic, Hebrew, and English. Palestinians who can speak in English do. I asked Ziad what language he used, he smiled and said, "You know, I never really thought about it, but I use English—I don't know why. I am usually so nervous about being allowed to pass without trouble. But I do think when I use English they become annoyed. They assume we are all stupid and uneducated." Speaking English, a lingua franca, signifies educational status and can be a means of maintaining dignity in an otherwise degrading situation. Speaking Hebrew indicates one's status as a worker or perhaps a former prisoner. A Palestinian scholar explored the complex power dynamics of language at checkpoints. "By refusing to use Arabic . . . I was refusing to allow any bonds of solidarity, or even interpersonal understanding through the language, to obtain between us. I looked at the soldiers as members of a foreign force that illegally occupies my country" (Suleiman 2004, 8–9).

Russian-speaking soldiers are distained. Palestinians note, ironically, "We speak better Hebrew than these Russians, and yet they have the right to live here, and we don't have rights even if we were born here." As new immigrants, many with a murky religious affiliation, Russians are thought to act tougher at the checkpoints. Likewise, female soldiers are assumed to be ruder as well, as they try to assert themselves in the macho military world. A Russian soldier boarded a bus leaving Tulkaram filled with internationals and Palestinians. After checking identity cards and asking in broken Hebrew what we were doing in this area, she pointed her rifle at passengers and muttered, "You are all trash."

Sulky young soldiers slouching against buildings or cement blocks at checkpoints is an iconic scene, as are scenes inside the offices at the checkpoints, where the male and female soldiers frequently flirt, joke around with each other, chat, or send text messages, indifferent to those who are waiting for permission to move, and conveying to Palestinians their insignificance and powerlessness. They do not even warrant a serious military demeanor. The casual flick of the hand, or a dismissive nod of the head, expresses their utter indifference. At a checkpoint on the eastern side of Jerusalem, a soldier, wearing sparkling gold costume jewelry with her long, tapered nails painted hot pink, automatic rifle slung across her torso, boards the bus and perfunctorily glances at identity cards but doesn't look anyone in the face. The male soldier working with her stays on the steps of the bus busily sending text messages on his cell phone. To the side of the bus, lined up quietly in a barbed-wire-topped, fenced walkway, stand well over a hundred Palestinians waiting under the scorching sun to enter Jerusalem.

On a bus traveling near Jayyous, we stop at a flying checkpoint. The post-adolescent soldier, his sagging pants revealing colorful cartoon-themed underwear, studiously licks a dripping ice cream cone at 9:30 on a scorching morning. He saunters onto the bus, cone in one hand, the other on his rifle, collects identity cards and hands them to another soldier, while we wait in the heat. Fifteen minutes later he reappears—without his ice cream cone—returns the documents, and mumbles "go." He never searched the bus or anyone in it. The behavior of the soldiers is simultaneously ordered and idiosyncratic. Needless to say, there is a detectable logic to the one experiencing it: journeys interrupted, the humiliation of being subjected to the whims of others, perpetual fear, and the absence of recognition as a full human—in short—the disrespect of indifference. These experiences go to the heart of human cultural capacities and trust in the predictability of everyday routines.

The lack of predictability breeds an anticipation of violence and sometimes near gratitude if it does not materialize. Does one say "thank you" at a checkpoint? Does saying "please" and "thank you" raise the question of participating in one's own subjugation, and signal acquiescence? Silence registers a refusal to normalize and legitimize by denying the polite verbal exchanges that ordinarily confer recognition and respect.

Rites and Arbitrariness

Jumana, a young chemistry student, said,

> Once I waited at the Container for eight hours—there was a soldier—eighteen, nineteen years old. He had unzipped his pants—you could see his genitals. He had his arms up in the air and he was shouting. This crazy guy held us up for eight hours—women, children, and pregnant women, people who needed to go to work or to home.

Checkpoints are encounter spaces characterized by unpredictability and petty cruelties. They set in motion at once a ritualized sequence of actions and encounters, but, unlike traditional rites, they can be quite arbitrary. This seeming incongruity, however, is resolved by the intent and outcome: immiseration, restrained and filtered mobility, and a constant state of ambiguity and thus a population in a perpetual state of anxious anticipation. As we have seen, documents are slipped into the pockets of soldiers, who then disappear into the guard post, sometimes returning quickly, sometimes hours later. Often, they simply carry them around while their owners wait. Oddly enough, the guards often do not check the cars themselves or do so perfunctorily.[10] Given the lax security, waiting seems to be the issue.

Even with her Jerusalem identity, Arwa dreads checkpoints and avoids them when she can. "I have a feeling of panic as I approach them, as though I can't breathe, and all my muscles tense up." When I pressed her as to why this panicky feeling overtakes her, she responded, "I think because I feel a loss of control, a complete loss of control. I feel as if I am not a human being. I am without dignity or respect—as though I am a big bug, as if I am stripped of human existence. Once I am out of the checkpoint, I relax. I feel physically different." The anxious anticipation of the impending encounter, then the liminal state of being temporarily "stripped" of human status followed by a state of relaxation conforms loosely to the elements of a rite of passage although there is no celebration of a new status, simply passage from one space to another. However, passage is ritualized—that is, repetitive and symbolic—a context of pronounced hierarchy and subordination. Indeed, just about any movement beyond immediate locales mandates participation in these ritualistic enactments of power and subordination. Yet despite ritual's sequenced actions, there is a remarkable degree of randomness. Not surprisingly, it is in this uncertainty that the analogy to ritual reaches its limit. People worry: Will I be detained, or arrested, or beaten, or insulted and humiliated? What is in store for me? How long will it take to pass? Will it close before I pass? Habituation to ritual does not signal acquiescence. The capriciousness of the day's orders, as well as of the personnel's whims, makes Palestinians hypervigilant and filled with trepidation. Jumana complained, "Every time you go through a checkpoint it is different even though you have exactly the same papers. At some checkpoints, they even reject permits they issued to allow entrance to Jerusalem, for example. You see—it is just like this! You never know why these regulations or orders come about. Why is it like this today, and another day like that? It depends on their moods."

Repetitiveness is expected to produce a self-disciplining body, accommodating constrained movement, pervasive monitoring, and a shrinking sense of space, whose control over time is limited. By 2006, as part of the "civilianization" (Havkin 2011) of checkpoints, which included outsourcing to private-security companies, the following large, yellow signs, in Hebrew, Arabic, and English, were posted at Qalandia:

> Welcome to Atarot Checkpoint. You are entering a military area, to make your transit easy and to avoid unnecessary delays please read these instructions and follow them. Please prepare your documents for inspection and approach an inspection point when it becomes vacant. Follow instructions of the inspector. Please wait your turn. Entry is one by one. Have a good day.

Passage is made to appear contingent on compliance and following instructions. The responsibility for delays rests with those seeking passage, not the checkpoint regime. In other words, checkpoints are didactic spaces in proper comportment with associated rewards or punishments.

The specific contours of randomness are unknowable, but the unexpected is always anticipated. An incident in late 2006 is illustrative. I was in line in the enclosed, metal-fenced path to enter Qalandia, when, without warning, a lone, wild-eyed soldier, rifle drawn and finger on the trigger, rushed toward a family of four that was standing a few paces ahead of me. Everyone in the line turned to see what was going on. The son, no more than five or six years old, was carrying a small, child's suitcase. The soldier grabbed it and with one hand opened the clasp. All the contents fell to the unpaved ground, which was muddy after an early morning rain. As he poked through the child's belongings with his rifle, the boy's parents stood by silently, unable to do anything, too fearful to even ask what was going on. Terrified by the soldier's actions, and witnessing his parents' impotence, the child was stunned. Finally, satisfied that there was nothing of interest in the suitcase, the soldier abruptly turned and walked away, leaving the shaken family to retrieve the suitcase's contents from the mud. All this took place in silence. The soldier neither addressed the parents nor asked their names or where they were headed; he didn't even check their identity cards. Government bureaucracies require that their demands be recognized as authoritative and embed them in a repetition that is "not obscured but highlighted" (Feldman 2008, 14–15). The sheer repetition of colonial power, its embeddness in everyday movement and activities, from the mundane to the spectacular, displays and produces state power for both the colonized and the colonizer. Yet the effect of repetition and compulsory participation reveals the fragility of power, and the need for its constant iteration.

In this world of ambiguity, it is obligatory to follow orders and accept arbitrary decisions and indignities. A futile attempt in 2010 by a group of Palestinians and European academics to visit the Samaritan community near Nablus is illustrative.[11] Our guide, a middle-aged Palestinian academic, had been in contact with the community leaders, who were waiting to receive us. Our driver steered our small bus up the precipitously steep and rocky mountain leading to the compound, which was located next to Bracha, an Israeli colony. The checkpoint was adjacent to a military base just outside Bracha. The driver had called ahead and been told by the community leader, "The soldiers are very moody today. They might not let you in." So we were prepared. As we approached the checkpoint, two soldiers quickly appeared and ordered us to park the van. After they checked the driver's identity card, they said that they had to call the Ministry of Interior to get permission for us to enter. We waited between twenty and twenty-five minutes, only to be told, when the soldiers returned, "Only Palestinians can enter this road, no foreigners." This was clearly an arbitrary statement given that Palestinians were typically not allowed to use a road so near a colony. We asked if we could park and walk in. They were emphatic: "No, the Ministry has forbidden you to enter." Yet only two days before, the same Palestinian driver and guide had entered without problem. The guards told us to go to another entrance to the Samaritan compound, on the other side of hill. Our guide was on his cell phone talking to the community leader, who was on another phone with the Ministry trying to get us permission to enter. As we approached the Bracha colony we saw its neatly arrayed detached houses, surrounded by tidy stone walls, well-tended lawns, and colorful flower beds. An armed private-security guard stood in a small guard booth at the entrance.

While we waited, Israeli cars and buses drove at a brisk pace in and out of this ultra-gated community. In the meantime, the guard had called for reinforcements. A jeep with three soldiers raced up and parked in front of our bus to block its path. Then the soldiers sauntered over and spoke with the guard, then to our driver, and then waited while the security guard made phone calls. Gruffly, they told us to go back to the first checkpoint or to call someone with a car with Israeli license plates to drive us in. Our request to proceed on foot to visit the Samaritans was met with another resounding no. This tactic, telling us to go back to a previous checkpoint, is one I had heard about repeatedly. Our guide said as we left, "They are afraid of foreigners traveling with a Palestinian guide; if you had come with an Israeli guide, they would have let you in. They don't want foreign visitors to see what is going on or talk to certain people."

Within Israel there is some opposition and criticism of the checkpoints. For example, members of Machsom Watch position themselves at checkpoints to witness and document abuses, and, occasionally, they intervene when they witness the abuse of Palestinians. The assumption is that their presence will compel better behavior from checkpoint personnel. Not surprisingly, they have little actual power, except in their ability to document egregious behavior and, perhaps, some degree of moral persuasion.[12] Palestinian opinions on the group are mixed; some find their presence somewhat reassuring, knowing the worst abuses will at least be witnessed and recorded. Others are not so sure their presence does any good at all. Once, traveling to Salfit with Randa, we were stopped at a checkpoint where we saw three middle-aged women from Machsom Watch busily writing notes on their clipboards. Randa commented sarcastically:

> Their presence is negative. They monitor the behavior of the soldiers. They should be working against the occupation. How can you be against checkpoints and yet stand there monitoring soldier's behavior? They are trying to protect and enhance the image of the soldier. They legitimize the occupation and the checkpoints. Once they asked me, "Are things okay?" I just responded flatly, "I am okay." They are not the ones to save us. This is occupation.

Gender, Age, and Appearance

"After sixty years, they know us and our culture well," said Arwa. Visibly angry, she recounted her experience at a checkpoint that morning. "Sometimes this soldier calls me by my first name, implying that we know one another. I was horrified when he did this today. I feared people would think I was involved with him and getting special treatment. This is a way to create mistrust among us."

Arwa's comments reference what is known as *isqat siyassy* (downfall), "the use of the politics of sexuality—as reflected in the violation of societal codes of women's purity, honour, sexual abuses . . . for the soliciting of information" by the Israeli security apparatus (Shalhoub-Kevorkian 2009, 15; Shalhoub-Kevorkian et al. 2014). Arwa's fears were twofold: that any suggestion of having a relationship with a soldier would make it appear to Palestinians that she was a collaborator. In this, the state relies on twisted understandings of "Arab culture" and its imputed cultural complex of honor and shame located in women's bodies.

Settler colonialism's gendered dimensions are vividly played out at checkpoints. Women can be subjected to sexual harassment and abuse engendering a state of *isqat*; men are subjected to ritualized demasculinization. Paradoxically, for Palestinian men, enactments or expressions of masculinity, such as confronting soldiers or not complying with an order to maintain face and honor can be met with physical brutality, thus risking masculinity's very public undoing. The immobilized male body, sometimes stripped nearly naked and forced to wait, is in stark contrast to the hypermobile, hypermasculine, well-armed bodies of the Israeli forces.

In many respects, mobility is distinctly gendered and culturally grounded. When, how, and what sorts of spaces women can appear in and traverse operate in a field of local cultural complexes of gender, sexuality, mobility, and the nature of space. Female mobility is a distinct yet fluid construct contoured by class, education, region, state policies, household composition, religiosity, and the particular practices of individual families. Mobility is also linked to age; the movement of a postmenopausal woman is less monitored than that of an eighteen-year-old girl. The former's sexuality seemingly diminished, her public presence is perceived as less transgressive and hedged with danger. Young girls go to school and visit friends, but their movements are more closely monitored. Cell phones raise a question: Do they enhance efficiency in monitoring or do they allow women to elude it? In the post-puberty teen years, restrictions are activated to control for sexual infractions that could stain the family name. However, mobility is also structured by class. Women with professional jobs or from higher-income families can buy cars and thus enjoy a wider scope of mobility. Educated middle- and upper-class women who work with foreign NGOs often pass more easily through checkpoints, because they travel in cars with organizational logos and with foreign colleagues.

Protracted conflict has the potential to alter, challenge, and reaffirm gendered norms, behavior, and subjectivites. So what actually happens to women's mobility with closure? Conflict can provide an opportunity for the mobilization and emancipation of women, yet they can also face sexual violence, and a re-traditionalization of gender roles can unfold. Thus conflict opens up an uneven space in which conceptualizations of gender and gender relations may be reconfigured along multiple, often contradictory lines. Families' fear of soldiers' behavior at checkpoints, the inability to give precise times for arrival at home due to incalculable waits and recourse to multiple forms of transportation can activate and magnify traditional restraints on mobility. Families also restrict women's mobility in fear of detention which could involve sexual assault. However, high male unemployment increased mobility for some women as they became breadwinners. In addition, married women are assumed to move more easily and thus may be tasked with taking care of family business that involves crossing checkpoints.

Women face a duality of subjugating structures: a patriarchal system and and a colonial occupation. I was looking for a research assistant when a friend suggested I talk to her neighbor, twenty-year-old Layal, a Palestinian American with a US passport but no Israeli-issued residency visa that would allow her live on the West Bank. I arranged to meet her at a local café. I was unable to hire Layal to work with me because she did not have the requisite skills, but even if she had, her parents would not have allowed her to move beyond her immediate neighborhood. She complained, "I feel imprisoned—I have a US passport, but it is meaningless here without a visa, and my parents won't let me go anywhere."

At checkpoints there is little privacy. Security personnel can compel publicly repetitive, often intimate, gendered performances of hierarchy in which Palestinians are both actors and audience. Randa's description of passage at Eretz highlights the combination of sophisticated technology and harassment, and a gendered, voyeuristic field of view:

> Eretz checkpoint is the worst and it is the most technologically advanced. They use a scanning machine that sees through clothes so it is a problem for women. You are in this machine but there is no person—you have no contact with another human being. Suddenly a voice will shout from above, "That bra you are wearing—does it have underwire?" This is so humiliating! Most women, including myself, are terrified of this sort of bodily invasion.

This sort of spectacle reiterates an ethnicized socio-spatial order and the power of visualization with gendered contours. At checkpoints, the Palestinian body is socially profiled; characteristics such as age and sex (and religion) come into play. Sometimes gender is built into the physical structure. For example, some checkpoints initially had separate lines for women and men, making for a different experience—women's lines moved faster and involved less waiting and intensive searches. Sometimes the category is further broken down, as in the following encounter in which ideals of feminine beauty are overlaid with racialized aesthetics. Over lunch, Lana, a young science professor at Bir Zeit University, told me the following story about the Surda checkpoint:

I use to go through it every day, twice a day, coming and going from the university. Once the soldiers asked us to form two lines—one line for ugly women and one for pretty women. We were stunned and, of course, outraged. This was too much and so insulting. There was a woman who was confused by this order. She stood in the "pretty line." The soldier shouted at her, "Go to the ugly line!"

Age and gender overlap in the monitoring and control of mobility. During Ramadan, the Muslim holy month of fasting, I boarded a bus at Qalandia, headed for Jerusalem. As more people lined up to board, the driver called out, "Only those with Jerusalem identity cards or over sixty years of age are allowed." This age categorization was common, especially on Fridays, when practicing Muslims want to pray at Jerusalem's al-Aqsa mosque. Sometimes only older women were allowed to enter the city.

For the elderly, the discomfort of prolonged standing hinders mobility, as does the absence of toilet facilities. Um Fuad, who had always enjoyed visiting her husband's village in the north, complained that she could no longer make the trip because she couldn't sit in the car long periods without having access to a restroom. The terminals at Qalandia and Bethlehem now have bathrooms, although they are quite dirty. Indeterminate delays are grueling for women and men of any age.

Age garners neither respect nor kind treatment. Soldiers can be heard addressing elderly women as *hamara* (donkey) or *habla* (crazy). Seeing the elderly being humiliated enrages younger people, as does seeing handicapped or wheelchair-bound Palestinians waiting patiently for a gate to be opened by soldiers who are ignoring them. Postmenopausal women may be culturally freer to move, but they confront physical obstacles. It is difficult, if not impossible, for them to squeeze through narrow openings in walls, tramp up and down rocky hillsides, or jump over piles of stones or ditches. Sixty-five-year-old Um Hani had a complaint similar to her friend Um Fuad's:

Now I can no longer go to Jerusalem. The trip is too difficult. Going through Qalandia is like going through Allenby. It is the same thing. I have to take off my shoes, they spray something in my hair—hot air, I think. I shouted at those soldiers, "What are you putting in my face?" They put more hot air and told me, "Breathe, breathe." I told them, "There is something wrong with you. You are not normal." I have never seen a bomb or dealt with weapons. I don't know how to use a gun.

Males from age thirteen through their late forties constitute the potentially dangerous male Palestinian body. In an article on the first intifada, I wrote that the willingness to confront the occupier was understood as heroic, a sacrificial act akin to a rite of passage to manhood (Peteet 1994). With the second intifada, the heroic encounter has been supplanted by the humiliating encounter. As a viable resistance movement has waned, being interrogated, detained or tortured is less resonant of masculinity. Moreover, the "crisis in paternity" (Johnson and Kuttab 2001)—that is, men's inability to protect and provide for their families—exacerbates the demasculinizing effect of the checkpoint.

These spectacles of subordination and hierarchy infantilize and humiliate to the point of despair. My neighbor Sami complained bitterly about the young female soldier who humiliated him, "Who is she to treat me this way—making me stand there like a child!?" I ran into a visibly agitated Jumana on the street. She had just visited her distraught father and related this story: "My father was with his friend—these are men in their fifties. They forced my father's friend to take off his pants and shirt and go through the check point in his underwear. He pleaded with them, but they refused to listen; he's a bit overweight and was so embarrassed. My father came home and cried!" Lana saw a similar episode on her way to the university:

> In line at Surda checkpoint, I see one of my male graduate students. The soldiers stopped him and ordered him to remove his clothing down to his underwear. Everyone watched in horror as this scene unfolded. I was still in line when he turned and saw me. He could not look me in the eye until nearly the end of the semester. This was terribly humiliating for him and for me.

To be forced to undress in public, in front of others compelled to watch by virtue of being there, is a not infrequent occurrence, and the stories circulated in both hushed tones and with a sense of moral outrage. Whatever the tone, in making public an intimate, private act, the meaning is the same: an assault on masculinity, cultural notions of self and propriety, and the gendered social order. These disciplinary routines are designed to produce a gendered subject of compliance, an effeminization of the Palestinian male, immobilized and unable to protect or support his family.

A crush of people waits for Qalandiya to open, which could happen in fifteen minutes or hours later. Elderly women shout at the soldiers, trying to shame them into opening. It is 2004, and the checkpoint is still largely open-air and has less of the surveillance apparatus that will appear soon enough. Mothers with children alternate between entreaty and argument as they shove permits and sick children at soldiers. Trying to make themselves "invisible," sometimes they can slip through unnoticed. I have many times seen an elderly woman, in her richly embroidered dress, place a box of produce on her head, glance around quickly to make sure no one is paying attention and then, with studied nonchalance, walk through the busy Qalandia checkpoint undetected. This sort of manipulation of age and gender relies on culturally inflected expectations of female passivity and invisibility.

To move through Jewish-Israeli space and subvert the mobility regime by speaking to it in its own meta-language, Palestinians sometimes try to adopt Jewish dress and styles. For example, when Nasreen, whose presence in Jerusalem was "illegal," moved around the city, she would let down her hair, spritzed to hold her natural curls, and wear a short-sleeve top to mimic the appearance of a Jewish woman. To attempt to pass as Jewish youth in West Jerusalem, Palestinian boys got buzz haircuts and donned the tight T-shirts and wrap-around sunglasses, a look popular with ex-soldiers and private-security guards.

Randa commented on women's dress at checkpoints:

> Once I was feeling insecure but I knew I had to go through this checkpoint. The soldier asked, "Where are you going? What do you do?" When he found out I do counseling and psychology, he said: "Can you do counseling for us?" I was so scared but I felt the need to be strong. I said, "I only work with women." He said, "You are a pretty woman—sit and talk with me." So I am thinking, "what should I do?" They have power over me, and it was a lonely area. I was very afraid. So I thought of something to say. I told him, "Ask your boss for counseling, it is not my job." We had forty minutes of discussion. They like to talk to women, especially the unveiled ones. We are similar to their image of women, like Israeli women. I had to convince them to let me pass. You know, we have no one to help us if there is a problem. We can only be clever and try to deal with them. The *muhajibaat* [veiled women] are badly treated. In general, all of us are badly treated—but for the *muhajibaat* it is worse. For me, I can talk to them. They think I am not politically active. They think veiled women hate Israel and have a closed, narrow mentality. Sometimes they ask them to take off their jacket and turn around. Female soldiers are worse than males. They are so mean. They enjoy humiliating you as a woman. They shout, "Where are you going? Why are you working? Go back!" Maybe they have been abused by the soldiers so they take it out on us.

I did observe and hear numerous stories of unveiled girls being harassed with unwanted flirtatious behavior; for some young women donning the veil is a way to avoid harassment. Selma started wearing the veil to pass through checkpoints more easily. She said, "When I was not veiled, I stood out and sometimes soldiers would call me to come forward, then start flirting. I veiled to avoid this. I didn't want people to think I was loose or collaborating and start gossiping about me." Veiling in this instance may constitute a language of refusal. On one hand, it constructs a zone of privacy around the body and can confound the colonial as well as the male gaze. On the other, the veil can invite more scrutiny when the veiled woman is assumed to be political, which renders her a visible potential threat. Some observers, like Randa, contend that the veil heightens their vulnerability to harassment (Shalhoub-Kevorkian 2009).

Jumana, who moved around frequently for work and school, related several incidents that underscore the sexual politics of colonial occupation with its degrading and humiliating demands for bodily intimacy and exposure:

> I was in a van and the driver had on Arabic music. At the checkpoint, the soldiers came to windows of the van, and one of them said, "Turn it up louder. All girls get out and belly dance for us." When we refused, they said, "Park the van on the side there. You will not move until these girls belly dance for us." I was so humiliated—even if he threatened to kill me I still would not dance. The men in the van were so humiliated. You know, Arab men try to protect women. We are like brothers and sisters, especially in this sort of situation. I was so shocked and humiliated I could not speak. I was sitting next to the driver, so I got most of their attention through the window. I just went silent—so silent. We sat for three hours in the sun. Finally, he gave us our ID cards back and we left. That day I couldn't do anything. I was thinking, "What is next?"
>
> Another time at a checkpoint, a couple of soldiers came up and pressed their faces against the windows. They didn't ask for our ID. They just stared intensely at me and the other girl. A young man in the van finally blurted, "*ibn kalb*" (son of a bitch). The others tried to shush him, and we all told him not to speak because they are just waiting for a reason to start shooting. Finally, they let us go. The girl cried all the way to Ramallah. The men were so angry—their faces were red—we were all humiliated and embarrassed. No one spoke—there was absolute silence except for the sobs of the girl.
>
> Once a soldier asked me to kiss a guy in the car. I said, "I will kiss him because he is Palestinian and he is my brother." They think they know the culture but I turned it around on them.

Jumana's encounters hint at the ever-present possibility and reality of sexualized vulnerabilities and humiliation. These encounters go beyond the individual body; colonialism makes the female (and male) body visible, not just to Israelis but to other Palestinians as well.

Checkpoint encounters also reveal the fundamental cracks in the "patriarchal bargain," in which men retain power and women accept a normative, though often constraining, gendered social order, in exchange for support and protection (Kandiyoti 1988). The bargain is being unsettled by the same forces undercutting masculinity: immobilization, checkpoint encounters, and the diminishing possibility that they will be reliable breadwinners and protectors. Desperate for an income, Fatima, a forty-year-old mother of four took up paid domestic work. With long delays at checkpoints, she could rarely be certain when she would return home. Her husband, who had once worked in Israeli construction and was now unemployed, tended the children and home. This is an example of the management of ruptures in the patriarchal bargain.

Age and gender orders can become strained when women earn more and travel more easily than men, as well as when children witness their parents being abused and humiliated at checkpoints. Young girls and women are vividly aware of the negative impact of unemployment, immobilization, and humiliation on their male kin. They may sympathize, but they don't want to bear the brunt of their frustration. Amal, who came from the surrounded village of Walaja to study and work in Ramallah, explained:

> As girls we are denied our freedom from two sides: the occupation and our traditions. What makes me mad is the guys, mainly my brother. My father is really so nice and sweet with us. He never says, "You should do this, or you shouldn't do that. You can do whatever you want." In Walaja, it is normal for the soldiers to come to our home and say to my brother, "Come out of the house" or "Get down from the bus." It is not easy for my brother. But he is not denied freedom by society or the family. His encounters with the military make me nervous—I can deal with them myself, the anger and humiliation— but I don't want my brother to be angry because then he tries to control me to compensate, and this is a bad thing.

Relations with parents are changing as well in complex, uneven ways. Parents who fear for the safety of their daughters at the checkpoints are likely to restrict their mobility. Selma didn't tell her parents about an incident in which she was detained and interrogated at a checkpoint; she instead said that she was late because the lines were long. She was afraid they wouldn't let her continue to work if she told the truth. Yet, some parents accord daughters more freedom of movement, making a choice not to allow occupation to interfere with their education. Jumana recounted her attempts to complete high school:

> I remember my senior year in high school. I had to go to Hebron to study because the schools in the camps stop at the ninth grade. It took ten minutes by taxi to reach the high school. Then with closure and the checkpoints, it began to take six hours. I would get up at 3 a.m. and reach back home at 9 p.m. Soldiers would attack the school sometimes or declare a curfew. Once, they imposed a curfew, and I thought "Where shall I go?" I went through the checkpoint—it was me and about fifty other people. On the main street the soldiers stopped us and said, "Stay here. We are going to shoot you all at 7:00." We realized that if we moved we could be killed and if we stayed we could be killed. So we decided to crawl, like alligators, across the pavement. The street was full of settlers. I looked back and saw one of my teachers. She had a limp so she couldn't crawl easily. I went back and got her. I couldn't let her die. I helped her cross the street, and we survived. God wanted her to live and he helped her get out of there.

I asked Jumana if after this incident her parents considered making her quit school:

> No, my parents rented a house in Hebron so my sister and I could go to school. At the time of my final exams, soldiers attacked the house from 8 p.m. to

8 a.m.—nonstop shooting. My mother didn't know how to protect us. Bullets were coming in the window. Goodness! A test is nothing compared to this. My mother put me under her body and she said, "I won't let them kill you." Imagine that! We found another house in a safer area. Sometimes curfews were announced, and it was exam time. If you miss one exam, you lose the whole year. You can be under curfew, and then you hear an announcement on the radio that the exam is in four hours. How can you be prepared?! I have a friend whose father made her leave school because he said he could not protect her. He said, "I won't let my daughter be raped." She wanted me to talk to him. But he insisted, so she studied at home and passed her exams. But she missed high school and the social life that comes with it.

Girls hide things to avoid parental worry but also out of concern that parents will curtail their education or employment. Amal had an experience in Walaja when soldiers did not let her leave for five days, even though she pleaded with them every day that she had university exams in Ramallah. Now that the once twenty- to thirty-minute ride could take hours and entail passing through multiple checkpoints, her initially reluctant parents allowed her to live in Ramallah as long as she came home periodically. She didn't want anything to jeopardize this arrangement. Amal told me a story that she had kept from her parents. After a weekend at home, she and a friend had a confrontation with soldiers in a jeep, who had stopped them after they had trudged for two hours through the Wadi al-Nar (Valley of Fire), in the heat, to avoid a checkpoint on their way back to university. Drawing on hydraulic metaphors of containment, Israelis refer to Palestinians who walk in the hills or on old paths to avoid checkpoints as "leakers" or "drippers." In the course of the confrontation and argument that ensued when the soldiers insisted the girls reverse course, Amal boldly exclaimed in a fit of anger and frustration, "Fuck You!" (in English). She continued, "This soldier got down from the jeep and he said the same words back to me. He positioned his rifle to shoot me, but his friends prevented him." She herself was astonished that she had dared to utter such an insult, but she was so exasperated by the thought of being forced to walk back for two hours and possibly missing classes. She was emphatic, "I would never tell my parents about this encounter—not just because I was walking the deserted hills but that I had the nerve to speak to a soldier this way. I could have been arrested, shot, or beaten." Her audaciousness, though, gave her a momentary sense of satisfaction.

A setting of racialized and acutely asymmetrical power could be a recipe for sexual violence. In war, rape can be deployed as a strategic weapon to erode morale, compel mass flight, emasculate men, humiliate the nation via sexual assaults on women who often serve as its symbolic icons, sow chaos and fear, and display domination. Mass rape by Israeli military forces has not occurred on the same scale as in Bosnia, the Congo, or Rwanda, for example. However, this does not mean rape and sexual violence have not occurred. The ambiguity around the sexual is itself problematic, although this is eroding with the uncovering of records of the rapes of Palestinian women in 1948 through archival and oral history research.[13] The shame and stigma of sexual assault ensures that few women or men will speak of it.

Various accounts have been offered for why mass rape has not occurred: some have argued that notions of Jewish purity and racism compel Israeli men to avoid sexual encounters with Palestinian women.[14] However, across the globe, colonial militaries and race-based states have engaged in rape and entered into sexual relations with the racialized indigenous population (women and men), no matter how tightly drawn the lines of separation and imagined racial difference. In both Apartheid South Africa and the United States during slavery and under Jim Crow, there were well-defined, legally instituted mandates against interracial sexual relations, yet these relations, and white-on-black rape, were hardly infrequent.

The threat of violence against women may become part of the state's arsenal. Knesset member Ayelet Shaked's statement is telling:

Behind every terrorist stand dozens of men and women, without whom he could not engage in terrorism. They are all enemy combatants, and their blood shall be on all their heads. Now this also includes the mothers of the martyrs, who send them to hell with flowers and kisses. They should follow their sons, nothing would be more just. They should go, as should the physical homes in which they raised the snakes. Otherwise, more little snakes will be raised there.[15]

Shaked collapses the demographic threat with collective punishment and publicly iterates the threat coming from the heart of the government.

During the 2014 Israeli assault on Gaza, Professor Mordechai Kedar of Ben Gurion University seemed to advocate rape as a deterrent; he was reacting to the Palestinian kidnapping and killing of three Jewish settler youths when he baldly stated, "The only thing that can deter terrorists, like those who kidnapped the children and killed them, is the knowledge that their sister or their mother will be raped. It sounds very bad, but that's the Middle East."[16] Is this a call to openly incorporate rape as part of a military strategy to combat opposition?

I asked Jumana if she had been sexually harassed at the checkpoints.

Sometimes they claim they need to touch us. So there is harassment. They might touch your hair or arm or ask, "How old are you?" Part of our culture is secrecy especially about these sorts of matters. In this sense, our culture helps them. It is hard for parents to protect their girls from soldiers. If they feel they can't protect you, they may not let you go out. There are stories of girls being kidnapped and taken by unknown people. They speak Hebrew but dress up as Arabs and speak Arabic as well. I work with a friend whose sister was kidnapped. Six armed men speaking Hebrew-accented Arabic entered their house. They took his twenty-three-year-old sister, and she has never been seen since. She just disappeared. The parents went to the police, but who can do anything? No one talks about these sorts of incidents.

As noted earlier, conflict can reproduce gendered subjects and at the same time give rise to new gender relations and subjectivities as well as a strained patriarchal bargain, distressed male and female bodies, and emasculated males.[17]

The ability to navigate closure varies along class, regional, and residential lines as well as the level of connections with Israeli economic interests. For example, Palestinians with the blue Jerusalem identity cards can enter areas in which other Palestinians require a permit. For lower income people without cars, checkpoints involve long, arduous waits exposed to the elements, standing on tired feet. Those with cars at least can escape the extremes of heat and cold and the prolonged standing; they can wait in the semi-privacy and comfort of their heated or air-conditioned cars. Nor do they need to cart around heavy bags and children. Those wishing to cross the Allenby Bridge from Jordan into Palestine can pay extra to travel VIP (that is, in a small van rather than a large bus) and to sit in an air-conditioned room while their documents are processed more quickly. Palestinian Authority employees have VIP status and often pass through checkpoints after only a cursory inspection of their documents. In the years immediately following Oslo, Palestinians who were doing business with Israeli companies were given special permits that facilitated passage at checkpoints. The contrast with throngs of Palestinian workers, queuing in long lines, before dawn, to enter Israel or Jerusalem is striking. Bethlehem checkpoint is a case in point (as was Gaza until 2005). Workers from Bethlehem (with work permits) who labor in colonies in the Jerusalem area line up by the hundreds early each morning and late in the afternoon to exit and then re-enter Bethlehem.

Collective Experiences, Narration, and Subjectivity

After a visit to her parents, Selma said, "When we get together with family and friends, all any one talks about is the miserable situation—how to get around, their experiences at checkpoints, problems with permits, and so on. Sometimes, I don't want to talk about it, and I say let's talk about something else." Sharing stories of daily tribulations generates empathy and outlines the boundaries of a moral community of suffering. These narrations underpin a complex range of subjectivities, both collective and individual. Selma elaborated on her feelings of helplessness and empathy for others:

> I hate it when I see someone treated badly. Once at Qalandia—there were a lot of people—one soldier ordered, "Line up one by one. There was a line for men

and a line for women. There was a young man—twenty-one or twenty-two-years old. When he did not respond quickly enough, this soldier runs up, grabs him, throws him to the ground, and starts kicking him. Imagine this! I hate these things. I don't like to see them happen to others.

Some stories circulate widely in this terrain. In 2008, I heard this calamitous checkpoint story from several people; it remained remarkably consistent in the telling. Munira, the nurse who waited at the checkpoint to meet the patient, related:

A woman in a wheelchair, accompanied by a female relative, arrived at Eretz checkpoint. Once the two exited the main part of the checkpoint, they reached a set of cement blocks in the road—these are about three feet high—you see them everywhere. These were arranged in parallel rows, with about three feet between them. So, this woman had to rise up out of the wheelchair and hoist herself on top of the cement barrier. When she crossed to the second barrier, a couple of young men tried to help her. They put their hands under her armpits to gently help her down. She has just had a double mastectomy—an incredibly painful surgery that included the removal of glands under the arms. She was screaming in pain. Her companion was wearing a long dress. When she went to cross the double barrier, she slipped and fell between the two cement blocks. She panicked—she was stuck, like a turtle on its back that cannot turn over. The Eretz checkpoint is a masterpiece of what I call the "misery committee"! They are so cruel. Can you imagine making someone in her condition go through this!

Such stories embody themes of suffering, empathy, and the pragmatics of daily life. Voicing suffering and expressing empathy trace the boundaries of a fleeting and situational moral community, encompassing a complex range of articulations: ordinary conversation, where anecdotes and stories are exchanged; in artistic venues, such as in an increasing number of films about closure; in the occasional flare-up at a checkpoint and the constant commiseration with others, among others.[18] That sense of moral community is always present, however subtly expressed or acknowledged. Crises and disaster can be productive of new "communities of disaster" (Solnit 2009), although, I would caution, they are often fleeting. Randa echoed the atmosphere of sociality and community:

After going through the checkpoints twice a day, I was exhausted. So it became a social site. I tried to socialize. There is a bright side to Qalandia, you see. When we worked in the al-Ram area, we used to meet at the checkpoint every morning. We would gather together and socialize and exchange news. It was a sort of social scene. Instead of becoming frustrated with waiting, we chatted and tried to have fun. We would make fun of the soldiers and make jokes. We would do some of our shopping at Qalandia.

The ubiquitous cell phone facilitates another circuit of knowledge that joins Palestinians in a moral community. Using their phones, they share information about flying checkpoints, long delays, and unanticipated closings and tell family and friends where they are. In a long drive in a *service* to Tubas, the well-dressed young man sitting next to me called his wife before and after passing through each checkpoint to let her know he had successfully navigated it. Thus Palestinians are drawn into circuits of knowledge about mobility. Drivers of buses, taxis, and private cars constitute another link in the circuit of knowledge about mobility and, indeed, are often a main source of information about obstacles, which they share with others, often stopping to tell other drivers about conditions ahead.

The constant exchange of stories about navigating the terrain of closure also sheds light on the extent to which these routines are not normalized and the critical consciousness—the thinking through—that is brought to them. Repetition and routine neither manufacture consent nor dilute the desire for unencumbered movement at one's own pace. Palestinian commentary runs between "we're used to it" and "what can we do?" referencing an ability to resist through adaptation, in recognition of their limited room to maneuver, as well as acquiescence.

The moral community expands to include others who share the restraints of closure. Janet, a young American lawyer working as a consultant to the PA, said that her Palestinian colleagues were cordial but formal with her. Once she began to share her own first-hand experiences of closure—checkpoints, delays, rude soldiers—her colleagues became friendlier and began inviting her to socialize with them outside work. They also began to talk more openly about their own experiences in front of her.

Subjectivity, the "inner life and affective states" (Biehl 2005, 6), the kind of introspection in which Palestinians engage daily, and desires are deeply entangled with the colonial encounter. Colonial endeavors and their privileging projects prompt questions about what it means to be a human and the valuation of the self in face of an overwhelming control of daily life's contours, temporal rhythms, and spatial parameters. Arwa feeling like a "big bug" or Ahmad's statement that "they are gods and we are animals"—reference a heightened awareness of subjugating structures and constant engagement in critical analyses, and underscore being simultaneously inside and outside. They observe and learn from the petty indignities of the demands for bodily conformity and of the suffering of others, as they themselves undergo the same processes of inspection and funneling and the behaviors and demeanor they compel. This dual positioning situates Palestinians in a complex range of subject positions: observers and participants, critical commentators and analysts as well as sometimes enforcers of oppression as when taxi drivers refuse to drive those without permits to Jerusalem or when the Palestinian Authority police arrest militants on Israelis orders.

Public acts of conformity do not necessarily correspond to an interior state or disposition. Constant repetition of subordination through ritualized bodily practice, in an atmosphere where violence is an ever-present possibility, does contour subjectivity. However, silence and deadpan faces at checkpoint constitute both a language of refusal and dissimulation and acquiescence to overwhelming power and fear. Palestinians are skilled practitioners of the emotional distancing that undercuts a simple assignment of a subject position.

Silence can be emblematic of distancing and subjectivity. Aside from being a tactical means of maneuvering, silence is a language of refusal. Palestinians cultivate silence and emotionless faces during encounters. These skilled practioners of dissimulation combine silence with critical awareness, analyses, and reflection. Such micro-practices require conscious deliberation. Closure's contradiction crystallizes at the checkpoint: the colonizer's desire for an immiserated, unidirectional, mobile Palestinian (out of Palestine) and a fractured community has nurtured in its stead another chapter in a saga of shared suffering, a narrative that transcends geospatial boundaries. In other words, these collective experiences and subjectivities heighten a sense of belonging to the larger community of Palestinians.

Most importantly, the adoption of *sumud* (steadfastness) at the checkpoint undercuts both a colonial subjectivity and habitus, as Palestinians formulate and reformulate the meaning of their own behaviors and dispositions. Khalil, a mild-mannered banker in his early forties, strove to maintain his dignity by refusing to accept dehumanization, perceiving this as a "form of resistance." He says, "Checkpoints are a challenge. I have developed a special way of talking to the soldiers. I use little tricks, like joking with them. I smile in their faces. This is a mission for me. Sometimes soldiers refuse to let me pass. I wait until their shifts change and try again."

Khalil's persistence and dissimulative smiles are a language of refusal to acquiesce to subjection. *Sumud,* that most essential of Palestinian political and psychological qualities in face of colonialism, fashions an arena at the checkpoint encounter in which a different sort of subjectivity takes shape. The steely and defiant silence that demonstrates *sumud* is a language of active refusal, or what anthropologist Lena Meari (2014, 548) astutely notes is the "unmaking and remaking of the self, the continuous practice of desubjectivation." Being steadfast, proceeding through the checkpoint in spite of humiliation and delay is both a state of being and a state of potential. In this zone of intimate contact, the Palestinian continues to move against the odds. The subterfuge—the sneaking through, the use of others' documents—are forms of *sumud,* as is the constant state of alertness to uncertainty and a readiness to quickly shift strategies in face of ever-mutating obstacles.

Palestinians' subjectivity is also conditioned by desire and absence— what they don't have: the ability to enjoy ordinary things, a "normal life" with unhindered mobility, security, and safety with a measure of predictability, an expansive sense of space, and human rights. Their subjectivity is anchored in the demands of others, and they are quite conscious of the others' lack of absence, of what the other has because of what the Palestinian has been denied—they can see the colonies, with their green spaces and parks and swimming pools for children, and compare that with their own lack of the same.

The elaborate and ritualized encounter of power and subjugation at the checkpoints which infantilizes and punishes the Palestine are not in line with Bourdieu's (1977) habitus, which entails unconscious dispositions. The identity card as a prosthetic and sequencing through the checkpoint may be automatic embodied responses, but the critical consciousness that accompanies them and the verbal analysis and critique that ensue belie any uncomplicated and retooled notion of habitus.

Conclusion

At checkpoints, the state's structures and protocols for mobility are vividly displayed, publicly enacted, and viscerally experienced. Checkpoints are structured around an embodied and sequential course of movement with corresponding demands on demeanor and speech. Movement is ordered by a disciplinary and ritualistic, although often ambiguous, sequencing. Enacting the script publicly reaffirms and reproduces the formula of subordination and domination, yet its strangling effects have prompted resourcefulness and improvisation, what Allen has described as "getting by" rather than large-scale resistance (Allen 2008).

Palestinians complain yet accommodate; they talk of being content to stay in Ramallah, which "offers everything," even as they long to move freely. They speak of suffocation and imprisonment, of the desiring of a "normal" life: "We want to enjoy the simple pleasures of life—go to movies, to a café in Jerusalem, to travel, to feel safe."

Technologies of surveillance, from the rudimentary to the hi-tech, compel a forced visibility encounter that concurrently renders Palestinians invisible to the Israeli public. The wall and the immobilizing checkpoints keep Palestinians out of the line of sight so effectively that most Israelis and foreign visitors to the country can legitimately claim to be clueless as to what is happening nearby. However, checkpoints have become flashpoints for violence. In June 2015, for example, soldiers shot and killed an alleged stone-throwing youth at Qalandia; a Palestinian woman stabbed an Israeli police officer at the Bethlehem checkpoint. Qalandia is the site for demonstrations and stone throwing.

Checkpoints assume an aggregate, unitary Palestinian body defined by its collective potential for opposition, and thus they violate international law prohibiting collective punishment as well as freedom of movement. Security is the fetishized rationale in which Israelis cast immobilization: "We do this because they are terrorists." In the post-9/11 world, mobility has been securitized and subjected to ever-evolving surveillance techniques. As part of the WoT, mobility is now a matter of national security globally, reaching an extreme in Palestine where the ability to move is openly and unequivocally distributed according to ethno-religious and national identities. The inequitable allocation of mobility and space crafts an expanding Jewish space/time and a shrinking, fragmented Palestinian one. Israelis move with ease, echoing Virilio's speed and power equation (Virilio and Armitage 1999), while the spatially constrained Palestinian only moves with permission. Checkpoints' immobilizing effects have seriously eroded their ability to produce space. Human mobility figures prominently in the way landscape is produced, reproduced, and endowed with meaning. A new lexicon of topographic names and spatial locators peppers daily conversation: checkpoints, flying checkpoints, terminals, underground passages, gates, Areas A, B, and C, and bypass roads. Landscape is constantly being reconfigured through interdictions of access and mobility, new forms of the built environment, and linguistic changes, evident in Hebrew signage, that can render it nearly unrecognizable. In other words, landscape is always in an emergent state, produced by human design ranging from the banal and subtle to the grandiose and spectacular.

If place acquires definition and meaning through the social activities people engage in and the social relationships they craft and pursue in them, then Palestinians are increasingly constrained in their place-making capacity. They can only craft and give meaning to place in very delimited areas. In spring 2010, Arwa, her mother, and three sisters, hearing that passage at the Huwarrah checkpoint had eased, decided to go from Jerusalem to Nablus for the day. The mother remembered visiting Nablus often before the time of closure. Her children had never been. Arwa was so excited when she told me with a big grim, "I went to Nablus. Imagine, I have lived here all my life, so close to Nablus, and yet I have never seen it." Their visit fell during Ramadan. They spent the day walking around Nablus and ate lunch at a Christian-owned restaurant. On the way home, they were confronted with a flying checkpoint and a jovial soldier, who exclaimed, "You must be Christians!" Before they could reply, he asked if they ate in Nablus. When they responded in the affirmative, he was pleased with himself, "I knew it! I knew you were Christians. None of you is wearing the veil and you ate during Ramadan." Insulted and dismayed, Arwa told me, "You see, this is how they try to divide us. They make us aware of religious difference. If we were veiled, would he have been so pleasant? The soldier made it seem as though he was so cheerful and nice because we were Christians and somehow got better treatment. Her mother's memories of driving to Nablus and her own are remarkably different. Her mother remembered the straightforward route north on the Al-Quds-Nablus Road and visiting Nablus as a Palestinian rather than as a Christian. Arwa remembers the road being blocked, being compelling to drive a roundabout route, and a checkpoint encounter that marred the day by seeming to privilege one community over another, by a third community.

The next chapter details the temporal rhythms of closure. It asks what a highly calibrated system of control over mobility means for time, livelihood, family and social ties, health care, and sense of place and familiar landscapes? What kinds of disorientation and world view attach to restricted mobilities? What happens to the collective memory of shared space when the scale of movement is severely obstructed and the landscape reconfigured to not just exclude the indigenous but to denativize them and indigenize the colonists?

4 Waiting and "Stealing Time"

Closure's Temporality

On a visit to hebron, Arwa and I encountered an iconic scene. Two Palestinian youths, not more than seventeen or eighteen years of age, were squatting, in the blistering sun, their backs against a cement wall, waiting while the three young soldiers manning the small but tightly controlled pedestrian checkpoint at the entrance to the Tombs of the Patriarchs horsed around. The contrast was striking: the Palestinian boys were at the mercy of soldiers their own age. The soldiers were friendly to foreigners seeking entrance to the Tombs, though, and seemed to want Arwa and me to linger and talk. Not wanting to appear oblivious to the boys' detention, we kept the conversation to a minimum. When we passed by the checkpoint again several hours later, the boys were still there, their bodies still squatting, backs against the wall.

Time is "an artifact of power" (Peteet 2005a, 37) and in the space of Palestine-Israel, there are polyrhythms, just as there are multiple spatialities and sovereignties, and each one a means of ordering power and relationality. Waiting, with the body in prolonged stasis, publicly performs and displays state domination over the minutia of daily life. Like space, Palestinian time is subject to control and appropriation, a visible and embodied mark of distinction, where the biological and the social connect in "a medium of hierarchic power and governance" (Munn 1992, 109).[1] As we have seen, in Palestine's reconfigured landscape, moving through time and space is an exercise freighted with power and inequality. At checkpoints, Palestinians' control over the timing and rhythm of their movements through space is suspended; in the time of closure, the space of the checkpoint marks the intersection of distinct temporal orders as well. The checkpoint is a structural and experiential object, I contend, that mediates time for Palestinians. Pivotal for colonial domination over the minutia of everyday life, for Palestinians the temporal has become a realm of shared experience, a marked category, objectified and immediate in individual and collective subjectivities.

Through the lens of mobility's temporal rhythms, or "rhythmanalysis" (Lefebvre 2004), I explore how time and space intersect, an intersection succinctly and elegantly captured by the Palestinian writer Raja Shehadeh (2008, 173) when he describes a walk taken in the West Bank. "When we climbed up again the whole scene of the new construction lay bare before our eyes. There was so much up-heaval, it was as though the entire earth was being reshuffled. It was as though the tectonic movements that had occurred over thousands of years were now hap-pening in a matter of months, entirely redrawing the map."[2] Israeli time moves on a "tectonic scale," undoing thousands of years of time. He was describing the literal enactment on the ground of Soffer and Bystrova's (2005, 47) warning that "the demographic clock is working against Israel, rapidly and frighteningly, and threatening it in the time span of no more than another decade." Separation and closure, along with accelerated Jewish settlement, are meant to be a panacea for the ticking demographic clock.

This chapter probes temporality, rhythms, and relationality in the time of closure and their impact on the fabric of quotidian life. It identifies waiting as a primary embodied aspect of the rhythms of closure that surfaces at the intersec-tion of time, space, and energy or, for our purposes, movement (see Lefebvre 2004). The chapter takes a brief foray through the terrain of time and political claims, elaborates Palestinian estrangement from home through a brief exami-nation of language and signage, and wraps up with an overview of how, in the first decade of new millennium, obstructed mobility and deceleration severely hampered the ability to participate in, nurture, and reproduce kinship and so-cial ties embedded in networks of obligation, reciprocity and sentiment. In ad-dition, health care was seriously compromised, education was impeded, and the economy was devastated.

Not surprisingly, Israel joins a host of colonial enterprises that have appended native time to the colonizer's time (see Merry 2000; Cooper 2005), resulting in polyrhythmia. In colonial regimes, new temporal orders were often associated with demands for a regulated and disciplined labor force. In addition, colonial regimes often imagine the native as occupying an alternate time zone, distinct from "modern" time. Palestinians and Israelis occupy distinctly hierarchical and active relational spatiotemporal zones. As a consequence, the hierarchical social order is etched in time as well as space.

A related facet of time in the colonial present is the notion of the "tempo-rary." As a discursive device and psychological weapon, the "temporary" compels an indeterminate, protracted state of anticipation. In international law, occupa-tion itself is an "interim measure" of governance "in the period between armed conflict and a peace settlement" (Dugard 2007, 2). When the Palestinian occupa-tion began, it was declared "temporary," but actions on the ground, particularly the building of colonies, soon belied that claim. Closure, imposed as a temporary measure—"until further notice"—in March 1993, has yet to be lifted. The wall's $3 billion price tag vitiates any notion of its "temporariness," as does its concrete-ness, conveying permanency hiding in plain sight. The wall was presented to the world as a temporary security device. Laws that constrain Palestinian human rights are also cast as "temporary" (see Gordon 2008, 244). In other words, claims of temporariness have been wielded to manage the occupied population and quell resistance (ibid., 24–25).

Anthropology emerged in a context in which "faith in salvation" was replaced by "faith in progress and industry" (Fabian 1983, 17). The occupation operates in this framework but also consciously creates the conditions to thwart Palestinian progress by slowing time. Fabian's "physical time" can become "political physics," or what I will call in this ethnographic context the "physics of mobility," whereby the colonial occupation deems it "impossible for two bodies to occupy the same space at the same time" (ibid., 29). Carrying this formula further, the physics of mobility in Palestine illustrates the intersection of time and space, and how obstacles to mobility produce space diluted of natives, space that can be then recategorized and imagined as Israeli-Jewish.

Waiting

About the Palestinian experience of time, the writer Leila el-Haddad wrote:

> Always waiting. For this is what the Palestinian does: we wait. For an answer to be given, for a question to be asked; for a marriage proposal to be made, for a divorce to be finalized, for a border to open, for a permit to be issued; for a war to end; for a war to begin; for a child to be born, for one to die a martyr; for retirement or a new job; for exile to a better place and for return to the only place that knows us; for our prisoners to come home; for a time when we no longer have to wait."[3] (el-Haddad 2009, 4)

Indeed, waiting does seems "to be the neglected Achilles heel of modernity" and, I would contend, is only marginally present in the literature on (im)mobilities (Bissell 2007, 277).[4] However, waiting in Palestine is hardly equivalent to the mundane waiting of ordinary life, whether in line at the post office, going through airport security, the grocery store, or the bus stop. Indeed, waiting in Palestine severely disrupts everyday life. "Occupation time" (Meneley 2008, 20) prevails, in which Israel determines the scope and speed of Palestinian mobility through temporal engineering; the wall, checkpoints, and permits slow down Palestinians' mobility. "Occupation time" obstructs their participation in modern industrial time and yet also "interferes with the seasonal rhythms of old. It is its own temporal category" (ibid., 21). In occupation time, speed, that quintessential signifier of modernity, is decelerated through prolonged and capricious waiting. The control of Palestinian time fashions a particular kind of body and subjectivity and slows down development, work, education, and social life while enabling the scope and speed of the colonial society. If time, like space, is in great measure produced through action and mobility, we need to ask what happens when time is appropriated and subject to restrictions.

El-Haddad's inventory of waiting positions it as a constituent component of the Palestinian national condition. Palestinians waited to return home following the mass displacement in 1948–49, believing their temporary exile would end when the violence subsided. In the camps, refugees live the paradox of protracted temporariness—trying to construct normal lives in what are by design temporary abodes. The right of return, so central to Palestinian politics and national sentiment, suggests a state of suspended time, a protracted period of waiting for a right that remains out of reach. Under occupation, Palestinians face interminable waits at checkpoints and for permits. All wait for solutions, for justice, for recognition, and security. A sense of crisis suffuses most Palestinian lives in anticipation of the next restriction, the next moment of violence, and the next disaster.

In a world where time is wielded as a weapon, questions arise as to how is it experienced, conceptualized, and negotiated. After hours spent trying to reach Nablus to visit friends, Muna's lamentations—"we are masters of waiting" and "our struggle will be a long one"—conveyed an expansive and contradictory view of time. They know that colonists are swiftly moving in and have the privilege of traversing bypass roads, unencumbered by permits and checkpoints. They watch with heavy hearts as each day brings new indignities. Nevertheless, they know that the situation can only be sustained for so long; they, too, wait for the proverbial tipping point when violence will erupt. Both Israelis (see Ochs 2011) and Palestinians wait—for the next explosion, the next round of fighting, the next peace initiative that both know will amount to nothing. This reminds us of anthropologist Victor Crapanzano's (1985, 42) depiction of white South Africans, as they "wait for something, anything, to happen. They are caught in the peculiar, the paralytic, time of waiting."

In waiting for a permit, to arrive home, for a doctor's appointment, or to visit family, the immediate future is contingent less on the modern accoutrements of time, such as schedules, clocks, watches, and agendas, and more on the checkpoint opening, the queue starting to move, the soldiers arriving and swinging open the gates. Palestinians wait to pass inspection. They wait under the hot sun or in the freezing rain. The cell phone is a constant presence, relaying information about estimated times of arrival and warning of delays and flying checkpoints. Arriving late to work after a weekend spent at home in Jenin, Ziad sighs after a series of long delays at checkpoints, "We are patient," but "we can only tolerate so much. At some point, it will explode." Needless to say, just beneath the surface of compliance a seething frustration and bitterness saturates the atmosphere at checkpoints, communicated in the angry muttering of those in crowds moving at a snail's pace, if at all.

Waiting is an embodied state of simultaneously contained movement and stasis. When faced with inexorable waits, the body decelerates, often to a standstill; a heightened state of alert and agitation takes over as Palestinians wait for the line to inch forward, for the rattling sound of a turnstile starting to move, for the grunts of a soldier's order to "go!" They fidget, shift from one foot to the other, talk on cell phones, turn to one another to exchange information about alternative routes or just to complain, commiserate, or mutter or curse quietly; sometimes they get angry and leave, but most often, they are just still. Their bodies sweat in summer and shiver in winter; they hold their bowels, wait to eat and drink; their legs and backs ache. Eventually, they lean against a wall or sit on the rough, often dirty pavement. Mothers hush crying babies and young children squirm. Yet this is not ordinary waiting, this is state-enforced waiting as a form of punishment and control. The sheer physicality of waiting engenders an acute sense of time.

This objectified sense of time is magnified by the randomness it inflicts on daily rhythms and agendas. "They are stealing our time. Everything takes so long!" Muna exclaimed angrily. She had just been granted a twelve-hour permit to travel ten kilometers (six miles) to Jerusalem. An otherwise mundane event, a book reading by a friend, had become a major endeavor. She arranged a taxi driven by a Palestinian Jerusalemite, whose Jerusalem identity card and Israeli license plate allowed him to ferry people through the checkpoints as long as they possessed the requisite permit. Hers was for the day only, so she had to be back in Ramallah by nine o'clock that evening. It had taken five days from submitting the application to actual issuance of the permit. "Stealing time" captures the materiality of closure: a concrete, objectified sense of time, the actual minutes, hours, and days that accumulate while waiting. Sharply contoured by an interlinking repertoire of mechanisms of containment, Palestinian time is a tangible material thing that can be granted or denied, or, as Palestinians see it, stolen.

As we have seen, obtaining a permit such as Muna's, requires advance preparation: a trip to the Palestinian who is the liaison with the appropriate Israeli office, then days or weeks of waiting, followed by a trip, or perhaps several, to pick up a permit. Like a child, she (and all who seek permits) must request permission and then wait for "approval." At lunch a few days before a hoped-for visit to her children and grandchildren in Jerusalem, Muna expressed the uncertainty of those days, evident in her constant use of the phrase "if I can go." Would she receive a permit or would she have to cancel a visit her family eagerly awaited? On top of such preparation, checkpoints temporally stretch out the actual trip. Having one's time yoked to a dominant other infantilizes and subjugates. Protracted waiting affirms that a Palestinian's time is without value and that the space within which they desire to move is not theirs. They live in a state of prolonged time-out, a common form of discipline for children.

When time does move faster than anticipated, Palestinians may feel that things are improving; yet they are quick to chastise themselves for feeling this way, as Ziad did when he exclaimed, "Look at us! We are happy when the checkpoint becomes more regulated and predictable, or they put in a bathroom. We see this as a pleasant thing when really they are just throwing us a crumb and trying to normalize the checkpoints." In an atmosphere of anticipated discomfort and expectations of stalled mobility, any improvement is welcomed, though it is not without such sharp critiques. There is also an awareness that what can be given can be taken away in this punitive atmosphere.

Returning to work on a Sunday morning, Ziad complained about his boring weekend, "I just sat here. I just want to see the sea. We are trapped like animals in a cage unable to move this way or that. Young people elsewhere can travel and have opportunities we will never have." Ziad envisions a fast-moving world he is locked out of. It is worth noting that his laments reflect global problems affecting young people, who are a growing demographic, as young men and women all over the world languish in the face of high unemployment and diminished opportunities. Young people like Ziad are suspended in time with a keen awareness of being cooped up, made worse because of a vague memory of a time of less impeded mobility.

Waiting is a deeply sedimented way of being. Palestinians wait to be scrutinized and validated, and then granted, or denied, permission to move. Paralysis can set in as Palestinians hunker down in their enclaves, avoiding movement if they can, unwilling to risk the indignity and the uncertainty that await them at checkpoints. But this can have a cost. As Um Fuad complained about being unable to visit her husband's village, because the trip was too long without access to toilets, her son Fuad chimed in, "Making people suffer like that is part of their humiliation, and it is a way to get our land." Um Fuad added, "We own a lot of land around Toubas—it hasn't been confiscated yet. If we can't visit there and tend to it, they will take it."

Time/Space Intersection and Relationality

On a crowded bus that was inching along the road next to the wall, an elderly man started loudly badgering the driver about why the bus was moving so slowly. Eyeing the man in his rearview mirror, the driver shouted, "Fly! Take an airplane if you don't like it." The passengers burst into laughter, finding dark humor in the reality of time slowed down. Now and then, when the road went over an incline, we could see Israeli cars zipping by on the other side of the wall. In this context, time, like space, is decidedly relational as well as polyrhythmic. Piece by piece, an infrastructure that immobilizes Palestinians and enables Israelis to move with relative ease and speed has taken shape. While "people can live within and think in multiple temporal frameworks" (Deeb 2009, 243), Palestinians are yoked to "occupation time," a decidedly unique temporal order, and to the rhythms of the

Jewish calendar. Curfews, common since 1967, are a good example of both the relational intersection of time and space and arrhythmia. Arrhythmia can be a "pathological situation" (Lefebvre 2004, 77) where de-synchronization is "morbid and then fatal" (ibid., 78). Curfews impose prolonged waiting on Palestinian communities where mobility is strictly forbidden except for a few hours a day, and people are, in essence, incarcerated in their homes. Often declared during Jewish holidays or after an incident of violence toward colonists or the military, curfews completely seal off the OPTs or certain towns, such as Hebron, which is well-known for the numerous days it has spent under curfew. A mass lockdown ensures that Jews move with ease and relative speed while Palestinians are more or less stationary. Nasreen complained angrily, "Every Jewish holiday my husband and I are apart. I have to sleep at my parents in Ramallah because of the complete sealing off of Jerusalem." Aside from easing the restrictions on entry to Jerusalem for the elderly and women, Palestinians' mobility during their own sacred time is accorded little recognition. Randa was fuming on the eve of the end of Ramadan, the Muslim month of fasting:

> You know, the evening before this Muslim feast day—everyone is trying to go home to be with family. So, I arrive at Qalandia, and it is closed. A big group of us waited for four hours in the cold. There were many elderly people and women with small children. Everyone was so angry. I couldn't stand it! I was so hungry and getting thirsty. I went to a small shop near the checkpoint and kept eating sweets and smoking—this was the only place a girl could smoke in public and no one would criticize her. I needed to smoke. We waited for hours from four until eight o'clock. I needed to go home. I needed to go home and prepare for the feast. I could barely stand up I was so drained, but I kept thinking. I need to go home and cook and clean and be with my family.

Conceptualizations of distance unfold at the intersection of the spatial and temporal. Palestinians measure distance less in kilometers and more in equivalent times—"We could have been in London or Paris by now!" Distance is calculated by the number of obstacles that will be encountered and the temporal rhythms they impose. When I asked Ziad how far it was to Jenin, he replied, "Five checkpoints—maybe four or five hours from Ramallah." Before closure, distance was referred to temporally and spatially, but that intersection has been distorted, if not ruptured.

Colonists read their maps to find out how to get from place to place. Tellingly, Palestinians rarely use maps as navigation tools. The colonial map is an artifact of foreignness; it signifies a lack of topographic knowledge and of intimacy with the terrain that is gained from a lifetime of living there. Israeli maps pinpoint colonies, bypass roads, police and military posts, and emergency telephones, and warn of areas of possible danger.[5]

Virilio's concept of "dromocracy" can be applied to Palestine, where those who command speed rule (Collins 2008, 9–10). Slow Palestinian time can be juxtaposed to hyper-speedy, smooth, and unobstructed Israeli movement. Drones and F-16s can attack without warning; military vehicles move at a rapid pace along the well-paved, lightly traveled bypass roads. In this case, command is premised on unhindered mobility and speed. The direct corollary of ease of movement is that Palestinian space shrinks and Palestinian time slows. In other words, in this violently imposed social order, time and space have become arrhythmic and distorted.

Deep Time: Signs on the Landscape

The bald statement by former Israeli prime minister Ariel Sharon that "we are going to leave an entirely different map of the country that it will be impossible to ignore" resonated in my conversation with Kareema, a student studying in the United States. In 2010, Kareema had just returned from a trip to visit her family in a village just outside Nablus.[6] Over lunch in New York, she told me:

> I want to tell you a story about going home last summer. On the small bus going toward Nablus, I looked out the window and did not have a clue as to where we were. I used to know the area quite well. There were signs everywhere, but they were in Hebrew. Roads to the villages were closed or blocked by cement slabs. Everything looked so different from what I remembered. Checkpoints blocked the road. I felt very disoriented and unsure of where I was. I kept asking the driver "where are we?" This is what they have done to us—imagine! I grew up here but I was lost.

A terrain dotted with physical obstacles and Hebrew signage triggered a sense of being lost and disoriented in a once familiar landscape.

Over the past century, the landscape of Palestine has been radically transformed to conform to a Zionist-nationalist narrative. To effect deep time by evoking an imagined ancient past, naming has played a critical role in crafting "anachronistic time" (McClintock 1995, 40). In the endeavor to bring deep time into the present, the natives are out-of-place, now foreigners in an increasingly unfamiliar and unknowable land- and name-scape from which they are excluded; the native is consigned to another time and space.

Naming is closely entangled with claims to space and reflects the capacity to make these claims a present reality. Indeed, dwelling and naming may impose the most basic features of place-making. The practice of chronomastics, "a discourse about names highlighting an awareness of times past," renders names "social objects that articulate contemporary and past classifications" (Brink-Danan 2010, 385). The "new political systems, and the symbolic systems that accompany them, engender reclassifications that rely on the ability of old signifiers to signify something new or of new signifiers to signify something old" (ibid., 392). When Israeli cartographers Hebracized place names and topographic features, they were laying claim to what they believed belonged to the Jewish people in a "supreme act of national self-assertion whose aim was to draw up a contract of ownership, a linguistic title deed, to legitimize the claims of the Jews while at the same time delegitimizing the rights of the Palestinians" (Suleiman 2004, 212–213).

Both a symbolic intervention and a performative act, naming registers claims to sovereignty and attempts to confirm the meaning of place. In this case, naming saturates present time and place with signs redolent of a mythico-historical past, seamlessly knitting together past and present. In contentious settings, naming can also be part of "political annihilation" (Bodenhorn and vom Bruck 2006, 1). In this orbit of relationality, naming maps Israeli-Jewish sovereignty and concomitant rights while attempting to un-map and de-indigenize the Palestinian. Accordingly, these linguistic strategies have a dual purpose. First, they are attempts to nativize Israelis by consciously and methodically cultivating a historic-religious identification with place. Second, they work to efface the Palestinian presence and history. Like Kareema, who felt lost when she returned to her village near Nablus, Palestinians are increasingly disoriented as they traverse terrain that was once familiar through a lifetime of use.

Colonization and claims to territory are starkly visible in the road and street signs. The imposition of Hebrew and the erasure of Arabic names and signage in the West Bank mimics the process the Israeli Names Committees undertook, after 1948, to rename Palestinian villages, towns, and natural features of the pre-1948 landscape. Erasing Arabic names and replacing them with Hebrew names removes the traces of the indigenous and unsettles their memories of place, while bolstering the mythico-history of Jewish claims to a minimally populated Palestine. To erase and rename is a relational undertaking, an act of simultaneous appropriation and denial. In short, naming is an act of intervention, a way of organizing and giving meaning to place that draws lines of exclusion and inclusion. Palestinians continue to use Arabic place names and thus to contest appropriation and actively insist on their own linguistic landscape.

Upon entering the West Bank from Jordan, one is met with the symbols of occupation, from the blue-and-white Israeli flags to the ubiquitous signage in Hebrew. Indeed, few Arabic signs appear until one reaches the outskirts of Jerusalem. Signage levies meaning visually and cognitively, announcing presence, sovereignty, and exclusion. Hebrew signage proclaims Israeli-Jewish space, with its associated exclusivity, and warns about trespass. Walking down Nablus Road in East Jerusalem in fall 2010, on the blue-and-white street sign indicating the Palestinian neighborhood of Sheikh Jarrah, the Arabic script had been blacked out with spray paint. Israeli colonists had begun occupying Palestinian homes here in 2010, often evicting the residents with little notice. A small group of colonists were gathered in a circle, listening attentively to a young man holding a clipboard, who was issuing what seemed to be a set of instructions. About thirty IDF soldiers stood nearby, ready to protect these new colonists. The blacked-out road signs and the presence of the colonists portended, in no uncertain terms, the intensified colonization of this Palestinian neighborhood. The linguistic erasure of the Arab presence on the signposts paralleled the effect of the evictions in transforming the neighborhood's demographics. In Jerusalem, it is not uncommon to see blacked-out Arabic script on the street signs. This linguistic blacking underscores the uncertainty of the colonizers' claim—as if it cannot withstand the inclusion of other narratives of place and belonging—and resonates with philosopher Judith Butler's (1997, 9) contention that "the threat begins the performance of that which it threatens to perform" and "seeks to establish, through language, the certitude of that future in which it will be performed."

On Jaffa Street in West Jerusalem, there are no Arabic signs on any of the buildings or shops; when Arabic script appears on street signs, it is small and inserted in the middle, between the Hebrew and English. In response to Zionist demands, in 1922, the British promoted Hebrew to an official language, equal to Arabic and English (Suleiman 2004, 144–145). Under Jordanian rule (1948–67), Arabic and English were the official languages; Arabic was on top on street signs, and English was underneath, reflecting its status as a linga franca and the language of the Mandatory power (ibid., 189). With the occupation, most Jerusalem street signs are now written in three languages; the order was reversed with Hebrew on top, often in its own frieze.

If signage is a device of spatial orientation, the erasure of Arabic road signs and their replacement by Hebrew signs is intended to produce spatial unfamiliarity and shrink temporal depth. Roads in the occupied territory are navigable to those who can read Hebrew. As one drives north from Ramallah on the al-Quds-Nablus Road (Route 60), almost no signs indicate the proximity of Nablus, a major Palestinian city with a population of around 250,000. There are, however, intermittent signs in Hebrew, Arabic, and English indicating even sparsely populated colonies. A new system of transliteration from Hebrew into English rather than from Arabic (the Hebrew *ha-* replaces the Arabic *al-*) has appeared. Arabic signs all over West Bank are written in transliterated Hebrew. For example, Jericho is transliterated in Arabic as Yerhico, not Arihah (or Jericho), further iterating the strangeness at home.

The landscape is becoming simultaneously strange and familiar, but, ultimately, the once-taken-for-granted will be overtaken by this sense of estrangement. The knowledge transmitted from one generation to another will form a memory of what cannot be experienced first-hand. What happens to the memory of shared places and space when movement is severely obstructed and the landscape begins to vanish before one's eyes? The immobilized body minimizes its sense of spatial expanse and inherits a memory of a past time, when space was expansive and time had not yet been appropriated. Memories take shape in particular places and with immobilization become meaning-laden. New inscriptions of place will eventually color memories in a palimpsest, where colonies and checkpoints jostle with former names in referring to place. Palestinians have incorporated a dominant foreign presence in the landscape—they have to move around its spatial formations daily, and their lexicon is now littered with new topographical names of colonies and checkpoints.

Temporality and Making Claims

Calibrating the temporal is closely linked to creating facts on the ground. Both Israeli and Palestinian national narratives draw on past time to bolster contemporary political claims. French philosopher Gilles Deleuze's (1995) insightful assertion that "negotiations sometimes last so long you don't know whether they're still part of the war or the beginning of peace" resonates in the framework of conflict management that has replaced peace seeking. Israel delaying negotiations is premised on a set of conditions that are always in motion: initially, it was claimed there were no Palestinian people, or they had no representative. Their representative, the Palestine Liberation Organization (PLO), was declared a terrorist organization, and the state does not negotiate with terrorists. Then Israel declared Palestinians were not partners for peace; the ever-present condition to be met before negotiations can proceed is that Palestinians must renounce violence. Now, Israel demands recognition not just as a state, which the PLO has done, but as a Jewish state. Multiplying conditions forestall negotiations and facilitate creeping expansion and annexation. As Israel rachets the conditions for negotiations ever higher, Israeli bulldozers are busily clearing space for new or expanded colonies and bypass roads.

US-Israel negotiators have consistently deployed a strategy of seeking interim agreements on current pressing issues, such as Oslo, deferring to a "later" time the critical issues of refugees, settlements, borders, and the status of Jerusalem. In this scenario, the 1948 *nakbah,* the 1967 occupation, and continuing colonization are treated as faits accomplis. Politically, deferral positions Palestinians in a state of perpetual beginnings. In short, as contemporary issues dominate political discussions, the core issues deriving from 1948 and 1967 recede further into the background. This state of deferral and perpetual beginnings "mete[s] out promissory notes that are not exceptions to their operation but constitutive of them" (Stoler 2008, 193).

The Zionist narrative traces a direct spatiotemporal link between biblical time and the present, collapsing the intervening years along with the presence of other populations: Caananites, Philistines, Romans, Greeks, Byzantines, and Arabs, among others.[7] Although there has been a small Jewish presence in Palestine for thousands of years, the region has been continuously populated by others as well. In this discursive orbit of collapsed time and vacated space, the past presence of a Jewish community in Palestine has endowed contemporary Jewry anywhere with rights denied to Palestine's indigenous Arab inhabitants. Indeed, for Palestinians, rights are in large part delineated by a spatial-temporal framework hinging on a "where were you when" formula; for example, according to Israeli regulations and law, Palestinians absent from their normal place of residence in Palestine on or after November 29, 1948, did not have the right of return, and as "absentees," their land could be seized (Fischbach 2003, 21–23). Similar strictures from 1967 govern Palestinian residency in the OPTs, fixing rights in an imagined demographic, spatial, and cultural past. That Palestinians are recent migrants from surrounding areas and thus can relocate to the wider Arab Middle East was long a standard Zionist argument,[8] one that ignores complex regional patterns of habitation, exchange, and mobility under successive empires over several thousand years, as well as ethnic and religious diversity and modern nationalism.[9] Thus one temporal moment is privileged over all others, eliding not just history but the modern system of human rights and international humanitarian law as well.

In this orbit of telescoped time, where do the indigenous fit? Palestinian and Zionist narratives recognize some of the same recent temporal markers, but their meanings diverge radically. Palestinian narratives highlight continuity of loss through time and collective trauma: *al-nakbah* (the catastrophe) was followed by the 1967 occupation, leading to the most recent stage of colonial domination in the form of closure and separation. In the Zionist narrative, these same temporal markers are to be celebrated. If 1948 is marked as a catastrophe by Palestinians, a moment of radical rupture and a trope for ongoing suffering, for Israelis it serves as a watershed moment in the desire for statehood and renewal.[10]

In remaking the space of Palestine, present time and space have been refashioned to conform to an imaginary time. For example, the pastor of a church in the United States recounted to me a conversation with a senior military officer who had baldly commented that a "small number of Palestinians will be kept in Jerusalem to provide local color for the tourists." "Local color" suggests a vestige of an exotic past, to be frozen in time for tourists' consumption. In this time/space formulation, the Bedouins of the Negev, for example, serve as a backdrop, ethnographic artifacts called forth to display and perform cultural diversity. This begs the question, do living human artifacts have rights and where do they fit in the state? The Palestinian "cave dwellers," agriculturalists and pastoralists living south of Hebron, provide an example of "live ethnographic prop[s]" (Lagerquist 2008, 2). In elaborate legal proceedings, ethnographic exotica outweighed, if not masked, the process by which these folks came to live in these caves. Until recently, they had dwelled in modern concrete houses adjoining the caves. When the ruins of a synagogue were uncovered beneath their houses, the occupying authorities evicted the inhabitants and demolished their homes. They then took up residence in the caves that had once adjoined their homes. Yet the *New York Times* ignored the evictions and house demolitions, noting only that "Ancient Susiya contains the ruins of a synagogue dating from the Roman period, attesting to a long and robust Jewish presence here. Jewish settlers started moving in again" after 1967 (ibid., 9). What is a "long and robust presence"? "Moving in again" sounds as though they had been gone for a few months or years. Lagerquist documents the legal process by which the residents attempted to reclaim their lands: their lawyer adopted an "ethnographic argument" (ibid., 10), while the government adopted the nomadic defense, in which Palestinians are cast as nomads rather than settled agriculturalists and pastoralists with an attachment to place as well as ownership, to undermine a long history of residency. The government "offered to regulate the time the Arabs could spend there, allowing them to work the land during planting and harvesting season, and Jewish holidays" (ibid., 11). Lagerquist astutely notes that "what was being promoted was the right . . . to be ethnics, bearers of a culture outside history" (ibid., 12). Residents were forced to live outside time; they could cultivate their crops on a state-regulated time schedule, and their presence was only legitimate if they were artifacts within a finely managed landscape.

As we have seen here and in chapter 3, closure consigns Palestinians to arrhythmic conditions, a temporal mode from another era. This unraveling of their ability to navigate the terrain poses a severe challenge to many aspects of daily life.

The Geography of Health and Sociality

This section explores two other areas impacted by closure: medical care and sociality, as they unfold at the juncture of temporal appropriation, fragmented space, and restricted mobility. If dense webs of reciprocity and sociality weave people and communities together across time and space, immobility has a profound effect on the fabric of social life. Closure and waiting also impede access to health care. Critiques of a "productivist" means-ends approach to waiting often oddly fail to give any serious attention to power or the state (see Bissell 2007). Waiting, I contend, is a tactic in a strategy of population management and a means of exacting collective punishment. Waiting is, in fact, part of calibrated abandonment. Darryl Li's (2008) compelling description of Gaza in the wake of Israel's self-designated "disengagement" or "withdrawal" in 2005 summarizes a calibrated humanitarian crisis that has become a regime of governance. In reference to Gaza, which is a more extreme case of what transpires in the West Bank, Israeli architect Eyal Weizman (2011, 85) alludes to another kind of suffering and "subtle form of killing . . . undertaken through degrading environmental conditions to affect the quality of water, hygiene, nutrition and healthcare . . . and by making it difficult for patients to travel."

A brief mention of the economy is in order. Occupation's intensification under closure has been a preemptive assault on Palestinian development, seriously undermining the potential for economic growth, in fact producing continuing de-development (Roy 1995; Meneley 2008), leaving the economy in shambles. The movement of goods and labor in the OPTs is subject to stringent regulation, and employment opportunities in the OPTs and Israel have shrunk. A multitude of factors can be identified that have negatively affected the economy of the West Bank, but "it is generally undisputed that the sweeping restrictions on movement . . . are a major reason for the deterioration of the Palestinian economy and the increase in unemployment and poverty."[11] Echoing the temporal framing of occupation and closure, most restrictions are said to be "indefinite in duration."[12]

In the 2000s, the UN Secretary General's Personal Humanitarian envoy reported "a crisis of access and mobility" in the health sector (Bosmans et al. 2008, 104). Siege-like conditions in Gaza provided the most compelling evidence for the adverse effects of closure on health. Acute shortages of food, energy supplies, and medical and sanitation equipment fueled the emergence of "chronic nutritional diseases, including stunting or excessive underweight," as well as high levels of anemia in women and children.[13] The completion of the the wall in the West Bank "will cut off a total of 71 clinics; 41 clinics were already totally cut off. Some 450,000 Palestinians will be directly affected, and a further 80,000 indirectly."[14] A UN study said the area was "on the brink of a humanitarian catastrophe." Between September 2000 and September 2012, Israeli forces in the OPTs killed almost 7,000 Palestinians; about 500 Israelis were killed by Palestinians. During this period, 1,335 Palestinian minors were killed, and 44 Israeli minors were killed.[15] Israel has carried out 238 extrajudicial executions, and in doing so killed 186 bystanders. Add to these figures the more than 2,100 Palestinians killed in the 2014 Israeli assault on Gaza.

Life and Death

A series of conversations with Nabil, a lively thirty-five-year-old paramedic and ambulance driver for the Palestinian Red Crescent Society, and his colleague Mohammed shed light on the devastating impact of constrained space, time, and mobility on access to life-saving health care:

> In early 2008, we were taking a patient to Tulkaram and returning back with two patients from a traffic accident. We went through twelve checkpoints.

These were all flying checkpoints—from Ramallah to Tulkaram. When we returned we faced fourteen. It took six hours and that was actually fairly speedy given the number of stops. I was counting them in my head 4, 5, 6, 7, and so on. At each one they checked the ambulance, and then they checked again, over and over.

When I inquired as to the distance between Ramallah and Tulkaram, he replied, "It is seventy to eighty kilometers (forty-three to forty-nine miles)—maybe one hour of driving." Mohammed chimed in with dark humor, "We could have flown to Europe!" underscoring how distance and time no longer meaningfully intersect and further demonstrating the pathology of arrhythmia.

At Qalandia, the capriciousness of control as well as petty cruelty was clear in early spring 2007, when Nabil and Mohammed were taking a patient who had a permit to enter Israel for cancer treatment:

Two soldiers come to check the identity card of the patient, and they made him get out of the ambulance. Luckily, it was sunny day, not too cold. I hear the older say to the younger one, "Give them their cards and let them pass." But the young one puts them in his pocket. So we phoned the ICRC [International Committee of the Red Cross]. They called the checkpoint, but still this guy would not give us the identity cards. So, we waited with an ill patient for a couple of hours for no apparent reason, other than this guy wants to show who is the boss.

Access to medical care is mediated by occupation authorities who determine who and what can pass through checkpoints and at what speed. Many villages are served by small primary health-care clinics, and residents are denied unimpeded access to medical facilities in larger towns, such as Ramallah. If the wall divides a town, and the hospital is on other side, patients may have to drive for hours, often over bumpy back roads and through multiple checkpoints to reach a hospital that is only a few miles away. By 2006, there were well-over a hundred documented cases of denial of access to medical care at checkpoints leading to death, including of infants. Moreover, Jerusalem's six specialized hospitals are off-limits to West Bank Palestinians who don't have a permit to enter Jerusalem.

In a protracted settler-colonial setting, the local civilian population faces frequent exposure to stressful, often life-threatening situations. Home itself and social life are battle fronts subject to military incursions and control. Demolition is a prime example. Between 1967 and 2012, over 28,000 Palestinian houses were torn down (Schaeffer and Halpern 2012, 1). While body counts may dramatically show how violence suffuses ordinary life, the quotidian, seemingly mundane details of everyday existence, particularly chronic micro-aggressions such as humiliating encounters are stressful too (Barber et al. 2013).

Palestinian conversations are laced with stories of the ill and incapacitated trying to get through checkpoints. Once at Qalandia, I observed a wheel-chair-bound, middle-aged woman and her daughter try to cross. The younger woman, permits in hand, waited at a metal gate next to the turnstile, waving her hands to get the attention of a couple of soldiers, so they could open it. They studiously ignored her and continued chatting. After about fifteen minutes, one of the soldiers unhurriedly walked over, gave a cursory glance at their permits, and without saying a word, opened the gate and waved them through. Palestinian ambulances are not allowed to enter Jerusalem; at the checkpoints, patients must be transferred to an ambulance with Israeli plates; this means that patients may have to walk across crowded checkpoints, with the usual lengthy waits that entails.[16]

Nabil had been on the front lines of emergency medical care for over a decade, first as a driver and then as a paramedic during the second intifada (1999–2011). When I saw him at his mother's house or when I happened to run into him in Ramallah after he finished work, he told me stories of what it was like ferrying the ill and injured in an ambulance through a checkpoint:

> First we wait, always waiting. The soldiers open the doors—front and back. They check everyone's identities, including the patient's. They look at the equipment. At Qalandia—it is hard. They delay you no matter what the condition of the patient and they call the DCO office. There is a woman there, Rachel; everyone knows her. Sometime she refuses to let you pass. Once she did not let me pass because the patient, although critically injured, did not have a permit.

Nabil confirmed the rampant stories, and my observations, of ambulances being made to wait in line at checkpoints and being boarded by military personnel. He explained that soldiers get in to check the wounded; they may order patients to walk or be carried through the checkpoint to take another ambulance on the other side, or even deny them passage. Sometimes soldiers will declare a patient not ill enough to pass—the "younger soldiers are the worst—the older ones are readier to let them pass. Once a young soldier asked a patient, 'How do you feel when I am searching this ambulance?' Then he asked for his identity card. Later, we laughed over such an absurd question. We have to try to keep a sense of humor just to get through these situations." Another time, a soldier denied a patient passage, and said, "Get your treatment somewhere else!"

Decisions about the urgency of the need for medical care are sometimes made by soldiers at the checkpoints or from a distance via telephone by DCO personnel, known simply by their first name, such as Rachel. It is hard to miss the cruelty, indifference, and callous disregard for the lives of Palestinians in these medical emergencies. Nabil told me of two instances when, in his opinion, people died as a result of denial of access to medical care:

The military called us and said, "We have shot someone and you need to go and pick him up." We searched for hours! From 9:00 p.m. to 1:00 a.m. The Israelis could see us and kept calling and telling us, "Go right. Go straight. Now down." Finally, from the hill opposite us, they turned on a spotlight and showed us where the body was. The guy had been shot five times. He had a big hole in his back and you couldn't see his knees and his face was half gone. He was bleeding all over the ground. Maybe if we had reached him right away, he would have lived. It was like a game for them.

Another time, the ambulance crew was ordered to the Beit El checkpoint to pick up an elderly man with heart problems. "When we arrived at the checkpoint, they made us wait ten minutes. I kept telling them it was urgent. The soldier said he would check. I could see the older man across the checkpoint with a younger man supporting him. When they eventually let us cross to take him—nearly forty-five minutes later—he was dead."

Curfews and chronic delays at checkpoint, as well as the difficulty of obtaining permits, mean that hospitals and clinics are often short of staff who cannot get to work. Medical personnel have been detained and beaten. For example, Nabil, Mohammed, and several of their emergency medical technician (EMT) colleagues were detained for months without charges during the second intifada. They had gone to the *muqa'tah* (headquarters of the PA) in Ramallah to pick up some wounded. Mohammed described what ensued:

As we were leaving, the soldiers stopped us, made us get down and ordered us to line up against the wall. They shouted, "Put up your arms." Then, they tied our hands behind our backs. The wounded were put in a car and driven off. The rest of us, including two wounded guys, were taken to Beit El. It was raining and very cold. I was separated from my colleagues and kept outside. I felt I was between the earth and the sky. After that night, they took me to Ofer prison, where I waited outside in the cold for two days without a blanket or jacket. They kept moving me from place to place. Sometimes I would go for two days without food. I was unable to bathe for eleven days once. I remember I counted thirty-three days without drinking anything hot, just water. Most of the time we ate matzo—an Israeli cracker. No one went to the bathroom. We asked the doctor to give us something. After thirty-three days at Ofer, I was transferred to Naqab prison. This was my first time in prison. They asked the same four questions over and over, "Where are you from? Who are you? Where do you work? Are you married?" And then they let me go. When they released us, we remained, with our hands tied behind our backs, waiting over fifteen hours. We waited like this to be transferred anywhere. I was there sixty-six days, always waiting. Finally, a judge saw me and told me to go—no charges against me.

Palestinians requiring treatment in a Jerusalem medical facility must obtain a permit detailing their medical condition and ascertaining that they have an appointment at a particular hospital and can only receive the appropriate treatment at that hospital. A study by Vitullo and colleagues found:

> In 2011, 33,285 patients (23,877 from West Bank and 9408 from Gaza Strip) referred by the Ministry of Health required Israeli permits for access to hospitals. Of these referrals, 24,168 (73%) were within the oPt, and 4,764 (14%) to Israel and 4,350 (13%) to Jordan. 175,228 patients and their companions in the West Bank applied for permits for health-care access in 2011; of these, 32,678 (19%; range 8–30% in 16 district offices) had their access permits denied or delayed. Data for the first quarter of 2012 showed the most frequent reason given for denying patients was security (680 [42%] of 1,622 denials). No criteria could be identified for denials on the basis of security. For the 1,053 staff who needed permits to travel to work in hospitals in East Jerusalem, 986 staff received permits for 6 months, 46 for 3 months, and 21 were denied permits. All permits were restricted by mode and route of entrance to East Jerusalem. Only on 49 (5%) of 1,074 occasions were ambulances permitted to enter East Jerusalem. In 2011, 1,082 (10%) of 10,560 applicants in the Gaza Strip had their access permits denied or delayed, with no reason given, and 197 (2%) were called for security interview. Patients aged 18–40 years had the highest rate of denied or delayed permits . . . Interviews with Gazan families of patients who had their permits denied or delayed showed that six patients died while waiting for the permits. (Vitullo et al. 2012)

Having a permit does not alleviate petty cruelties and delays. The doctor treating Selma's cancer-stricken elderly grandfather, Abu Ali, recommended chemotherapy treatment in Jerusalem. Abu Ali applied for and got a medical permit, but his wife and children were denied permits to accompany him. His family took him to Qalandia, where he was made to walk across the checkpoint to a waiting ambulance. At the end of the day, he had to reverse the process. To go for such treatment without a member of the family is culturally inappropriate, and as Selma said bitterly, "just plain mean."

When I next see Nabil he is downcast. He and a colleague were called to the Surda checkpoint, on the route to Bir Zeit University. Unattended by trained medical personnel, a woman in labor who was trying to reach a medical facility in Ramallah was forbidden to pass. By the time Nabil and his colleague arrived, the woman had delivered the baby behind a large rock, and it had died. Modern warfare targets women in specifically gendered ways. Rape and sexual atrocities come to mind, but with closure, denial of access to reproductive health care has endangered pregnant women and rendered their infants vulnerable. In an area with a relatively high (5.93) fertility (Giacaman et al. 2005, 129), women's access to maternal health care is critical. Over the past five decades, childbirth in medical facilities had become the norm, and home births were increasingly uncommon. In 1999, 92 percent of births occurred in hospitals (ibid., 134); by 2002, home births increased from 8 percent to 33 percent.[17] By "early 2004, the Palestinian Ministry of Health had documented at least 55 cases of women giving birth at checkpoints, and 33 cases of babies who have died after delivery because of delays at checkpoints" (ibid., 135).[18] As home births and births in small clinics increased, maternity wards in urban hospitals were delivering fewer babies. Compounding the problem was the inability of family to provide traditional support and caregiving upon the birth of a baby.

A report by the UN High Commissioner for Human Rights drew attention to the economic, medical, and psychosocial consequences of closure for pregnant women. Between 2002 and 2004, these included an increase in the number of induced labors and in the caesarean delivery rate, which increased from 8.8 percent to 12.4 percent. Women who know they will have to cross a checkpoint to reach a medical facility sometimes try to schedule their deliveries, hence the rise in C-sections and induced labors. Ghada, a twenty-five-year-old accountant in Ramallah, was filled with anxiety as her delivery date approached. It was her first pregnancy, and she wanted to deliver in Jerusalem, so the baby could have a Jerusalem identity, as she did. Her husband worried that she would go into labor in the middle of the night and have to go through Qalandia. She tried to reassure him, "Don't think about it, God will take care of it." Late in her eighth month, however, she decided that she did not want to be at the mercy of checkpoint personnel when she went into labor, so she scheduled a C-section and went to stay with relatives in Jerusalem. Her husband had a West Bank identity card and therefore could not accompany her. Palestinians without a Jerusalem identity card can schedule a procedure in a Jerusalem hospital and then apply for the required medical permit (Wick et al. 2005, 175). But the system is especially burdensome for pregnant women because the permits are only valid for a day or two and delivery dates are uncertain. Women in the last stages of a pregnancy therefore must go to the DCO office every day or two to renew their permits.

Closure has made childbirth a source of anxiety for women and their families. Stories of women in labor being compelled to undergo the indignity and danger of delivering in public, without medical assistance, and of infant distress and death at checkpoints encapsulate the horrors of occupation. Painfully suspended in time and space, the immobilized and laboring body epitomizes the repressive nature of closure and its inhumane disregard for life. Indeed, the potency of these stories brings to the fore Israel's demographic anxieties about a high Palestinian birth rate. This anxiety was initially registered in public discourse when then Israeli prime minister Golda Meir pronounced, "I cannot sleep at night for worry of all the Arab children being born that same night."[19]

The concept of dignity hovers over the encounters between Palestinians and occupation authorities. If we ask what constitutes dignity, then recognition, being seen and treated as an individual with personal autonomy and worth, comes immediately to mind, as does respect for personal space. The Universal Declaration of Human Rights declares, "All human beings are born free and equal in dignity and rights." Here, dignity precedes rights (Mann 1998, 31). Challenges to Palestinian dignity occur daily—the checkpoint and the permit system infantilize and deny autonomy and are a potent recipe for humiliation. Personal space, by definition, is violated repeatedly at checkpoints, where they, and their things, are searched, scanned, and often man-handled, and during home invasions and house demolitions.

With many occupation personnel safely ensconced behind plexiglass at large terminals like Qalandia and Bethlehem, there was little direct contact. However, at the smaller checkpoints, there still was face-to-face contact, and humiliating scenarios. In discussing humiliation and dignity, Rania related:

> Sometimes I feel I should smile because I need to get through the checkpoint. If you look at them too directly or with any other emotion on your face, they will likely say, "You, why are you looking at me like that? Get down and come here!" And they make you sit there. Sometimes it is not easy to keep my eyes down. Once, there was an Ethiopian soldier checking the bus. We just looked at each other. I thought, "I hate you and you know that." And later, when he saw me through the window looking at him, he ordered me, "Get down, come here now." So I had to get down—I was the only one who had to get off the bus—and sit there. So it was not easy—I was thinking "I hate you, you are in the wrong place." But I couldn't say that. They can kill you, your friends, or the ones you care about, and you have to act normally, without any feelings.

Prolonged exposure to political violence, particularly humiliation, has a measurable impact on well-being (Barber et al. 2013). The emotional landscape of occupation and closure is one of chronic micro-aggression, insecurity, and fear, fertile ground for anxiety and depression. The impact of "living in an environment characterized by severe, sustained, institutionalized and repetitive violations of individual and collective dignity is likely to be substantial" (Mann 1998, 34). Physician and health-rights activist Jonathan Mann argues that biomedical research was on the cusp of identifying this "hitherto unrecognized pathogenic force with a destructive capacity" (ibid., 36). Chronic humiliation led to increased fear and insecurity, depression, and "feelings of being broken or destroyed" (ibid.).

Kinship, Marriage, and Intimacy

"What the eyes do not see, the heart does not mourn," said Muna, with an air of resignation. This Arabic proverb evokes the visuality of landscape, sentiments of loss, and compromised social relations. It is the Arab version of the English proverb "out of sight, out of mind"; however, it doesn't always ring so true. In-stead, it may reflect the actual fear of losing the capacity to know a place and, as we shall see below, its material reality. Muna talked about an old friend who lives in Beit Hanina, a suburb of Jerusalem, which in pre-closure times was a ten- or fifteen-minute drive from Ramallah. Her recourse to the proverb conveyed the strain put on social and kin relations, which, however much lamented, are not yet forgotten:

> She lives in a different country. The occupation was better than this [closure]. I am not saying it was a blessing, but at least we could live. We could move to all areas and we could connect with each other. We could go to Gaza. But now we are all fragmented, we are psychologically fragmented. Everyone is depressed. Closure is affecting everyone's psyche. Under occupation, the only structure that functioned was the family. Now the family is fragmented—as a support system it is now failing. If our families cannot see how we are suffer-ing, they can't help us. Each family is taking care of itself. This proverb is about distance. If they are far away, like my son, they don't understand what I need to live here, for example, what electricity costs each month. It is harder for him to pay my expenses while I am here. It would be cheaper if I lived with them in the US. So the whole support system is affected by the distances between people. My son is married to a girl from Jerusalem. When I was in the States, my daughter-in-law gave me a gift and a birthday card to take to her mother in Jerusalem. It took them over a month to come here to get the gift and card. I cannot go to Jerusalem so they had to come here. It was not easy for them. They live behind the wall. They had to backtrack and everything had changed and they did not know where they were and what road to take. The landscape had changed so radically. They left their house and encountered the wall and they found out they would have to go a very long way around. It took them one and half hours to get here. Normally, it takes fifteen minutes.
>
> Many people with Jerusalem identities don't come here because of the humiliation. There is no certainty and this is very stressful—who wants to move around when you are never sure of where you are going or if you can actually get there. There are flying checkpoints, so you never know. I just stay in Ramallah most of the time. I can't go anywhere unless I leave the country. The Israelis are very creative—they are geniuses in devising ways to make us suffer. They are projecting their own experiences on us. They blame us for their experiences.

Sawsan, a middle-aged woman taking care of her elderly mother in East Je-rusalem, is the sister of an old friend. I asked if she had seen any other family members recently.

> I don't go anywhere—to Ramallah or anywhere. I am afraid I won't get back into Jerusalem. I take care of my mother, and if I were delayed at a checkpoint or didn't make it for some reason, she would be left alone. There are two large

checkpoints between here and Ramallah—Beit Hanina and Qalandia. I don't visit my niece in Beit Hanina. She lives near the checkpoint, up the hill. I am afraid to go. Before, I would have gone anytime. Now with these checkpoints, I don't visit Beit Hanina. We have family in Bethlehem—I haven't seen them in two years. Some of our family meets in Beit Jala because it is outside the checkpoint. It is difficult for people to visit these days because it costs a lot of money to take so many vans and buses. People in the West Bank say we are lucky to have the Jerusalem identity. But we can't go anywhere. Yes, we can go to West Jerusalem, but where else? I feel that if they know I am an Arab, anything can happen. I am afraid they will detain me and make me wait or take my identity card and make me wait, and then my mother will be alone.

Both Sawsan and Muna illustrate the geography of strained kin relations and sociality and the subjectivities it fosters. Obstructed mobility hinders the physical closeness necessary to sustain kin relations. Family support networks, sedimented in networks of reciprocity, are compromised by the inability to attend life-cycle events: marriages, births, deaths, celebrations, or even the simple but meaning-packed and emotionally satisfying visiting that nurtures ties with kin. There is a retreat into the immediate nuclear family or, sometimes, enhanced ties with family members living in proximity.

Closure also affects the decisions young people make about romantic relationships. In the Middle East, marriage slots people into expansive networks of affiliation. Arwa and a young man from Bethlehem were discussing a potential relationship. She told me in tears one day that she liked him and was interested in a relationship that could lead to marriage but exclaimed, "I can't marry him! I would lose my Jerusalem identity card if I live in Bethlehem. Then I wouldn't be able to enter the city or see my family or friends." She said, "I have a good friend who is in love with a young man from Nazareth but she decided not to marry him because according to the new Israeli law, she would be forbidden from living in Nazareth with him." Major life decisions are made under the shadow of an occupation that allocates mobility to different categories of identity card holders and imposes "juridical borders" on relationships (Johnson et. al. 2009, 29).

Rania's wedding illustrates marriage in the time of closure and at the height of the second intifada, when Israel was entering cities and towns in Area A. Military incursions and checkpoints disrupted the traditional sequence of marital events and their location, and the joyousness that usually attends a wedding. In a terrain fraught with uncertainty, Rania's family members tried to arrive in time for the wedding.

I was married in 2002. At that time, the situation was so bad. It was so difficult for us because I am from Beit Jala and my husband is from Ramallah. The marriage is supposed to be at the husband's home. At that time, it was horrible to come from Beit Jala to Ramallah. We faced many, many checkpoints.

The problem is my family—half of them have the West Bank identity card, and my mom, one of my brothers and I have Jerusalem identity. My father, my other brothers and all the rest of my family, they have West Bank identities. So they couldn't get to Ramallah easily because of the checkpoint at Qalandia.

I was so nervous. Girls who are getting married are supposed to be interested in what they wear, the party, the flowers, the food, and all of this. Me—the only thing I was thinking—how can my family, especially my father, how can he enter Ramallah in order to be with me. Imagine, it is my wedding! How can I get married without my father?

It was awful. When we reached the checkpoint, the soldier didn't want to let my father and my grandfather pass—these are older people—they didn't let them pass. I was crying and I showed the soldier my dress. At the checkpoint, in front of all these people, I opened the bag. I told him, "It's my dress. It's my wedding tomorrow. He has to enter." The soldier shouted at me, "No, he doesn't have a permit. So I don't care, go and get married alone." I said, "Why? It is my wedding, at the least my father should be with me." And he saw the dress and all my things. But he didn't care. I stayed there for one hour trying to convince him. This was at Qalandia. He did not accept to let him in so my father and grandparents decided to go around, through another road, through the mountains, through horrible roads. My grandparents, they are old, it was so difficult for them. Finally, they entered Ramallah.

But I still feel so sad, until now, that I did not leave from my father's house, the place I grew up in. I went out from my mother's family house here in Ramallah, near Qalandia. It is tradition for a bride to prepare herself at her house and then leave for the church from her father's house. This is the tradition and it is the most important thing at a wedding.

We had a small party after the wedding, and during this time the Israeli army was entering Ramallah. There was shooting, and then a curfew was imposed that night. There was a lot of shooting, so we ate cake quickly and went home. We were stressed the whole time. You hear the bombs and shooting and, at the same time, you want to live your life, to have fun on your wedding day. But you can't. You are stressed and nervous and you are thinking about what is going on outside. What can we do?

While in Amman, I paid a visit to Amin, a mild-mannered, high-level bank employee, and his wife and daughter. I had known Amin's family, the Nijims, for over twenty years. Amin and his immediate family had been involuntarily relocated to Amman. The process by which their movement unfolded is emblematic of the state's demographic and population-control policies, stalled time, the differential legal identities of Palestinians, and the permit system. Born in Amman to a West Bank family, Amin carried a Jordanian passport. Soon after Oslo, he joined his extended family still living there, including his mother and siblings. His wife Yumna had a West Bank identity card. Newly married, they bought a house, furnished it, and settled in Bethlehem, where their families reside and both were employed. As a Jordanian passport holder, Amin had to apply to the

Israeli embassy in Amman for a visa to enter the West Bank, and then apply to the Civil Administration offices at Beit El for a work permit; sometimes it was granted for a couple of weeks, sometimes for a couple of months, sometimes for six months, the length of time always unknown until it was actually stamped in his passport. So he would go back and forth between Amman and Palestine, renewing the visa each time. In 2002, for reasons never made clear, his request for a West Bank identity card was denied by the Israelis. Then, in Amman, he was denied a visa from the Israelis and forbidden to return home:

> In 2003, I had my work permit renewed for six months. Before it expired, I came to Amman with an overnight bag planning to spend two days getting my visa from the Israeli Embassy. But they did not reply to my application. They didn't say yes or no. I tried to follow up the matter, and some contacts told me, "They are not issuing visas for anyone, even if you are legal and they have nothing against you. So don't waste your time." When I would call the embassy, the operator would tell me they still have no answer. A simple "no answer." So I would call every day and they would say, "We have no answer." I even paid the fee for the visa and got a receipt. But still there was no reply. Days passed. I requested a vacation from the bank. I kept asking them to extend it. That was in August, then September came, then October and my passport was still at the embassy. Still no reply. It was obvious that I was not getting a visa.

Later, over dinner, he continued telling me about the events that had led Yumna and their four-year-old daughter, Sahar, to move to Amman:

> I just kept waiting. They didn't say, "Your application was rejected"; they just said, "There is no reply." The fact that they didn't say "your application is rejected"—this is what bothered me—the not knowing, the uncertainty. I was fifty years old and suddenly found myself stranded, unable to go to my home or family. I was not prepared for this strange feeling. So I kept hoping the visa would be granted, but it wasn't. I went the following year in late winter and took my passport from the embassy. There was no rejection and no acceptance—there was no reason. I was very, very frustrated. It's like being wounded and left in the open. My wife had a good job in Bethlehem and Sahar was in preschool. All our family is there, our social life as well, and, most importantly, my job. By September, I had used up my annual leave. My employer kept giving me unpaid leave, but after a couple of months they said, "We sympathize but it cannot go on like this." So, I had to resign—they were good—they gave me compensation, but it was so difficult.

It took Amin nearly a year to find work in Jordan. Yumna continued working in Bethlehem and her family helped with the baby. She said, "We had a new house and furniture. We had just finished paying for it." Eventually, when it was clear Amin would not be allowed to return, Yumna moved to Amman. She had been going every couple of months for short visits. Sahar, she tells me, "had been fearful when Amin traveled to Amman that she wouldn't see him again. She cried and was anxious about traveling in general. You know, she knows all about visas and passports. Imagine, a child of that age who understands such things! We lost our home, our jobs, and our families. What can we do? Israel controls these matters." Yumna misses her family, "I'm so lonely some days," she says plaintively. "I know almost no one in Amman. We can't even go out to dinner or a movie because we have no family to take care of Sahar." When I had Friday lunch with Amin's mother and brothers in Bethlehem, they lamented his absence and said sadly, "Even at Christmas and Easter, we are no longer together." As their mother aged, they felt keenly the loss of one brother's presence and assistance. Amin and Yumna are keeping their house in Bethlehem, certain they will return one day, "We have the big key, you know, Palestine is ours," Amin quipped. Amin and Yumna's story is suffused with waiting, uncertainty, ambiguity, and, ultimately, the straining of kin ties. They understood what happened to them as part of population thinning. "They just want fewer and fewer of us," Amin responded when I asked why he thought his visa was not renewed.

In a society where kin ties and networks of family and friends, near and far, are the cement holding together the social order, closure has had a serious and observable impact on the ability to sustain, perform, nurture, and reproduce these relations. Patterns of reciprocity and mutual assistance among kin that were part of a deeply sedimented system of obligations and rights that tied people across spatial distances can be stretched thin in protracted crises. Yet it is at precisely such moments that people turn to these networks for assistance. Thus it may be more fruitful to identify a continuum of mutual assistance in which ties are simultaneously weakened but other ties are reinforced or new ties are created. With its emotional nurturing and provisioning of financial and social support, as well as it maintenance of the networks of social relations that link each individual to an ever-expanding array of others, family is indeed often hailed as the one social institution that has continuously facilitated resilience in the face of occupation. With closure and separation, family contours are being reconfigured. The extended family's obligations and expectations of assistance to kin are diminishing as face-to-face contact with family ebbs. Spatial constriction compromises the family's ability to perform the work of nurturing and reaffirming social ties. The nuclear family may be shaping up as the basic family unit, but even that can be unsettled by closure.

Nasreen's life and relationship with her husband were so strained by the complexities of living in Jerusalem "illegally," and by her husband's fear that if they left Jerusalem, he would lose his Jerusalem identity card, that she was at a breaking point. In exasperation one day, she cried, "I am thinking of divorce. I love him, but I can't live like this. He must give me the baby—I'll just take a bit of furniture and that is it." She had already described herself as a "captive" whose husband had to drive her everywhere in his yellow-plated car; even so, they feared a document inspection at a checkpoint that would end their lives as they knew them. Nasreen's family life is another illustration of the pathology of arrhythmia.

Rania relates how visiting her family in Jerusalem, Bethlehem, and Beit Jala is now constrained by checkpoints and her husband's inability to go there. When she wants to visit her family, she goes with her eight-month-old daughter:

> I have the Jerusalem identity card, so it is somewhat easier for me to come and go. Because most of my family has the West Bank identity card, they just come here once a year. I go to their house twice a month. My husband has a West Bank identity card, so he can't go to Beit Jala with me to visit my family. So when I go to visit my family, I go alone with my daughter, who is eight months old. It is very hard to travel like this with a baby when you are alone. It takes hours at the checkpoints. She needs to sleep, eat, and have her diaper changed. To go to Beit Jala, I go from my house in Ramallah to Qalandia checkpoint by bus, or my husband drops me there. Then I walk across Qalandia and take another bus to Jerusalem. It is often a different road. It depends on which road is open, because sometimes they are closed. If it is closed, you turn around and try another one. So I go to Bab al-Amud in Jerusalem, from there to Beit Jala to the school, where there is another checkpoint. I walk across this checkpoint—you can't cross by car. From there, I walk to my family's house. It is supposed to take twenty-five minutes. Now, it sometimes takes more than three hours. Sometimes, you decide to go and then Qalandia is closed. So you can't plan your day. I am too stressed out by this. When I first came here I was always nervous and crying because I wanted to see my family. I wanted to be in touch with them, to be able to come and go to them. To live like normal people live. The first period of your marriage—you are still so close to your family, because it is a new life. You want your family to be close to you. So I used to cry every day. I wanted to go to my family's house. But Qalandia checkpoint was always closing, and it closed at seven at night. There was a curfew at that time. It was so difficult.

Rania and her husband felt there was a distance between her husband and her family. He said, "I don't really know them well because I don't see them often."

The Fayyad family relations also shed light on what is happening to family networks and relationships. Hasan's mother lives in Abu Dis, on the West Bank side of the wall. Even though she was born and raised in Jerusalem, she does not have a Jerusalem identity card, and thus cannot enter or live in the city legally. In the pre-wall era, Hasan visited her daily in her house, just few hundred yards from his. After the wall, visiting became more complicated. Sometimes if his permit had expired or was not recognized, he feared going in and out of Jerusalem, preferring to lay low at home until he could renew his permit. Sometimes when he did visit, he would go through the *bab*, or jump point, and hope that no soldiers were stationed there when he returned. Eventually the *bab* was sealed. Because she is a West Bank resident, his aging mother cannot visit him or live in Jerusalem, so now he seldom sees her. She is bereft of the assistance and companionship of her son and his family. These are not unusual cases. Palestinian marriage networks were once fairly expansive but now entail a certain level of calculation and risk. If one is caught living for any length of time outside Jerusalem, even if it is to live with a spouse, one can lose the right to reside in Jerusalem. Palestinians with West Bank or Gaza identity cards are forbidden residency, or even entry, to Jerusalem. Even if they marry Jerusalem identity-card holders, as Hasan and Nasreen did, they cannot legally enter or reside in the city.

Hasan's cousin Samir is married to Rihan; she has a Jerusalem identity card, and lives in Shufat, on the Jerusalem side of the wall. Samir lives in Abu Dis, on the West Bank side. Rihan works in Ramallah every day. After work she takes the kids to the last *bab* in the wall to try to see their dad. She is exhausted and fed up with this daily routine. They have two houses now, two rents and utility bills, not to mention taxes and a strained marital relationship. If she lives with her husband in Abu Dis, she risks losing the Jerusalem identity. The police monitor Palestinian-Jerusalem households to make sure everyone with a Jerusalem identity card is accounted for. Those whose residence in their officially registered homes cannot be ascertained risk losing their Jerusalem identity card and thus the right to reside in the city. In this way, the Arab population of Jerusalem lives in fear of losing residency if they work or live outside the city.

In talking about family visits, Fatima, Hasan's wife, told me:

> Now we only visit the very close family. I visit just my mother and father and my sister, who lives near them, and my aunts. That's all! Before, we used to visit all the extended family and friends from college. Everyone lives in a different place, and I haven't seen them in such a long, long time. When we finished college, we used to visit each other easily. I don't even dream of visiting my best friend. She lives in Nablus. We talk on the phone and dream of seeing each other. We have never seen each other's children. We have family in Gaza, Jenin, Hebron, and Nablus. But we never visit them anymore at all. They cannot come, and we cannot go.

Munir's description of his experiences of delays and waiting at checkpoints captures his now diminished interaction with his family:

> Without checkpoints, it takes about thirty minutes to reach my family's village. Now there is a minimum of six checkpoints I must pass through. Sometimes it takes me two to three hours. Once it took me eight hours. I used to visit my family almost every day. Our parents are aging, and only my sister remains in the village to help them. My brothers and other sister should be helping, but because of the time it takes to get there we often can't be of much

help. I have a brother and sister in Nablus. It is almost impossible to visit them—it can take more than eight hours. I can't wait like that at checkpoints with my children, so we just don't visit. Recently, I missed my niece's wedding because I was kept waiting at the checkpoint for so long!

Life-cycle events can be severely hampered by immobility. Fatima, who also missed her cousin's wedding, explained, "We used to go to the family events of the aunts and uncles and all the extended family—weddings, births, funerals, and graduations and on holidays. Now, no! Our children, they don't know what the large family is anymore. They don't see their relatives. People are getting used to this. It is frustrating."

Muttering about families being unable to see each other and a murky sense of solidarity, what Fatima described as "everyone for himself," is somewhat tempered by the heightened significance of relationships with neighbors and friends who are nearby but who are less bound by the reciprocal obligations of kin ties. For example, when the salaries of the PA employees were cut because Israel had withheld tax revenue due to the PA, it became common to borrow money from friends and neighbors. Munir lent money to a neighbor who hadn't been paid, whose sick wife needed medication. However, there are limits to how much both kin and non-kin can provide. "I can't keep lending money, or soon I will be out of money. People are trying to feed their children, and they haven't been paid in months. Everyone who is receiving his salary is being asked by friends, neighbors, and kin to lend money," he explained. Thus the impact of crisis and the multiplicity of ways people respond are hardly uniform. Some social ties are ruptured, others given new meaning and purpose. People turn to friends and neighbors for the sorts of assistance and support once provided by family.

Conclusion

Not surprisingly, spatial fragmentation and constriction are replicated in the arrythmatic temporal domain. Hemmed in by temporal deceleration and spatial constriction, Palestinians are suspended in a time/space formula in which they wait and anticipate. This spatial constriction and decelerated mobility engenders a sense of strangeness in the landscape. As we have seen, signage is a performative and productive act that at once erases, claims dominion, and remakes place. New signage expedites Jewish mobility and familiarity, simultaneously instilling a sense of unease in Palestinians.

For Palestinians, time and space can no longer be taken for granted; they have become heavily marked categories, objectified yet convoluted and subject to uncertainty. For Palestinians, the illogic and discontinuity of space are transposed to time. For Israelis, contiguous space between Israel and the colonies and among the colonies, renders time far less problematic as it intersects fairly neatly with space.

As J. M. Coetzee wrote in *Waiting for the Barbarians* (1980), colonizers live in a state of perpetual anticipation of the barbarian's violence. Yet for the subjugated, violence and impermanence are lived realities, their anticipation is often borne out as they go about the routines of quotidian life. Time is another arrow in the quiver of modern warfare. Temporal rhythms are saturated with consciousness, from the fretful anticipation of moving forward to the frustration of deceleration. Closure operates through temporal and spatial ambiguity and uncertainty, hardly the makings of habitus. When the outcome of waiting is not assured, the sense of its length and misery heightens. When control over time is appropriated, and unpredictability follows in the wake, trust in the immediate present or future is difficult to sustain. Waiting, that nervous suspension in time and space, mimics a state of prolonged liminality, between here and there, now and then, but without certainty as to outcome—will "there" and "then" be realized?

The organization and routinization of time through the schedule is often associated with modernity and industrialization; in the time of occupation and closure, controls over time are disciplinary, an aspect of risk management by the state security apparatus as well as a means of immiseration. The potent combination of high-tech biometric and surveillance technologies with the low-tech wall and checkpoints impede Palestinians' control over the mundane routines of their daily lives.

In Palestine-Israel, time is blatantly and visually relational: Palestinians wait, Israelis move. Closure, and the relentless march of colonists and their speedy mobility, is rapidly transforming the landscape and its natives' temporal rhythms. For now, Palestinians watch and wait, stranded in enclaves. They live in a state of alert, waiting for the next disaster to unfold—more colonists and the violence they increasingly inflict, land confiscations, military incursions, fragmentation of space, and economic devastation. After his olive grove has been uprooted to make way for the wall, seventy-five-year old Abu Bilal states with quiet dignity, "God will right this wrong. They will be punished. Injustice can't last forever." The anticipation of justice and a future, a time beyond occupation and closure, is apparent in his words of hope and dignity.

Fragmented space, stretched time, and prolonged waiting are components of a subjectivity that binds Palestinians across multiple borders, as do the miserable and deteriorating conditions they endure. Waiting and the trepidation it generates are shared experiences for Palestinians, whether they are in exile in Lebanon, Syria, Palestine, or Iraq, indelibly highlighting a shared feature of the Palestinian condition. A sense of the future is constrained by the blocking of opportunities to travel, to find employment, to marry freely without consideration of identity cards and residency, and to live where one chooses. The question to be posed and researched, with strong empirical data, is demographic: will the rapid expulsions and the flight of 1948 and the denial of return be replaced by slow-motion, voluntary migration, or "quiet transfer," in face of misery?

I passed through Qalandia one evening as the sun was setting. To the side of the pedestrian lane, I saw about fifteen Palestinian males, young and old, kneeling on flattened cardboard boxes, praying amid the tangled coils of barbed wire and debris. It struck me that they were publicly imposing their sacred temporal rhythms, rituals, and sounds on an encounter space that ordinarily appropriated their mobility and time and deprived them of dignity. They had, momentarily, stepped out of occupation time and were crafting their own temporal space, however ephemeral. The prayers reterritorialized the checkpoint; the praying bodies broke the Israeli-imposed momentum by confronting bodily restrictions through embodied ritual. This appropriation of time and space and refusal to acquiesce, this small gesture of taking back time and space, sets the stage for the concluding chapter on resistance.

5   Anti-Colonial Resistance
       in the Time of Closure

"We are like trees. Every time they cut our heads, we grow again," Maysun said in response to my rather mundane question, "How are things in Jenin these days?" She continued, "It is hard these days. People are sad, but we are used to living this life, so we find ways to overcome these barriers. Look, I am here today [in Ramallah] in spite of all the obstacles." A new normal will not easily prevail. This concluding chapter tracks the opposition to occupation, closure, and immobilization. Maysun's comments capture the hope, despair, and resilience that suffuse daily life and shape subjectivities. She intimates that Palestinians will not so easily be pushed from a landscape in which they liken themselves to "trees," deeply rooted and not easily bulldozed away. Continuing spatial-temporal fracturing, immobilization, and ever-expanding technologies of surveillance and control that overcome space and time are met by new and pragmatic ways of coping, negotiating, and mounting opposition. Into the structural matrix of the occupation and colonialism that color daily life can be added Palestinian political rivalry and increasing political localization. National-level leadership (PLO/PA) is impotent, fractured politically, beholden to external donors, rife with corruption, and widely discredited for its role in ensuring Israeli security. Understanding this volatile mix requires investigating the new forms of warfare and population-management techniques in a late settler-colonial setting and the sorts of politics that take shape in this setting. This chapter hones in on selected facets of opposition activity in Palestine in the era of closure: *sumud* (steadfastness), direct action, and village-level protest. This is not, by any means, an exhaustive inventory of means of opposition.

With shrinking geo-social contiguity, the locus of anti-colonial resistance has become more multifaceted, fragmented, and at once localized and globalized. Probing resistance in this context of a regime of control over the rhythms of daily life compels a close mining of the minutia of seemingly ordinary, yet oppositional, gestures and means of getting by, what Palestinians call *sumud*. A host of cultural practices and behaviors, from hip-hop to the Boycotts, Divestment, and Sanctions (BDS) Movement to militant actions; joint-action endeavors with Israeli, Palestinian, and foreign participation; and theatrical demonstrations and protests make up an oppositional stance. Spatial fragmentation localized an opposition politics whose participants, interestingly, also include an assortment of foreign activists and Israelis who are opposed to occupation and closure. Palestinian resistance increasingly operates in a transnational space. This chapter focuses on two facets of resistance: *sumud* and cosmopolitan village protests.

Everyday Oppositions

As probably can be said of most people living under conditions of severe repression, Palestinians accommodate but neither accept as normal nor totally acquiesce to the continuing realities of occupation and settler colonialism. Shrinking, discontiguous space and more limited contact among Palestinians and between them and Israelis has had an impact on the resistance tactics, collective and individual, to which Palestinians have recourse. Within the matrix of control, resistance is scattered across space, unfolding at multiple places and on overlapping levels, ranging from direct action, with its ritualized theatrics, to petty subterfuge, evasion, sabotage, defiance, dissimulation, and avoidance to civil disobedience, violence, hunger strikes, visualization or looking back, and new forms of artistic expression, simply getting on with it or staying put. Palestinian studies offer insights into the rapidly changing empirical realities and conceptual frameworks for understanding responses to contemporary conflict management, where a host of practices encumbering mobility and generating confining spaces are pronounced "modes of control."

The conversation about resistance, a problematic concept to begin with, was significantly reshaped by political scientist James Scott in the 1970s and, in this region, dramatically thrust center stage with the 2011 Arab Spring. Questions arise about technology and politics. In the age of instant communication, social media, and virtual communities, the temporal and spatial parameters of resistance are being reconfigured in ways that are still opaque. What are the parameters of resistance in the contemporary era of ever-mutating technologies of surveillance, monitoring, and killing, and in the Palestinian case, population and spatial fragmentation and localization of political action?

It is worthwhile quoting the historians Howard Zinn and Robin Kelley, both of whom wrote on hope, action, and vision in discussing the success or failure of resistance, and whether their criterion are adequate means of evaluation. Zinn sagely wrote:

> To be hopeful in bad times is not just foolishly romantic. It is based on the fact that human history is a history not only of cruelty, but also of compassion, sacrifice, courage, and kindness. What we choose to emphasize in this complex history will determine our lives. If we see only the worst, it destroys our capacity to do something. If we remember those times and places—and there are so many—where people have behaved magnificently, this gives us the energy to act ... And if we do act, in however small a way, we don't have to wait

for some grand utopian future. The future is an infinite succession of presents, and to live now as we think human beings should live, in defiance of all that is bad around us, is itself a marvelous victory (Zinn 2002, 208).

Kelley (2002, ix) proposes measuring success by the "merits or power of the visions" rather than by success in realizing it, because it is the vision that inspires "new generations to continue the struggle for change." Palestinians continue to envision different futures. Zinn's words resonate strongly in Palestine: to "live now as we think humans should live . . . in defiance of all that is bad" is itself a "victory" of sorts. Zinn's insightful and prescient words echo *sumud*, a deeply resonant term across the geographic expanse in which Palestinians are scattered.[1] *Sumud* means staying put and getting on with life, registering a refusal to move in face of continuing repression and dispossession. It can also encompass accommodation and defiance and dissimulation. Its temporality is embedded in waiting, perseverance, and patience, which have been elevated to a national occupation and defining characteristics of being Palestinian. "We are a people who wait," Randa sighed as we waited in a long line at a checkpoint. *Sumud* raises the question: Can accommodation and coping strategies, and the political subjectivities they inform, be forms of resistance?

It is worth remembering that half the Palestinian population still resides in historic Palestine (Peteet 2005). This is all the more remarkable given the lengthy and well-organized campaign to dislodge them. In a settler-colonial project with displacing impulses, where the indigenous population serves little purpose, except perhaps as the ever-present other in a fractious state, staying put and not emigrating can be a political act. Is it a collective strategy or simply a means of getting by for each individual; do small individual acts of ordinary daily life accumulate in weight to give *sumud* potency, and how is collective *sumud* registered and recognized? Can small individual acts coalesce to form a systemic challenge; what is the tipping point? The memory of expulsion and flight, seared in the consciousness of every Palestinian, was echoed succinctly by Bassam. With arms stubbornly crossed around his chest, he said emphatically, "We are not leaving. On the contrary, we are determined to stay put. First, there is nowhere to go, certainly not Jordan or the other Arab countries. And second, we remember 1948 and won't make that mistake again, no matter how bad it gets."

The village of Iskaka (population 1,000), located near the Ariel colony, where the wall reaches fourteen miles (22 kilometers) from the Green Line[2] into the West Bank, was slated to lose about 1,500 dunums of land. A group of villagers, tired after a round of protest at the oil groves, gathered to sip sweet, hot tea in the late afternoon shade. Um Leith, mother of several teenage boys, commented, "We will stay here until we die. In 1948, they must have faced something very terrible that could make them leave. They didn't really know what was happening and what would happen." For Um Leith, participating in protests and staying put are acts of resistance informed by knowledge of past events, unequivocal statements that colonial enactments of dominion and ownership will butt up against the reality of the indigenous presence. Staying put, however, is exhausting work.

So, how do people adjust to, accommodate, and resist the constraints on daily life? To get by, they simultaneously accommodate, adapt, defy, sabotage, and, on occasion, engage in outright resistance through protest and refusal. A collective response can be hard to discern when there is spatial fragmentation, but individuals simply going about their business can be framed as collective action, particularly when Palestinians have an acute consciousness of the role leaving has played in their mass dispossession. Staying put and engaging in a daily routine in spite of the hardships, as Maysun and Um Leith mentioned, may not break the occupation but by necessitating constant vigilance for acts of rebellion, neither does it clear an easy path for it.

Randa, who moves about constantly for her job in the West Bank and to visit friends, was adamant. "They [checkpoints] are not going to stop me from trying to lead a life of some normalcy. To keep moving is a form of resistance because it shows that we will not be stopped." She gave me the proverbial Palestinian response to crisis and hardship: *shu bidna 'amal?* (what can we do?) and *al-hayat lazim tistameer* (life must goes on). I had first heard these plaintive phrases from Palestinians during the Lebanese civil war (1975–91; Peteet 1991); I continued to hear them in the West Bank in response to daily hardships. "What can we do?" alludes to the odds stacked against them and yet underscores that just carrying on with daily life constitutes a resistant response to externally imposed conditions. With its temporal steadiness, "life goes on" signifies not giving up, not conceding defeat. It is polysemic, however, depending on context; it refers to the idea of continuing with daily life against the odds and yet a recognition of and resignation to the little that can be done to change those odds.

Randa and many others who do take to the roads demonstrate the incomplete routinization of the abnormal. To go through the motions at a checkpoint, for example, is not to acquiesce or to consent. It is better to get by and to craft small spaces and relations of normality. That is why Palestinians will endure long and humiliating waits to move from one place to another. Indeed, Munir referred to mobility as a "challenge," which he takes in order to pursue his work in community development. He does not see it as acquiescence but as getting along and indeed resisting by refusing to be immobilized. Habitus operates here in the plural, encompassing acquiescence, subterfuge, and dissimulation. Arwa lamented that "there is little spontaneity in our lives, which is depressing. We can't just decide to go visit someone or accept an invitation without thinking, calculating how to get there, how much time will it take, how many checkpoints." Thus a conscious set of calculations hovered over the temporal rhythms of daily life.

As routines were constantly reconfigured and contingency plans readied, mobility began to resemble the tactic as "an art of the weak" (de Certeau 1984, 37). A tactic is "calculated action determined by the absence of a proper locus . . . it must play on the terrain imposed on it and organized by the law of a foreign power." As a maneuver it operates in enemy territory "in isolated actions, blow by blow" (ibid.). Operating without a base, it makes "use of the crack that particular conjunctions open in the surveillance of proprietary power . . . it is a guileful ruse." Indeed, there are a multitude of individual tactics for coping with deceleration and immobilization, ranging from the mundane to the risky. Selma, for example, left a change of clothing for herself and her daughter at her aunt's home in Ramallah in case she did not make it through the checkpoint. Using someone else's identity card was risky. Some tactics required interactions with military personnel, as we saw in chapter 3, in which petty bribery or sneaking around or through checkpoints was not uncommon. A variety of disguises or subterfuge and dissimulation were called forth in response to checkpoints. Lies about where one was going and why and stories of dying relatives and ill children were shared humorously, and like subterfuge, were artful tactics of getting by. Dissimulation was evident when girls borrowed each other's identity cards to more easily pass through a checkpoint, especially to enter Jerusalem. Alertness to and a cultivated awareness of the potential for violent behavior on the part of colonists and occupation authorities was evident when parents instructed their children not to point at occupation authorities or colonists, a precaution to avoid accusations of stone throwing. Bassam warned me of the cruelty of soldiers and the need for dissimulation: "You should never let an Israeli know any of your weak points or he will take advantage of them. For example, I have a bad leg and hip from an old car accident. If I were to complain to the soldiers that I can't sit for long periods because of pain and stiffness, he will make me wait even longer or even hit that leg." This reminds of a line in poet Ibrahim Tuqan's (1905–41) 1935 poem "People!": "People, your foe is not of the type / to soften or show compassion" (Hoffman 2009, 98). Repetitive confrontations with an asymmetrical power that suffuses something as ordinary as routine mobility can trigger dissimulative behavior—not revealing one's inner desires or an infirmity that might be turned against one—as well as alertness, a heightened awareness of vulnerabilities and potential violence.

In response to my question about how she manages in the face of closure, Fatima replied:

> I will tell you something. I used to work in Bethlehem, and every time I went, there was a problem on the way. The soldiers tell me, for example, "You have to go back because you cannot go to the West Bank side with a Jerusalem

identity," which is clearly not the case. Well, if I surrender to that, then I will never go. I would just stay at home. We have to find ways to go about our daily lives; otherwise we will die. Really, we would die from frustration. So we always try to have internal strength—we have to find ways. We have to find ways—that is how we deal with our lives. There is so much anger and frustration. The problem—what we are always afraid of is that we will let it explode on each other. That is the worst scenario.

Responding to the same question, Khalil said,

We have to adjust to occupation. We have two options: struggle or face the facts and leave. It is a challenge. For me, I resist everyday by working with youth, by empowering them. They can tell people in the US who can affect policy. We are giving youth the capacity to build the future. I see this as a form of resistance. We are working in a humanitarian mess. Every problem we have is not a result of the occupation only but our own social problems as well. Training is a kind of empowerment and helping these people gives them a chance.

Again, a sliver of hope and a vision of the future peek through the clouds of despair and work against leaving.

Ironically, checkpoints are now encounter spaces in which, although nuanced by class, religion, region of origin, or gender, West Bank Palestinians collectively experience closure and are compelled to witness its imposition on each other. They are now encounter moments and spaces, not just between Israelis and Palestinians, but among Palestinians themselves. This may be why many demonstrations and outbreaks of violence occur at Qalandia.

While Palestinians talk frequently of suffering and the violation of their human rights in the registers of both cynicism (Allen 2013) and hope, they also point to their resiliency and their sense of caring for others who are suffering. Sentiments of empathy with others are elements of human dignity. The capacity to care for others in the face of extreme cruelty, to maintain one's humanity, underwrites membership in a moral community. Public displays of Israeli brutality may convey the cost of disobedience, but they also nurture a sense of empathy with others. At the checkpoints, Palestinians are both audience and subject to the Israeli enactment of sovereignty, real and symbolic, over space and the Palestinian body. In these encounter spaces, indignities against the individual and collective body are witnessed by other Palestinians. So, how does *sumud* unfold at a checkpoint? What are the transformative limits of this conceptually expansive term? In an upbeat voice, Khalil explained how he uses patience:

Checkpoints are a language of power. They have the power. And they are legal according to Israeli law. As a Palestinian I have to be patient. I will not give up. If I do I will be defeated inside. I can't fight them but I have my will. I show my patience but eventually I manage to move. These checkpoints are a form of punishment of women, students, children, workers—of all of us. What is the message of the checkpoints? They want us to leave. Life won't be easy is the message. Some of my friends are leaving because they can't live like this.

Accommodation and resiliency were at work when vibrant markets sprang up at checkpoints, and venders sold everything from juice and coffee to socks and clocks (see Hammami 2004). Accommodation in the face of a displacing project, however, can be the very stuff of resistance when confronting the logic of removal and population replacement. Palestinians claim that experiences of humiliation and incarceration will not make them easily buckle and leave.

The constant exchange of stories about mobility and how to navigate the terrain of closure sheds light on the extent to which a routine may not have become normalized and calls attention to the consciousness people bring to these embodied encounters. Repetition and routine neither manufacture consent nor dilute dreams of unfettered mobility. Palestinians oscillate between "we're used to it" to "what can we do?" referencing an ability to resist through adaptation and quasi-acquiescence in recognition of limited room for maneuver.

In the repertoire of modes of resistance, petty tactics are multitudinous. For example, at Qalandia one day, young boys hurled buckets of black paint and fire torches at the cement watchtower, blackening it, but not causing structural damage. Ten soldiers soon appeared and lobbed tear gas canisters at the boys. When Amal walked through Wadi al-Nar (chapter 3), as a "leaker" or "dripper" to reach Ramallah, she exemplified a dangerous defiance; she shrugged her shoulders and said, "What can we do?" As the checkpoints tightened, many people took to walking to avoid them, often for long distances and up and down treacherous hills; Ziad guffawed, "We get our exercise this way." When Amal's village Walaja was surrounded and movement in or out prevented, she got up early every day, dressed for university, packed her book bag, and headed for the checkpoint. She was not allowed to cross for five days, yet she went to the checkpoint daily and pleaded with them that she had exams in Ramallah. At Qalandia in 2005, a woman with her young son in tow cut ahead of a line of men pressing forward and simply walked through while the soldiers were busy searching the men and boys. *Sumud* and these ostensibly petty forms of determination to carry on with normal life convey to the Israelis that their presence will not be normalized and that they will have to stay alert to provocations and acts of subordination. These actions don't change the occupation, but they impede its normalization and register a refusal to acquiesce. Such actions, however seemingly insignificant, also offer Palestinians some sense of dignity and facilitate day-to-day coping.

Adjustment, accommodation, and subterfuge are means of trying to pursue as normal a routine as possible under trying circumstances. Still, accommodation exacts a price. Muna requested and received a visa to enter Jerusalem for a few hours. On the way home on the bus, she lamented:

> We accommodate all these measures. If they close one road, we find another. But we are dying a slow death. From the inside, I feel myself slowly dying. We are being deprived of our basic and practical needs. Most of us just think about our immediate needs—how to go to work, how to bring food. They want to kill us in our own homes and lands. We have all adjusted ourselves to living in our villages or towns—we can no longer go anywhere or to Jerusalem.

Muna's phrase "slow death" captures the drawn out nature of social death. Akin to Fatima's "worst scenario," Palestinians turning on each other, it calls attention to the pathologies of immobilization and fragmentation. Muna's comments touch directly on the complex and contradictory components of subjectivities: accommodation, adjustment, and persistence—"if they close one road, we find another"—and the pathologies of anger, deprivation, and slow death.

Protests at Qalandia are not infrequent, for it is at this largest of the checkpoints that Israelis and Palestinians interact in an atmosphere of routine, yet unabashed domination, humiliation, and subjugation. Checkpoints are potentially sites of the next conflagration, or third intifada, triggered when injustice and humiliation reach a critical point and spark mass action in one of the few spaces where Palestinians gather en masse. Loaded with symbolic and material significance, protests at Qalandia have ranged from annual commemorations of "Nakbah Day," on May 15, to spontaneous protests by youths burning tires in the street and setting up makeshift barricades of whatever materials are available, often empty, unusable water tanks, ragged pieces of plywood, and wooden crates. These unarmed protesters are met with tear gas; rubber bullets; and the "scream," an auditory weapon whose high-pitched sound sends those in the vicinity running from its ear-shattering noise. Palestinian flags are waved; Israeli flags are burned. *Kufiyyah*-clad young men hurl stones by hand or in slingshots. Protests mark events such as Israel's periodic assaults on Gaza or International Women's Day. To claim that closure is producing a docile subject would be to assume the homogeneity of Palestinian subjectivity. Rather, it seems to give rise to a racing back and forth between hope, accommodation, and despair—despair at the degradation of life under occupation and closure and hope for a future, however remote.

Direct Action and International Solidarity

It remains for future observers to ascertain the role Palestine's two intifadas played as precedents for the symbolism-laden direct action of Iran's Green Revolution, Lebanon's Cedar and March 14 Movements, and the Arab Spring, regional events that indelibly marked the first decade and a half of the new millennium.

Historically, Palestinian popular resistance has ranged from boycotts, sit-ins, and strikes to marches and demonstrations, tax revolts, and hunger strikes (King 2007). It bears mentioning that Palestinians have engaged in armed struggle and the violence it entails, as has most every anti-colonial national movement of the past century. Moreover, it is worth remembering that the end of Apartheid in South Africa was achieved through popular resistance and international support in the form of the BDS Movement that operated alongside the militancy of the African National Congress.

Civil or popular resistance in Palestine, often overlooked, has elicited a violent response, as though it poses a grave danger to the occupying state.[3] Violence and direct action usually work together, rather than one to the exclusion of the other. Both have been met with an Israeli response that ranges from tear gas and rubber bullets to beatings with truncheons, the firing of live ammunition, and mass arrests. Emergent leaders and voices of popular and civil struggle are routinely detained and imprisoned. For example, Jamal Juma, a leader of PEN-GON (Palestinian Environmental NGO Network), and Abdullah Abu Rahman, an activist in the village of Bil'in, have been repeatedly detained for staging protests. Popular resistance may be responded to, in part, as a dangerous mode of action because it does not cohere with the dominant narrative of the irrational, violent Palestinian that is associated with a pathological Arab-Islamic culture and Israeli-Jewish victimhood. Indeed, the organized, sustained, and ritualized nature of popular resistance undercuts assertions of irrational, baseless violence. Moreover, it confronts the violent Israeli state response with the moral legitimacy of peaceful protest.

"Civil resistance" and "popular resistance" may be more appropriate terms than "nonviolence," which remains problematic. For outsiders to insist, as do a host of international NGOs, that Palestinians engage in nonviolence, is to position themselves as arbiters of how Palestinians should respond to occupation. Moreover, the term "nonviolent" implies that violence is the Palestinian default position, and that civil resistance is a a departure from the status quo of violent behavior. This flies in the face of a long history of civil and popular resistance (Norman 2010; King 2007), exemplified by the six-month general strike against the British in 1936 and decades of petitions and diplomatic appeals to international bodies, innumerable demonstrations, sit-ins, boycotts, hunger strikes, and refusal to pay taxes, among other acts. Starting with the 1936 strike, most of these efforts have been brutally suppressed. These acts of civil disobedience, as well as stone throwing by youth and Israeli violence, marked the first intifada (1987–93).[4] Grassroots organizations, particularly the Popular Committees, which included, among others, medical, education, agriculture, and women's committees, offered economic and institutional alternatives to the occupation and provided for some basic needs and critical services. In fall 1988, in the thick of the first intifada, residents of Beit Sahur refused to pay taxes to the Israeli government. By collecting taxes from Palestinians, Israel was, in essence, making them pay for their own occupation. The refusal to pay taxes, a widely recognized form of nonviolent popular resistance to unjust rule, was met with a harsh response by the Israeli military. Beit Sahur was put under curfew and besieged, blocking supplies of food and medicine. Leaders of the tax revolt were detained and beaten. Military forces raided the village, confiscating nearly $1.5 million in goods.

Popular resistance often takes the form of direct action in which the goal is to mimic the injustice of occupation and closure and publicly demonstrate that subjugation will not be normalized.[5] In addition, direct action builds a sense of community and allows new, often local, leaders to emerge. A discernible uptick in direct action in the wake of the violence of the second intifada indicated a shift in the Palestinian struggle. Popular civil resistance, with a strong dose of localized and international solidarity activism, was apparent as armed struggle, never a viable strategy on its own, receded. The second intifada was triggered by the continued building of Israeli colonies and the then prime minister Ariel Sharon's provocative visit to the Haram al-Sharif.[6] Direct action has ranged from highly symbolic theatrics of civil disobedience, to large-scale coordinated village protests, and flotillas attempting to break the siege on Gaza. An example of the former occurred in a seemingly minor gesture of defiance when a group of young people let loose bunches of red, white, green, and black balloons, the colors of the Palestinian flag, at Qalandia. On October 24, 2012, a flash mob at an Israeli supermarket near a colony in East Jerusalem reminded the Israelis that occupation is not normal. Eighty protesters, calling for a boycott of goods produced in the colonies, organized by the Popular Struggle Committee, a coalition of grassroots organizations, were confronted by fifty police, who used stun grenades to break up the protest. In late 2011, a small, coordinated group of Palestinians boarded Israeli buses serving the colonies. Drawing inspiration from the civil disobedience of the US civil rights movement in which African Americans protested their relegation to the back of the bus, these activists protested their exclusion from the bus. When they reached a checkpoint, where their identities were ascertained, they were forcibly removed.

Direct action is often ritualized and transgressive. It attempts to breach the enclosed spaces from which Palestinians are excluded and to reclaim them, however fleetingly. Moreover, direct actions are moral statements publicly showcasing the oppressive or discriminatory nature of colonialism and occupation. Some rituals reclaim space, time, and the body through public performances of the sacred, such as conducting prayers at checkpoints. In situ prayers, which also occur where the bulldozers clear newly expropriated land, enact fleeting counterhegemonic spaces through ritual action. In hunger strikes, which are highly visceral and symbolic direct actions, the body is the immediate and intimate site of protest. Palestinians across all factions expressed support for the large-scale, coordinated prisoners' hunger strike in 2011. A hunger striker I interviewed explained that the "hunger strike is a form of pacifism. It is peaceful, not militant. It is a direct action that expresses how hard the situation is. We are telling the world we are serious. There is a symbolism in it. A hunger strike is between death and life—the wall is a question of life and death for us." In this action, the individual body stands in for the aggregate.

With the International Solidarity Movement (ISM) and the BDS Movement of the 2000s the struggle for Palestine became more internationalized. The wall in particular was a rallying point for the ISM and BDS, as were increasing comparisons of Israel to Apartheid South Africa. The ISM defines itself as "a Palestinian-led movement committed to resisting the Israeli apartheid in Palestine by using nonviolent, direct-action methods and principles."[7] Palestinian and Israeli activists were coming together to provide support to Palestinians with "two resources, international solidarity and an international voice with which to nonviolently resist an overwhelming military occupation force." The ISM aims to provide the media with a different narrative of events, witness and document human rights violations, and show solidarity with communities increasingly isolated by closure.

In mid-2005, in the wake of the 2004 opinion issued by the International Court of Justice determining that the wall is illegal and the nonresponse it received in Israel and abroad, Palestinian civil society called for international support for BDS, modeled after the anti-apartheid BDS Movement. BDS calls for Israel to adhere to international law, end the occupation and institutionalized racial discrimination, and respect the refugee right of return (Barghouti 2009, 50). To compel such compliance, the movement calls for a boycott of Israeli products from the colonies and for divestment from companies that do business in the OPTs and provide materials for the occupation, such as Caterpillar bulldozers. It called for musicians to refuse invitations to perform at Israeli cultural events and for academic associations to boycott Israeli universities that have not condemned the occupation and that collaborate with the military. It does not call for a boycott of individual Israeli academics.

As evidenced in South Africa, a BDS movement can be a potent tool in a struggle against an opponent of overwhelming strength. It relies on sustained appeals to a moral consciousness and international law. The goal of the movement is to impose penalties in order to promote positive change. It makes legal arguments and appeals to morality, as well as compelling comparisons with apartheid. The international community has proven unwilling to hold Israel accountable for continuing violations of international and human rights law. BDS and the ISM emerged in this political void, where armed resistance had proved ineffective. These movements are attempts to gain leverage where little exists either militarily or in the international diplomatic and legal arenas.

The 2010 saga of the *Mavi Marmara*, one of a group of Turkish, Greek, Irish, and Algerian ships transporting humanitarian relief supplies for besieged Gazans, gripped the global media. In a stunning move, Israeli air and naval forces intercepted the ship in international waters, rappelled up its sides, and killed nine peace activists. The remaining seven hundred activists, from all over the world, were taken to Israel and then deported.[8] Flotillas continued to try to break the siege of Gaza; in October 2012, six Israeli naval vessels commandeered the *Estelle*, a ship carrying European lawmakers, a former Canadian Member of Parliament, three Israelis, and a number of European peace activists. These flotillas and a less well-known "flytilla" to Ben Gurion airport in summer 2012 were motivated by support for the Palestinian people and were not connected to any political faction. International waters and the skies had become new deterritorialized spaces of activism.

Foreigners and Palestinians alike share the experiences of passage at borders and checkpoints and participation in direct actions. Both have to comply with procedures that include intrusive questions, unexplained and unnecessary delays, searches, and sometimes denial of entrance. However, it must be emphatically stated that their experiences are hardly comparable.[9] The stakes are vastly disparate. The foreign passport holder may be questioned aggressively and turned back but is not denied access to home and family.

Another example of transnational direct action transpired in May 2011. Nakbah Day demonstrations in East Jerusalem and Qalandia were coordinated with attempts by Palestinian refugees and their local supporters to approach the Israel-Lebanon border, Syria's Golan Heights border with Israel, and Gaza's Eretz crossing. In the course of these border protests, thirteen people were killed and scores injured.

The arts have come to the fore as critical sites for political commentary and mobilizing international youth. They also point to the emergence of new political subjectivities among Palestinian youth. In this new arena of cultural production, political commentary is targeted not just at the occupation but also at the Palestinian leadership and cultural traditions.[10] DAM's popular music 2001 video "Who's the Terrorist?" is a rhythmic and pulsating inverted narrative of violence and its historical trajectory, and it made them Palestine's best-known hip-hop group. Music video is a new venue for political expression for a people who feel all but voiceless in the wider world. DAM's video upends the standard narrative of violent Palestinians/Israeli victims by vividly displaying the disparities in weaponry, between stone throwing and the military might of the state. Poet Rafeef Ziadi, a spoken-word artist, talks back to the media image of Palestinians as not valuing life with measured, but palpable, ire in her 2011 performance, "We teach life, sir." In the midst of the Israeli assault on Gaza, a journalist asked her, as a Palestinian activist, "Don't you think it would all be fine if you just stopped teaching your children to hate?" Her poem is a response to this question. Written and performed in English, it is addressed to the West and the highly fraught cultural politics of childhood, particularly in the media and in the talking points used by Israel's supporters, that traffic in assumptions about the violence of Palestinian children. British-Palestinian hip-hop artist Shadia Mansour says her music is "resistance through art" and the "last tool we have."[11] These voices are angry, didactic, and compelling, and appeal to a generation whose mode of communication, personal and political, leans heavily toward social media.

Watching back became a mode of resistance, a countersurveillance technique that aimed to challenge dominant scripts of Israeli military and colonist violence as responses to actual and putative Palestinian violence and to document Israeli human rights abuses. "Shooting Back," a project initiated by B'TSelem, gave young people cameras to record Israeli violence and then distribute it on the internet. At almost any protest, one can spot an Israeli photographer, whether in plainclothes or a military uniform, shooting photos of both Israelis and Palestinians. Walking through the Palestinian neighborhood of Sheikh Jarrah in East Jerusalem on a Saturday in fall 2010, I came upon a group of about seventy Israelis, protesting a recent expropriation of Palestinian houses, facing about fifty occupation personnel; an Israeli photographer in plainclothes was there, busily snapping photos. Protestors explained that he was either from the military or the domestic intelligence service.

Political activity in Palestine remains uncoordinated and fragmented, factionalized along a Fatah-Hamas axis and thus lacks a clear mobilizing strategy, a unified national vision, and cohesive leadership.[12] A former political leader eloquently explained:

> Under occupation we have to deal with an army and with settlers who represent a state. They are not here as civilians but as armed colonialists. The Palestinians have the right to choose how they resist. But it would be wise to do it with a unified strategy, and even wiser to check the effects of what we do—is it useful or harmful? These things have been lacking. There has been something scattered in the methods of struggle—there has been no monitoring, no checking of what we have been doing. Is it good or is it bad? In order to do that, we need a very unified leadership to be able to study what happened. To assess what we are doing so as to plan for the future. This was lacking, not because of a leader—this is nonsense—the Americans and the Israelis officials blame Arafat. The problem here is not the person but the pluralism, which actually means there is political competition. It is the contrary of what they think. In fact, there is no central decision-making; this is not an ordinary national liberation movement with a unified leadership sitting somewhere and planning.

It is a lot of factions who are competing with each other for public support and who can be more militant.

Many were worn out and apathetic as a result of years of hardship, violence, and misery and localization of resistance marked this era of closure; by late 2015, individual acts of violence against the occupation were proliferating as individual Palestinians stabbed Israelis or used their cars to run them over.

Localization and Joint Protests at Home

As the violence of the second intifada subsided, some villages became sites of direct action with a notable international and Israeli presence. Although village protests were intense and concentrated political action, they hardly signified a national political mobilization with a clear agenda and a unified leadership.[13] Indeed, village protests could be said to indicate the opposite: fragmentation, decentralization, and localization. As the orbit of social life contracted with closure, so did political activism. In the popular perception and in stereotypes, active resistance has often been associated with camp youth and towns such as Jenin and Nablus. A joke captures this perceived spatialization of resistance, regionalism, and stereotypes about the urban-based PA: An Israeli soldier stops three young Palestinian men. He asks the first one, "Where are you from?" When he replies, "I am from Jenin," the soldier beats him. Then he asks the second one, "Where are you from?" He replies, "I am from Nablus." So the soldier beats him, too. Finally, he asks the third young man where he is from. He replies, "I am from Ramallah." So the soldier says to him, "Here, hold my rifle while I finish beating these two." This joke plays on regional stereotypes held by both Palestinians and Israelis; Jenin and Nablus have been known as hotbeds of resistance, whereas Ramallah, now an urban center where the PA is headquartered, with upscale cafes, fine dining, and a plethora of NGOs, has the reputation of generating less militant opposition.

During the mid-2000s, however, it was villagers from Bil'in, Jayyous, Zawiya, Ni'lin, Walaja, and Budrus, among others, who mounted sustained protests, often joined by Israeli and international supporters, many from the ISM. Initially innovative, village protests became somewhat standardized events in the repertoire of popular resistance and have since lessened in frequency and intensity. Incorporating symbolic theatrics, direct action, and ritual, they were generally well-organized, peaceful affairs, although they sometimes devolved into stone throwing, and the military and police often beat up peaceful protestors and used tear gas and rubber bullets against them.

In the protests, the enclaved villagers engaged in resistance on their home turf, while those with greater ability to circulate, Israelis and foreigners, came to them, a phenomenon that itself mimics hierarchy and privilege. Protests against the wall began immediately upon its construction, starting in the northern village of Jayyous, in fall 2002. After months of sustained demonstrations, the villages of Budrus and Zawiya, close to the Green Line and some of the first villages to protest, succeeded in getting the Israelis to reroute portions of the wall, saving some of the olive groves and the Budrus cemetery. The village protests, which often bring together people across factional lines, achieve at a local level what is often missing at the national level. While the protests have not stopped the wall, participants argue that the protests, along with legal challenges, were instrumental in compelling the 2004 Israel High Court ruling against the wall in Bil'in. Most significantly, they have garnered international attention via social media, which was also part of the intent.

To convey the drama of the protests, I draw upon my field notes from June 2004 in the village of Iskaka. I and a group of women from the International Women's Peace Network were traveling from their apartment and media center in the village of Haris to nearby Iskaka. We walked to the road just outside the village, where we waited for a shared taxi to take us to another village, where we would catch transport to Iskaka. We had to take two taxis because of the blocked roads. Driving slowly into Iskaka, we saw that the main street was thronged with hundreds of villagers and a wide range of internationals. When we got out of the cars, we were in the midst of crowds of young boys carrying Palestinian and Communist Party flags. A few Democratic Front for the Liberation of Palestine flags and banners flew as well. Young boys had painted Palestinian flags on their faces. A round metal tray, full of small, steaming cups of sweet tea, was passed to the internationals from a house on the main road. Eventually, a regal-looking man dressed in starched white *jelubiyyeh* with a camel colored *abaya* over his shoulders, his head topped with a white *hatta* and an *aghal*, stood on a small platform on the side of the road.[14] Everyone came to attention as the *rais al-baladiyya* (head of the municipality), called the protest to order and spoke to the crowd, "This is to be a peaceful protest. We are gathered here to defend our lands and livelihood. No one is to provoke the soldiers. We do not want a violent confrontation. We will march peacefully and gather for prayers at the site where they are destroying the olive groves. This is a Palestinian demonstration—there are no factions here—we are united as Palestinians." His speech was followed by the crowd chanting *Allah akbar* (God is great). Then one of the village organizers hurried through the crowd saying that "internationals" should be in the front. The internationals pushed through the crowd to reach the front. As the growing throng of protesters picked up speed and marched toward the olive groves, adolescent and teen-aged boys kept managing to get to the front. The march seemed a cross-section of the village: old men with canes in traditional dress, middle-aged men in Western clothing, women in all manner of clothing, youth of all ages, as well as an assortment of foreigners, ISM activists, Israelis, and some foreign journalists. It was a slow walk under the sun to the fields the bulldozers had torn up. From the send-off speech to the organizers who kept going back and forth through the line to keep order, the march and protest were well-organized. Women, from the very old to the young, brought up the rear. Many carried pictures of Marwan Barghouti.[15] At the side of the road, about fifty men knelt in Muslim prayer. There was a concerted attempt to prevent children from provoking the soldiers. Some mothers were patting their sons' pockets looking for stones they might lob at Israeli forces; a young boy, his head tightly wrapped in a red-and-white-checked *kufiyyah* so that his face was hard to distinguish, was caught with stones by his mother, who held him by the arm as she emptied his pockets. Other villagers informed parents, "Your child has stones." At the olive grove, men and women assembled in loosely separate groups. Participants gathered around men and women who led them in chanting slogans. The grove was a scene of devastation; the uprooted olive trees or chopped off stumps littering landscape of overturned earth mixed with stones from the crumbling terraces. At the top of the hill, armed and helmeted soldiers and border police watched, poised to strike. Perhaps the presence of the foreigners would keep them from acting too harshly, I mused. Obviously, that was the thinking behind putting foreigners at the front of the march. Then someone wisecracked, "When the press leaves is when they will attack." The distance separating protesters from the occupying forces was about fifty yards. People mingled, chatted, chanted slogans, rested under the shade of trees, and wandered around for about an hour. I spotted one Israeli women wearing a tear-gas mask of the kind the Israeli government had distributed during the first Gulf War, in 1991. It was a peaceful gathering on this day. As we walked back to the village, a small group of men again gathered on the side of the road to pray under the olive trees.

In some of the protests I attended from 2004 to 2012, a few young boys threw stones in spite of pleas to demonstrate *silmiyyah* (peacefully). Um Leith's son was typical of such youth, although I had also observed him using his slingshot after protests were over. In Iskaka, the protest was over, and the soldiers were positioned down the hill, parked on the road. Villagers trudged back to the village still carrying the small olive branches they had waved at the soldiers, along with their small bags filled with lemons, onions, white face masks, handkerchiefs, and the perfume they used to help ward off the effects of the tear gas. I was walking with Um Leith's young daughter, when her twelve-year-old brother joined us. When we were fairly close to their house on the edge of the olive groves, he suddenly pulled from his pocket a homemade slingshot, roughly patched together from a standard Y-shaped wooden frame with two long black rubber strips on each side, joined in the middle by a small round pocket of well-worn leather. He retrieved a stone from his pocket, placed it in the leather, and swung it around rapidly several times to gain velocity, skillfully aimed, and let loose the projectile.

The stone flew several hundred yards. I said, "I hope no one is over there." With a serious face, he said, "The soldiers are there." He pointed, and I could just discern the jeeps in the distance. Just then his mother rounded the corner and saw what was going on. She scolded him and sent him home with a quick, light slap on the shoulder. At Um Leith's spacious home, we sat under an olive tree on her expansive stone terrace. Her daughters brought out tall glasses of cold water and then a tray filled with cups of steaming Turkish coffee. It was a pleasantly relaxed hour, as we chatted in the coolness of the coming evening. Children were playing in the garden. Her stone-wielding son was sent to chase a *sous* (chick) that had escaped from its coop. He chased it through the house, out the door, and around the back, and returned with it gently cradled in his hands. He then proceeded to bring out an armful of colorful cloth bundles filled with stones. He showed me how he loaded them into his slingshot. I saw him the next week at a protest, pockets bulging with stones, which he hurled at the soldiers with his slingshot. Without fail, tear gas and rubber bullets soon followed.

A week later, I made a visit to Zawiya, where Um Bashar, a middle-aged mother of six, described a recent protest:

> People were walking down to see what was happening to their lands. The army was preventing them from getting close. It was a peaceful gathering of people. Nobody did anything violent. Then they started shooting tear gas, rubber bullets, and using their batons. They fired live ammunition in the air. Then, before they left, they picked up the tear-gas canisters and took them away. That gas made people hysterical, with hallucinations and spasms that continued for days.

A village elder who was at Um Bashar's house that morning guffawed, waving a gnarled hand, "Every day there are protests—this week we had around four hundred injured people." He held up a list the municipality maintains of the names of those injured.

With a population of around 1,700, the village of Bil'in, four kilometers (2.4 miles) east of the Green Line and seventeen kilometers (ten miles) from Ramallah, has attained iconic status as a protest site. It had once been a fairly prosperous village, boasting a new mosque and many newly constructed stone homes with neat, walled gardens, a result of income from years of male family members working in agriculture, industry, or the food service sector in Israel and the marketing of local agricultural produce, but now Bil'in faced a severe economic crisis. Many of the villagers who worked in Israel had lost their jobs; the nearby Jewish colonies were expanding relentlessly; and the wall had wound its way through expropriated village land.[16] In 1978, around five hundred dunams had been expropriated to build the Matitayahu colony. In the early 1980s, some of the village leaders had actively participated in the Israeli-organized Village

Leagues, a Palestinian-Israeli collaboration, which nevertheless did not end the confiscation of village land (Tamari 1983, 47).[17] In 1991, another round of confiscation made way for a new colony, Kiryat Seifer. In 2004, more land was confiscated to expand the Modi'in Illit colony by adding a neighborhood called Matitayahu East; this, however, is actually a new colony with a plan to build 2,700 housing units on cultivated Palestinian land. Modi'in Illit has a population of about thirty thousand and is built on the land of five Palestinian villages: Bil'in, Deir Qadis, Kharbata, Ni'lin, and Saffa. By November 2004, bulldozers were busy clearing agricultural land in Bil'in to carve out a path for the wall. Between 50 and 60 percent of Bil'in's land (about 2,500 dunams) has been confiscated, leaving villagers with about 1,500 dunams. In the wake of closure and replacement labor, villagers had looked to village agriculture to earn a living. But these land confiscations have diminished this alternative significantly.

As immobility and enclavization made it more difficult for Palestinians to gather in public spaces outside the village to engage in opposition activity, rural spaces took on heightened significance locally and virtually. Palestine may have shrunk spatially, and Bil'in may have been in a state of semi-isolation, but its reach was global. Participants in the Friday protests came from across the globe, and a video of the protest was posted on Bil'in's colorful website each week. However, much of the on-the-ground strength of the protests derived from local configurations of clans, families, and political networks.

Closure opened new spaces for localized activism and, concomitantly, the emergence of local leadership; indeed, Palestinians in such places often critiqued the urban-based leadership because of its silence about the wall. Despite the presence of multiple factions of the Palestinian national movement, and fairly intense Fatah-Hamas rivalry, villagers with long ties to the same place and facing the shared threat of land seizure did come together to protest. For rural folks, the shrinking space of Palestine posed an immediate threat to their ability to sustain themselves. Anger was often poignantly expressed in metaphors of food and substance as well as invocations of deep rootedness and intimate knowledge of place. At a solidarity conference in the village, Yasser, a leader in Bil'in's Popular Committee, read this piece from his diary, "Our suffering is akin to my mother giving birth during the harvest. I grew up on this land eating its bread and olives. I know every part of it and it has always provided for us. There is a love between us. We are deprived when they take our land. We didn't believe they would until the bulldozers came and uprooted trees from the Roman era—perhaps Jesus and St. John sat under those trees."

The socio-political composition of the protests potentially presaged a new political space, where the immediacy of local issues temporally and situationally overrode factionalism. Indeed, the Israeli policy of fragmenting Palestine is, in part, intended to distance Palestinians from an urban-based leadership now confined to Ramallah and thus quell organized resistance. However, this is not a descent into the provincialism of the local. Bil'in activists consistently use the term "joint struggle" to refer to Palestinian, Israeli, and international participation underscoring the need to work in a politically expansive and inclusive framework. Nonetheless, some Palestinians are critical of the term "joint struggle," often used by Israelis and foreigners to describe the protests, as suggesting a "degree of equality or at least symmetry" (Alsaafin 2012, 5).

A leader of the national movement stated emphatically that decentralization and the absence of a coherent strategy of resistance could be traced to the regime of immobility while pointing to the potentially long-term consequences of localism:

> Inability to move from one place to another is a problem. It is very hard to coordinate between Zawiya, for example, and Jerusalem and other places. People can say, "I've solved my problem; the others are not so important." The struggle against the wall began with people who live next to it. But actually the wall harms everybody. Even if you live fifty kilometers [thirty-one miles] from the wall it affects you. This is very dangerous—the villagers who felt directly harmed, who were having their land confiscated, acted against the wall. But it confiscates the freedom of everybody. The wall divides us and fragments national consciousness. The West thinks we shouldn't have a national consciousness, so if we do anything on a national level, they are against it. But if it is local villagers who are struggling for their own land, the West understands. So really it is a struggle for our basic needs, yet it is made clear to us that we should not appear like a nation, like the French, like the Americans, like the British. There is no public space—only individuals struggling. That is how they want us to be—individuals and nothing more.

In some of the villages that have been severely affected by the wall, the traditional practice of village defense (*faz'a*) has been mobilized to meet the needs of the political present. A young activist I interviewed in Bil'in provided this insight, "We protest best when it is our land. Each village will try to defend their land and they are the best ones to do it. We don't want to go to other villages." Yet this raises serious issues about the possibility of effectively confronting occupation and colonialism. In a contrary register, as the head of the municipality in Iskaka a presciently reminded demonstrators, "This is a Palestinian demonstration—there are no factions here—we are united as Palestinians," underscoring the enmeshment of the national and the local in the space of the village.

The leadership of Bil'in's Popular Committee Against the Wall (PCAW), which planned and coordinated the weekly protests, was composed of male representatives from the four main village clans and an array of Palestinian political parties. The past surfaces in the leadership: some of them are the sons of former collaborators who, as Yasser related, "are trying to clear this past collaboration."

This collective village leadership, whether family or clan based, is connected by multiple cross-cutting political ties to the larger national leadership and to a transnational network of international activists.

I had met Yasser in Ramallah at the office where he worked part-time, and he invited me to the village for the Friday protests. He explained that the "struggle in Bil'in is on two fronts: legal and popular struggle." On the legal front, it began in late 2005 and ended in 2006. He continues, "We filed a petition against the wall and the expansion of settlements. The court ruled the wall had to be moved westward, yet a year later the wall is still in the same spot. There is a catch in the ruling. It says the wall must be moved 'in a reasonable amount of time.' The court also ruled that the land confiscated for the wall must be returned to the villagers. The Israeli government's excuse for not moving the wall: there is no money. Israel only budgeted to build the wall, not to move it."

What follows is an ethnographic account of a series of Friday protests in Bil'in (see figures 5.1 and 5.2). On my first Friday visit, I caught the van that runs between Ramallah and Bil'in. Just before reaching the village, the driver pulled over to the side of the road, turned to the three passengers who were foreigners—a Buddhist monk from Japan, a young Scotsman, and me—and told us that there

Figure 5.1 Friday demonstration against the wall in Bil'in. Photograph by the author.

Figure 5.2 Protesters marching in demonstration against the wall in Bil'in. Photograph by the author.

was an Israeli checkpoint up ahead that would turn us back. He advised us, "Walk through the fields to the center of the village. Don't go too close to the road or the soldiers will see you." We hopped out and began a fast-paced trek through the neatly planted terrain. Moving through the thick foliage, we kept our heads low and our voices muted; occasionally, we caught sight of the checkpoint. We continued to skirt the main road until well past the checkpoint and then entered the village. Just as we got back on the main road, a pickup truck approached, and the two men inside asked us if there were any other foreigners walking through the field who might need a ride. They were patrolling the outskirts of the village to find people walking across the fields to help them and avoid the checkpoint.

When I reached the village, I made my way through the teeming crowd and headed for a modest ISM apartment that was often used by visiting internationals. In the hours before the end of Friday noon prayers, the center of the village began to fill with protesters. The ground-floor apartment was empty except for the sleeping bags and backpacks lined up against the walls. A lone black piano, which had been wheeled to the wall for a concert a few weeks earlier, filled a corner of the room. On the street, youngsters hawked Palestinian-themed string bracelets, key chains, colorful flags, and cold drinks. In the crowd were a group of young French activists, a number of American Jewish youth on a Birthright trip, who had left their guided tour to join the ISM; a contingent of Israeli students and peace activists, young and old; and an assortment of internationals.[18] The latter hailed from all over the globe—Buddhist monks, French and Dutch students, a wide range of international peace groups, members of the European Union Parliament, Nobel laureates, and women's peace activists were just some of the participants. The Israeli groups Anarchists Against the Wall, founded in 2003, and Gush Shalom, a peace organization, were prominently represented. Seventy-year-old Lucy, an American Baptist from Tennessee, who was retired from an international medical organization, attended the weekly protests. One Friday, before we headed to Bil'in together, she helped me prepare a small plastic bag with eye goggles, rubbing alcohol, and big wads of cotton, which Israelis and internationals carry to minimize the effects tear gas. Some Palestinians say, "We are used to it, we don't need anything," but others come prepared.

On my second Friday in Bil'in, I went to a tree-shaded dirt field, several hundred feet from the fence and the observant military forces, where about fifty internationals and Israelis and I attended a PCAW half-hour training session to learn how to deal with tear gas and how to behave if the military and border police crossed the fence and began to beat or detain protestors. A young man from the PCAW instructed us in such techniques as raising the arms above the head in a gesture of surrender. He explained the effects of the tear gas, which included nausea, choking, and burning eyes and skin and showed us how to minimize these effects by covering the nostrils with alcohol-soaked cotton balls.

After I had attended several of these Friday protests, I began to discern a ritualized script, with consistent sequencing, tempo, and spatiality. In general, the protests began with the participants milling about the village streets, greeting each other, and getting signs and banners; this was followed by a call to order by village leaders, generally males in their twenties and thirties. As the crowd quieted and assembled for the march to the wall, there was a palpable sense of anticipation. The amassed group, usually several hundred deep, walked slowly to the edge of the village, where the wall and colonies loom. After fifteen or twenty minutes, it arrived at the barbed-wire fence and gate cordoning off the expropriated land. This sets the encounter with the occupation forces in motion. Escalation and chaos often ensue.

Once, while I waited for the protest to begin, I struck up a conversation with a young Israeli peace activist, who explained, "There is a generational divide between the young Israeli activists and the older ones, such as Uri Avnery.[19] The older ones often don't speak Arabic, and while they see themselves as the vanguard of protests, they are happy to go home at the end of the day. The younger generation speaks Arabic and works more closely with the Palestinians. The older generation are really just peace activists; whereas we younger ones are anti-occupation activists." Later, I speak with Yitzhak, an elderly, ponytailed professor from an Israeli university, who had driven to the village in his bright-red car filled with university students. "Sometimes," he explained, "we drive in on back roads on Thursday evening and sleep at the ISM flat. That way we can avoid soldiers and checkpoints." A self-styled coordinator of the Israeli groups, Yitzak claimed that the Israeli press does cover the protests, and for this reason, he said, he participates in them, to more forcefully bring the situation to the Israel public. Asked about the Israeli protesters' political stance, he said, "We are those who do not accept the Zionist world view. They, the Zionists, have accepted the Nazi view of the Jews as needing to be separated. They have accepted this ideology of separation. We are pragmatic. We know we live in a world of Arabs. We lived together in the past. When I was young, before 1948, we lived close to some Palestinian villages. We did not need anything to separate us like this wall. There was no need—we had good relations."

After the noon prayers, the village men emerged from the mosque and headed to the crowd, which now numbered well over three hundred. Placards in English and Arabic bearing slogans, such as "no to the wall" or "Israel is a criminal" were being handed out by PCAW members. The sights and sounds in the village streets as the crowd assembled brought to mind the Tower of Babel as a multiplicity of languages ran together—Arabic, Hebrew, English, Spanish, German, and French, among others. Village leaders converse easily with the Israelis in Hebrew, learned over years of working in Israel. Gradually, the procession takes shape as people find a spot in the crowd. A sense of semi-indeterminacy—a blurring of social boundaries as to ethnic, religious, and national affiliations—hangs in the air. Yet the categories are ever-present and, indeed, are integral to the strategy of the protests. Internationals and Israelis are encouraged to come to the front of the procession, again on the assumption that Israel's military forces will hesitate before attacking foreigners and Israelis. This does not always work as planned; Israeli forces will engage in violence against Israelis, particularly the youth. But activists on all sides generally agree that the Israeli tactics are often determined by who is participating; when it is only Palestinians, there is more violence.

In a demonstration of youthful masculine bravado, village boys often join those at the front of the march. Villagers, largely men, but also a few women and quite a few adolescents, take up the middle and rear. PCAW members with bullhorns, stride quickly alongside the gathering crowd, reminding people not to engage in violence and to remain peaceful, "*silmiyyah*," saying "throwing stones is forbidden" and "no one throw a stone." In a call for collective symbolic action, word spreads through the crowd that everyone should raise their arms over their heads, a symbolic gesture to show they carry no weapons and are of a peaceful intent and to dramatically both embody and display the glaring disparity in weaponry.

Slowly and deliberately, the mass of protesters moves down the road, their flags and banners bouncing above them, toward the fenced-off orchards and the site of the encroaching wall. Suddenly, the occupation forces come into view on the horizon—three or four jeeps have just parked, and out spill a dozen or so military personnel. A murmur of anticipation rippled through the crowd. The protesters continued their march, getting as close as possible to the occupation forces. It reminded me of accounts I've read of tribal warfare in New Guinea, where the two sides line up on opposite sides and edge toward each other, eventually throwing a spear or two. But the resemblance ended there. The occupation soldiers had their hands in their pockets, rifles slung casually over the shoulder, and they just stood around for over half an hour, their manner relaxed, indicating an absence of tension or fear. Other times, however, their hands are on their rifles ready to shoot.

As if on cue, the call goes up, "To the wall!" The younger protesters are off and running down the slope and through the boulder-strewn olive groves to the site of the wall. Groups of soldiers follow just as quickly. The sequencing of defining actions unfolds in tandem: the call to approach the wall and the soldiers readying themselves to attack: tear-gas canisters loaded, automatic rifles readied, positions taken. Three or four soldiers would catch a protester, throw him to the ground, and start beating him with batons and rifle butts. The international observers rushed to take photos. Three soldiers caught an Israeli youth and threw him down on the rocky ground fairly close to where some of us were observing the melee. Held down by his arms and legs, he thrashed around trying to free himself from their grip while they beat him with batons. Several internationals pleaded with them to stop and hastily snapped photos. The soldiers shouted for us to get back. When they finally let him go, his face was bloodied. He was helped by fellow protesters to a PRCS ambulance to receive first aid. His wrist appeared to be broken. I rejoined the older folks who had stayed at the top of the road with four or five soldiers. We watched the scenes below as tear-gas canisters were fired and the injured struggled back up the hill to the ambulance. The object of the violence seemed less to squelch the protest and more to subjugate the protesters, and to convey that not only would nonviolence not stop the occupation's progress, it would bring about violence. Some of the Israeli peace activists had remained at the top of the slope. They got right up into the faces of the increasingly agitated soldiers, alternately shaming and berating them.

"Observers" from various peace groups attend the protests as well. An American peace activist and self-described observer explained, "Observers are now present in large numbers because of past violence by the Israeli forces. Soldiers were beating and arresting Palestinians, yet once in court, they would testify that

Palestinians had instigated the violence and resisted arrest. So photographs and observers can bear witness that the Israeli forces initiated the violence." Photographers were ubiquitous, both Israeli and international. Israelis carrying rifles, in uniform or plainclothes, were also taking pictures. Based on these photos, they would enter the village in the dead of night and arrests participants. The videos of the protests go viral, as Bil'in's website posted them every week. Palestinian protestors often cover their faces with the *kufiyyah*, and young boys, attempting to disguise themselves but also in a display of budding masculinity, pull their t-shirts over their heads, covering their foreheads, and wear red bandanas across their noses and mouths, bearing their pubescent chests.

The protesters do not carry weapons, in stark contrast to the heavily armed Israeli forces, with their helmets, rubber-coated steel bullets, automatic rifles, stun grenades, tear gas, percussion grenades, and, more recently, sewage water and the "skunk," not to mention communications technologies that enable them to call for quick reinforcements.[20] Indeed, unarmed protestors sometimes stand in front of the soldiers, their arms up in the gesture of surrender, an intrepid and embodied act graphically showcasing disparity. A play of bravado by protestors willing to face possible military assault contrasts with the morally suspect stance of the soldiers, whose role is to enable the occupation and land expropriations. Arabic-speaking protestors use the shame factor, especially with Druze police and soldiers, screaming at them, "shame on you!" or "it is *haram* (forbidden) to uproot trees."[21]

Young village boys taunt the military forces. The most audacious was twelve-year-old Mohammed. With his muscles tensed, his face a dark grimace of anger, he stood, all five feet of him, just inches from the occupying forces, his head jutting forward. Staring a soldier in the face, he shouted, "Ya Abu Nimr, you snake! I am here, come and arrest me." Pointing his finger at the soldier's chest, he yelled, "You see me—my name is Mohammed, and I will resist!" He continued shouting while striking poses for the Israeli photographers. Small groups of male youth get so close to the soldiers that they are inches from their faces, trying to engage them in conversation or shouting at them as did young Mohammed. If the soldiers start to converge on a protestor and show signs that they are going to beat him, other protestors rush forward, especially foreigners, to surround them, trying to calm the situation and to physically obstruct the blows raining down on the protester.

Frequently, a few ten- to twelve-year-old boys with homemade slingshots and rocks in their pockets would break from the procession and start lobbing stones. Catching sight of their young sons' bulging trousers, mothers were quick to make them empty their pockets of stones. Other times, these intrepid youths rapidly gather stones, launching them boldly. Rock throwing is frequently met with close-range firing of tear gas. Using Israel's weapons against itself, young male Palestinian protestors, on occasion, grab the tear gas canisters and lob them back at the soldiers.

One seasoned international protester described the village leadership, now patrolling the edges of the crowd, as "pointer dogs," who have a keen sense of the balance of power—how many protestors, how many Israeli troops—and are always alert to changes in the physical stance of the soldiers, such as when they start loading the tear-gas canisters, conveying impending violence. After observing several protests, one develops the skill to detect when escalation is immanent: soldiers load tear-gas canisters, approach the fence, take aim, and fire.

Small victories can be had. Yasser's elderly father and I sat in the shade on a large boulder from which we could observe the melee unfolding below us. Two soldiers approached us and gruffly ordered Abu Yasser to get up and start walking. He refused to budge, saying softly but firmly, "I can sit here, this is my village." One of the soldiers nudged him with his knee and ordered him to get up. Then the command came again, this time in a harsher tone, accompanied by a nudge with the butt of his rifle. Abu Yasser refused to move. Everyone watched and waited in silence, expecting them to forcibly make him stand up. Finally, they gave up and walked away. Cheers went up from the small crowd that had stayed up on the hill for this minor victory, an act consonant with *sumud*.

Gradually, the protests come to an end. Participants straggle back to the village in small groups; ambulances ferry the injured to local clinics; and the Israeli forces leave. Back in the village, village women offer lunch or refreshments to foreigners; buses fill up with people leaving the village; and the villagers go home. Often, the local leaders meet to discuss the day's events and to post the photos on the website.

What accounts for the sustainability of Bil'in's weekly protests? First, the temporal dimension is critical. Bil'in organizers understood that mounting weekly rather than daily protests, as some villages, including Bil'in, initially tried to do, would circumvent the inevitable burnout that meant dwindling participation. Second, they were all too familiar with the media narrative of violence as a frame for reporting on protests. So, they engaged in theatrical tactics to generate questions about the wall. Often, the Friday protests had a theatrical theme with an element of the carnivalesque. For example, protesters handcuffed themselves to the fence with plastic toy handcuffs. Another time, they donned long, colorful snake costumes, reminiscent of a Chinese New Year's celebration, as symbols of the evils of occupation but also mimicking the wall's serpentine path. Soccer matches between teams of local and international youth, as well as musical concerts have taken place near the wall. One Friday, a group of protestors dressed up as avatars, in costumes and make-up straight out of the movie *Avatar*, which portrayed a conflict between colonizers who were seeking natural resources and the attempts by the indigenous population to stave them off. In a symbolic and historically resonant gesture, a young boy donned a Native American headdress. These symbolic theatrical gestures attract media attention, and their peaceful- ness encourages local participation. Third, Yasser explained that the village has been able to sustain active opposition, in part, because "there are four clans in this village and every political faction is represented. We all coordinate together for the protests. No one clan or organization is dominant." He emphasized that nearly every family had lost some land to the colonies. The village is known for having a strong Fatah and Hamas presence, but nearly all Palestinian political factions are represented. Cross-cutting kin and political ties in the village fa- cilitate sustained protests. Last, social media facilitated coordination among all participating groups, garnering admiration and support for the well-organized protests.

Transgressions and Cosmopolitanism

Palestinian villagers are locally situated, rooted, and cosmopolitan as they team up with Israelis and international solidarity groups to protest, deploying the nor- mative discourses of human rights and universal justice. These enclaved islands are not completely adrift, without communication. Indeed, the internet has facil- itated the sharing of knowledge about how to organize and mobilize. For exam- ple, in 2004, in one fairly small, isolated village in the central West Bank, with a blocked entrance and exit and no paved streets, a room in an apartment rented to international peace activists was a buzzing multimedia center with global reach: multiple television screens, video transmissions streaming to all corners of the globe, internet, e-mail, and fax service. This was the pre-Twitter era, and texting was still emergent. Bil'in had a multilingual website that posted videos of the weekly events and provided background information on the village.

Protests dramatized a partial subversion of the segregationist purpose of the wall and illustrated that closure can be breached. Ze'ev Jabotinsky, forefather of the Likud Party, coined the term "iron wall" in 1923. His formulation of an "iron wall which the native population cannot break through" (quoted in Brenner 1984, 75) is inverted by Israeli participation in the protests. The "iron wall" refers to an impregnable Jewish military force that would unambiguously signal to the Arabs their inability to weaken the Israeli state and, most significantly, precludes any concessions to the Palestinians. Jabotinsky's iron wall included military might and a refusal to concede territory or sovereignty.[22] Peace would come through the complete acquiescence of the Palestinians. Jabotinsky, and his followers, did not foresee Jews making a "breakthrough" by joining the Palestinians in struggle against occupation and separation.

Internationals, Israelis, and American Jewish protestors transgress the boundaries, triggering "a collusion of classifications," which calls for "plate tectonics" rather than a "static geology model" (Bowker and Star 1999, 31). The will and capacity to overcome separation is dramatically and sometimes dangerously enacted during the protests. Protesters transcend and disrupt the imposed spatial arrangements of closure and separation, confound the narrative of irreconcilable Jewish-Arab enmity, hint at and fleetingly perform an alternative view of the polity and belonging. Further, they challenge unidimensional notions of space as fixed or simply relational. In a colonial expansionist state, space can simultaneously be fixed, relational, and moving. The protests could be cast as what geographer Martin Jones (2009, 489) calls a "phase space," which "acknowledges the relational making of space . . . *but* insists on the compatibilities between, rather the mutual exclusivities of" relations or networks and more fixed notions of space. Phase spaces bring together the two notions of space; Bil'in's space of opposition is an example.

For Israeli Jews, prohibited entry into in Area A by their government, participation in the protests constituted an illicit encounter, and unsettled the Zionist narrative of insurmountable differences between Arab and Jew. In coming together on the basis of shared political sentiments, the contours of a dangerously heterotopian possibility, and thus subversive space, came into focus, however opaquely. The social composition of the protests unsettled overly rigid binary conceptualizations of and presence in space, standard narratives of Palestinian-Israeli relations, and the ethnic-national classificatory system with its associated privileges and subjugation. With their global reach via the media, the protests became a public stage on which hegemonic notions of identity and communal belonging were contested and transgressed. Traversing these boundaries upsets the rules of interaction based on ostensibly dichotomized Arab-Jewish identities and loyalties. In coming together for protest, a liminal spatiotemporal zone and moment, effervescent and highly charged, crystallized. In so doing, a fleeting sense of *communitas* emerged, as did a moral community based on cross-linkages that undermined dominant narratives of fixed, singular spaces and identities.

These transgressions can be situated within an anthropological tradition. Joint Palestinian-Israeli-international protests constitute situational and fleeting cosmopolitan spaces and moments; the constitution of these heterogeneous spaces can be framed at the theoretical intersection of state classifications and the spatializations of populations and anthropologist Mary Douglas's slightly modified classic formulation of "matter out of place." Matter out of place coincides with vigorously monitored and policed classificatory orders and their associated spaces—in this case, Jews in Israel and its colonies, with Palestinians marooned in enclaves and subjected to controlled and calibrated mobility. While binary conceptualizations have been vigorously critiqued, there are instances when such classificatory orders remain a material and cognitive reality. In elaborating on "matter out of place," Douglas argued that it "implies two conditions: a set of ordered relations and a contravention of that order." Israelis who cross the lines of separation by visiting Areas A and B illuminate the way transgressive actions can begin to unsettle classificatory orders. This resonates with Douglas's (1966, 3) proposition that what constitutes "matter out of place," or "dirt," is an analogy "for expressing a general view of the social order." Dirt is "essentially disorder," which "offends against order and convention." Eliminating it works "to organize the environment" and make it "conform to an idea" (ibid., 2). Douglas's notion of "matter out of place" coincides with broadly conceived categories of a classificatory scheme of spatial ordering. I insert the phenomena of mobility or shiftingness into Douglas's formulation; in Palestine, the spatial is simultaneously fixed and in motion, as Israel's eastern border expands through the colonies as Palestinian territory contracts. In addition, the permit system for Palestinian workers was flexible enough to allow Israeli employers to continue using Palestinian labor, despite the mechanisms of closure. As Israelis settle in the OPTs, it becomes cleansed of "dirt," or "matter out of place," and then redefined as Jewish. When Israelis cross into to the Palestinian zone to protest, they undermine these spatial arrangements and their ideological underpinnings. In describing how they reached Palestinian villages, Israeli participants spoke of "crossing over" and trying to avoid detection by Israeli forces. And, indeed, their actions are often equated with disloyalty to the state and the Zionist project.

The concept of "matter out of place" alone is not a sufficient framework for understanding spatial transgression; it describes but doesn't take into account structures of power and the active rejection of fixed categorization. One way to frame these issues is by fleshing out the relationship between matter out of place and cosmopolitanism. Cosmopolitans "cast doubt" on absolutist notions of communitarian belonging (Rapport 2006, 24). These geopolitical and social spaces *in-between* register future possibilities. At these joint protests, a "demotic cosmopolitanism," (Mandel 2008, 314) distinct from the worldly cosmopolitanism of urban centers, comes into relief. In this risky and transgressive coming together, which ironically inverts Israeli cultural ranking between the ostensibly cosmopolitan Israeli and the provincial Palestinian, a moral community of opposition to occupation crystallizes that temporarily transcends national, ethnic, and religious origins and dilutes the supposedly bounded spatial categories of nation, ethnicity, and religion. In other words, in this setting, matter is all over the place—unleashed, so to speak.

A problematic concept at best, cosmopolitanism suggests a sense of belonging to a world wider than that constituted by narrowly defined and locally based primordial communities and identities. It is an orientation, an "openness toward divergent cultural experiences" and an involvement with other cultures "to some degree on their own terms" (Hannerz 1996, 103). The interest here is in cosmopolitanism's potential to express alternative visions of the socio-political order.

It registers openness to multiple narratives and visions instead of insistence on monothetic categories and socially homogenous spaces. In short, it points to the emergence of a polythetic sense of community.

Rarely is cosmopolitanism analyzed as a transgressive challenge to state sovereignty and a colonial endeavor. Cosmopolitanism as manifested in these popular joint actions fractures lines of exclusion and, in so doing, raises questions about the nature of the national narrative, state-citizen relations, and culture. Cosmopolitanism "does not mean that one does not have a country or a homeland" (Turner 2006, 64) but, rather, that one has a "certain reflexive distance from one's own culture," which produces a "humanistic skepticism toward the grand narratives of nationalism and modernization" (ibid., 62, 64). Most significantly, vernacular or local cosmopolitanisms are oppositional practices that expose fractures in the national narrative.

I use a spatially centered approach to cosmopolitanism, which shifts focus to the local and rural, and in so doing, dislodges the concept from its traditional moorings in urban space; rarely has cosmopolitanism been associated with the rural and local. Hence I would argue that cosmopolitanism is not an endpoint on a scale of dualities of cosmopolitan/urban and provincial/local. Nor is it a fixed quality. One can be a cosmopolitan and local simultaneously, having what Appiah (1998, 91) calls a "rooted cosmopolitanism." Cosmopolitanism is about imagining and acting on the possibilities for a future in which the lines of belonging and rights are more inclusive.

The violence wielded by the occupying forces at protests may be less a response to the peaceful actions of unarmed demonstrators and more to the blurring of the classificatory order and its categories, or matter out of place. Peaceful, theatrical protests with a discernable mixing and mingling of social categories may incur violent reactions, not just because they protest state actions, but also because they subvert the order of things. For the Israeli forces, the taxonomic order comes undone and cognitive dissonance sets in. Their world view of Jewish-Israeli rights, and their role in protecting those rights against pathologically violent Palestinians, is upended, and an alternative vision performed. Israeli attacks on peaceful protests convey a starkly unambiguous message: peaceful civil opposition will not be tolerated. Nonviolence, and, perhaps especially, joint Israeli-Palestinian action, goes against the grain of standard, hegemonic representations of Palestinians as inherently violent and thus may trigger violence. While matter out of place usually engenders discomfort, anxiety, and confusion, in this case it may arouse violence intended to obstruct slippage through and around boundaries. The highly symbolic nature of the protests and the violence they elicit point to the way symbolic challenges are conceptualized and responded to as real threats. In this topsy-turvy world, largely peaceful actions are understood as violent assaults on the prescribed social order.

In the long run, do these joint protests, like a host of direct actions and every-day tactics, have any efficacy in confronting settler colonialism? While they may draw attention to the colonial process, it nonetheless proceeds apace. On June 30, 2004, the Israeli High Court of Justice ruled that the route of the wall should be changed in the Beit Suriq area (Zertal and Eldar 2007, 428). On July 9, 2004, the International Court of Justice in the Hague rendered its advisory, nonbinding ruling on the illegality of the wall, which, the court concluded, amounts to collective punishment of and undue hardship for the Palestinians. On September 4, 2007, Israel's Supreme Court ruled in favor of villagers in a case they brought to reroute the 1.7 kilometers (nearly two miles) of the fence that prevented farmers from reaching their fields. A day later, the same court ruled to legalize the Mattiyahu East colony, built on land belonging to the villagers of Bil'in. So, did the protests have any effect on these determinations? It is hard to know. They certainly brought some international attention to the wall. In the past decade and a half, Bil'in attained the status of a pilgrimage site for international visitors concerned with human rights and the occupation, a phenomenon some Palestinians refer to sarcastically as "political tourism," drawing a subtle connection of protests with consumption of the other. The protests are fleeting moments, even if highly charged, particularly for Israelis and internationals who can retreat to the security of home and state; or, as anthropologist Ulf Hannerz (1996, 104) so astutely noted, "The cosmopolitan may embrace the alien culture, but he does not become committed to it. All the time he knows where the exit is."

Ultimately, village protests cannot confront the military machinery of the state, and that is not necessarily their goal. Rather, it is to insist that occupation and closure will be confronted, that they will be costly endeavors in terms of moral standing, and that the state must be ever alert to challenges to their rule. Moreover, they ensure that colonists will live under a cloud of uncertainty and constant reminders of their status as colonizers. In other words, occupation and dispossession will face opposition that can bring heightened levels of international scrutiny. Unfortunately, opposition actions feed the politics of fear (see Ochs 2011) so deftly cultivated by the state.

Conclusion

These protests blurred the standard categories of the violent Palestinian and the peace-seeking Israeli and, most significantly, challenged the narrative framework of Palestinian/Israeli enmity and irreconcilable difference. The usual positioning of Palestinians as perpetrators of conflict was unsettled when foreigners and Israelis participated in these protests. Although protests blurred the classificatory order, the participants were vastly unequal in power, resources, and access to protection. Internationals and Israeli Jews can return to the safety of their homes and the legal protections afforded by citizenship, while Palestinians face home searches, arrests, physical violence, and have limited access to legal services. In these inclusive practices an alternative future was imagined and acted upon. They embodied the hopes for a future vastly different from the present.

It remains to be seen the extent to which the direct action in Palestine that began in earnest in 2003–4, with its theatrics and lack of a dominant faction, may have set the stage for the protests of the Arab Spring, and for how the now defunct Arab Spring initially influenced the subsequent direction and flavor of Palestinian resistance. Fragmentation and isolation do present obstacles to mounting sustained opposition to an expansionist state. In face of dwindling public spaces of interaction and collective memories of place, can there be collective movement to regain space? At some point, sustained political mobilization has to be territorialized. Despite communication technologies and social media and the public sphere they craft, space matters. Tahrir Square and the US Occupy movement were spatial moments of unity, however ephemeral. Communicative technologies and virtual communities can overcome geography and immobility, but what does this observation mean politically?

Conclusion

Occupation and closure resemble an octopus-like monster extending its tentacles ever deeper into every aspect of Palestinians' daily lives, strangling their ability to lead lives of dignity and equality with some measure of certainty. Israel's sovereignty extends from the Mediterranean Sea to the Jordan River. Pockets of semi-sovereign, discontiguous enclaved Palestinian entities are scattered throughout this territory. In this territory governed by Israel, half the population lacks citizenship. Palestinians under occupation live in the territory of the state, however ambiguously defined, but they are not of that state. They are subject to an inexorable and complex regime of immobility, incarceration, surveillance, forced visibility and invisibility, and disciplinary order. In the shrinking spaces of Palestine, access to resources, from land and water to mobility, is allocated along racialized lines of ethnicity and nationality. For these reasons, attributions of an Israeli-Jewish and Palestinian binary can easily surface. Reality is more complex than first meets the eye. The identity card, the permit system, checkpoints, and the segregated road network do seem to affirm a binary. However, this binary is fragmented on the Palestine side of the divide, as it is the Israeli side, although to a lesser degree. Each side of the binary is internally differentiated; Palestinians are splintered into those from Jerusalem, Gaza, and the West Bank, each group having its own type of identity card, rights, and mobilities. Israel's internal ethnic fracturing hinges on the Ashkenazim, Sephardim, Mizrahim, and the Palestinian Arab, a category itself further divided by religion. In addition, within Israel, there is a pronounced Jewish secular-religious divide. In this world of hierarchically stacked identities and rights, to be without citizenship and belonging to the socio-political as well as religious order of the state situates the Palestinian on the receiving end of the colonial endeavor. Having unsettled the strictness of a binary, it is useful nevertheless to remember anthropologist Patrick Wolfe's (2013, 257) critical engagement with the scholarly discomfort with binaries in a settler-colonial context when he asks why the "spectre of binaries, so disturbing to non-Native sensibilities, should be less troubling to Natives?" Could it be, he suggests, that the "repudiation of binaries represents a settler perspective?" In other words, those who live in a world of segregated spaces, whose temporal rhythms are not of their own making, and who have few rights might indeed conceptualize theirs as a world in which binaries hold sway. In short, the Palestinians sense of a Jewish-Israeli and Palestinian binary coheres with Wolfe's assertion of binaries as "less troubling" to the indigenous population.

Palestinians understand the mobility regime as part of the logic of an ongoing settler-colonial project designed to encourage the evacuation of Palestine, thus making the land conform to a narrative in which Palestine, largely void of an indigenous population, could become a safe haven for Jews seeking refuge in a world they perceive as rife with persecution or its possibility. Since 1948, that watershed moment in mass displacement and demographic transformation in Palestine, the logic of displacement and replacement has been pursued relentlessly. Palestinians understand what Ahmad dubbed the third stage as a phase in a temporally stretched out, historically dynamic process of settler colonialism. Zionism has envisioned a state with a minimum of Arabs and a maximum of Jews, an exclusivist state. Removing the land from people would eventuate in the removal of the people from the land in this quest for demographic supremacy and unbridled access to local resources. Now rapidly colonizing Jerusalem and the West Bank, the Jewish-Israeli colonialist-settler movement envisions itself as the forward guard in this quest.[1] In extending sovereignty to the Jordan River, a demographic equation remains in the forefront: to winnow the Palestinian population by incarcerating them in enclaves, closely monitoring and regulating their mobility with an ever-expanding repertoire of technologies of surveillance and control.

Colonial rule in Palestine initiated a transformation of relations among people, place, rights, and territory in which one community has been privileged over the other. Indeed, this privilege is contingent on the negation of the other; for if the other is recognized as a rights-bearing person with a history of rootedness in place and place-inflected identities, what becomes of the exclusivist state built on a scaffolding of a religious-nationalist myth of linear historical presence, ownership, and belonging? I first encountered the Tunisian-French-Jewish writer Albert Memmi in a class on colonialism in the early 1970s. His work has served as an intellectual foundation for my grappling with the Zionist project in Palestine. His astute observation that the "deprivations of the colonized are the almost direct result of the advantages secured to the colonizer" (Memmi 1965, xii) succinctly and poignantly captures what in this book I have often referred to as *relationality*, a concept that frames Jewish-Israeli privilege and rights with the denial of the same to Palestinians. Memmi refers first and foremost to the economics of colonialism and quickly segues into its social and psychological dimensions. At its most basic, relationality involves the diminution of an indigenous Palestinian population both discursively and demographically in order to advance the presence and claims of Zionist Jews. These visceral and tangible asymmetrical relations, in significant part, form the context in which contemporary Palestinian subjectivity takes shape: the desire for normal lives, the absence of disorder, some measure of predictability, and the sense of dignity that comes with recognition of one's humanity—phenomena Palestinians observe characterize the life of others. Relationality in this lopsided situation hinges on the negation of one to produce the rights and capacities of the other. Indeed, it is that "descent into the ordinary" that can restore a sense of agency to the marginalized (Das 2007, 7). Built on an edifice of violence and domination, the violation of international law, and a mythico-history, as most nationalisms are, it is always at risk of coming undone. Not surprisingly, Palestinians, their narratives, and their claims for justice engender anxiety for Zionists; Palestinians are a thorn in the side of Zionism, their mere presence poses a challenge to its legitimacy and narrative.

In the new millennium, talk of the "transfer" of West Bank Palestinians and of the Palestinian citizens of Israel circulates among the Israeli right-wing currently holding the reins of power, and has aroused little international alarm. Such talk channels the momentous events of 1948 when the bulk of the Palestinian population (around 750,000) was displaced and subsequently denied the right of return stipulated in UN General Assembly Resolution 194. That denial remains a pillar in a set of legal, political, discursive, and demographic technologies of exclusion to render the Palestinian absent and the new Israeli as not only present but also the rightful owners. That initial denial of return established a barrier or wall of sorts that delineated the boundaries of inclusion and exclusion in the state, as does the cement wall currently winding its way through the West Bank, along with a host of laws and military orders, land expropriation, the permit system, and the vast network of checkpoints and bypass roads that work to immobilize, immiserate, and incarcerate the Palestinian population.

The wall, the structural hallmark of exclusion and separation, I contend, follows a logic similar to that used to the deny the right of return to displaced Palestinians in 1948 and to then confiscate their property. Confinement and obstructed mobility are stripping Palestinians in the West Bank of the economic, social, and civic life that mobility makes possible. In the colonial present, two walls, one cement and one paper, and a mobility regime facilitate the expansion of state and sovereignty and the continuing marginalization of the Palestinian population. In effect, the policies of separation and closure may be constitutive of a slow-motion ethnic cleansing through the quest to extend the boundaries and sovereignty of the state. Land emptied of Palestinians is land that can then be settled and transformed into Jewish space. Negation of a Palestinian presence has also been achieved by a renaming project that produces a landscape in which Jews appear as a historically deep presence and thus the natural and rightful owners. Overall, the systemic logic of Zionism has marooned Palestinians in the ever-shrinking remnants of Mandate Palestine. In crucial respects, the wall also signals a sealing off of Israel and a pivoting westward, away from the larger Arab Middle East in which it is geographically located.

The mobility regime and the enclaves signal a spatial approach to containing those excluded from the socio-political order. The inhabitants of the enclaves are neither refugees nor internally displaced persons, which highlights the limitations of current concepts in forced-migrations studies and the international law on refugees. The result of a protracted, multipronged strategy of displacement and occupation, enclaves in Palestine are hedged with ambiguities as to their spatial parameters, international responsibility for their inhabitants, and sovereignty over them. With their ambiguous borders, they constitute legal and political gray zones, in contrast to the more distinctly demarcated Bantustans, refugee and detention camps, and reservations that elsewhere have contained the displaced or those deemed marginal to the socio-political order. Inhabiting a gray zone renders Palestinian life even more unbearable and, ultimately, more vulnerable. As such, they add urgency to the need to reappraise existing conceptual categories. Both refugee camps and enclaves work to distance and contain those deemed not to belong to the Israeli state. Refugee camps in Lebanon, Jordan, Gaza, and Syria (pre-2012) warehouse Palestinians, while the enclaves contain and immobilize them. They bring to the surface questions about spatial devices used to concentrate and manage the excluded and undesirable, and thus join a coterie of devices from the colonial era to the present. Camps and enclaves are, I have argued, in conversation experientially and theoretically (Peteet 2016). Enclaves and refugee camps are narratively situated by Palestinians as sharing historical continuity and intent. There is a discernible continuity in effect and experience between refugee camps and the enclaves, but also, it must be recognized, there are qualitative differences. In this gray orbit it behooves us to explore new conceptual frameworks arising out of ethnographic and empirically grounded work. There is a pressing need to pursue new historically situated, ethnographically rich paradigms to make sense of the spatial devices used to contain the displaced. In other words, the enclaves point to the need for new theoretical, empirical, and lexical categories that well exceed our current frameworks. For now, "enclaves," with all its ambiguities, will have to serve as a point of departure until more precise terms surface, either in the Arabic vernacular or in Hebrew, the language of Israeli policy. The very grayness of these spaces captures the unstable sense of betwixt and between, neither here nor there, that prevails in Palestine.

In occupied East Jerusalem there has also been an attempt to reduce the Palestinian Arab population through the construction of Jewish-only housing, confiscation of Palestinian property, denial of residency and building permits, and a generalized atmosphere of violence toward Arabs, that is increasingly incited by the government and is carried out with impunity (Abowd 2014; Thrall 2014). As Palestinians are displaced, replacement proceeds apace in the city.

The occupation and the influx of colonists profoundly transformed the landscape of the West Bank. Twinned with a regime that prohibits access to spaces and re-inscribes the landscape with new forms of architecture and linguistic referents, the strict routing that funnels and filters Palestinians through massive centralized nodes, renders the once familiar now strange and imbued with danger. For Palestinians, once familiar places have been so transformed as to be unrecognizable. In the shifting landscape, temporal notions of distance have become distorted. It is clear that "who can remember and who can be made to forget, is, fundamentally, an expression of power" (Bisharat 2007). It may be anticipated that transformation of the landscape precludes a Palestinian return to a knowable place where belonging derives not just from a long presence but equally from memories and feeling at home and the capacity to move from place to place at a rhythm corresponding to a time/space interface. Making the landscape unknowable is another technique to denativize Palestinians and is coupled with techniques to nativize the Jewish-Israeli. Bypass roads provide speed and connectivity with Israel and among the colonies; in this geography of speed and mobilities one is hypo-mobile, the other hyper-mobile. In a distinctly colonial temporality, in keeping with the relational organization of inequality and privilege, Palestinians wait endlessly to go about their daily lives. For the Israeli the time/space interface is smooth; for the latter, the temporal is no longer synchronized with the spatial. In a world of calibrated unpredictability and disorder, Palestinians live in a state of anxious anticipation, trepidation, and waiting. Controlling mobility's speed and scope, coupled with sophisticated surveillance technologies, has become a prime component of the apparatus of modern colonial population management.

In Israel-Palestine, horrific rounds of violence are interspersed with the periodic "peace negotiations," which predictably fail to change the status quo. State violence is fairly widely perceived as a correct and rational approach to security threats, while that of the Palestinian nonstate actor is perceived to be driven by irrational hatred. Adding insult to injury, Palestinians are blamed for the violence inflicted on them. In this vein, in a letter published, in 1984, in the *Anthropology Newsletter*, anthropologist Stephen Pastner wrote that Palestinian "cultural values make them collaborators in the perpetuation, even the genesis, of their own misery" (quoted in Deeb and Winegar 2016, 134). Rather than seek long-term, sustainable political solutions, Israel and its supporters exhibit a readiness to accept persistent low-level conflict, with the periodic requirement to "mow the lawn," the Israeli metaphor for their actions in Gaza in 2008–9, November 2012, and the summer of 2014. For the Israelis, this policy is relatively painless, generates marginal internal dissent, and has met with few if any consequences from its external supporters, mainly the United States and Europe. Some have depicted how national mobilization around perceived threats may nurture internal cohesion (Ochs 2011). In 2014, the violence, both physical and rhetorical, against Palestinians reached new levels during the assault on Gaza. Knesset member Ayelet Shaked exclaimed during that time, "This is a war between two people. Who is the enemy? The Palestinian people."[2] Shaked's statement is a not-so-veiled reference, if not an incitement, to ethnocide and collective punishment, which rests on wholesale demonization. Her statement does not go against the grain of Zionism. Its displacing logic and racialized system of exclusivist privileges can incite just such a binary.

Palestinians, like Israelis, live in a heightened state of alert with a vivid sense of the historical continuity among a colonial past, present, and future in which the constant threat is punctuated by deadly spasms of violence. This climate of fear and insecurity calls forth reserves of resiliency and adaptability. *Sumud* may be an overused term, but it does retain a potency of meaning precisely because the simple act of staying put takes on heightened meaning when the goal is displacement.

A colonial spatial regime feeding a fractured subjectivity in a heightened state of alert in face of daily demands for deference recalls Lefebvre's (1991, 143) contention that the essential purpose of space is to "produce subjects obedient to spatial rules . . . prescribing and proscribing gestures, routes and distances to be covered." As Nabil sadly remarked:

> People have been taking drugs for stress. They are not always aware of what they are going through. They are so busy trying to survive and tend to their families and livelihoods that they don't always stop to analyze their own reactions. We are getting used to this way of life. We have bent, but it is not normal. It is not normal to be humiliated everyday—to be humiliated as a routine part of daily life. Is this normal? We react with stress and anger and frustration. Yet few of us take the time to catch our breath and try to figure out what is happening to us and to ask what closure and the wall mean for the future?

Closure and its obstruction of mobilities have fostered a constantly in-motion geography of subjectivity. Subjectivities, always multifaceted and laced with contradictions, shift as Palestinians move through different spaces, proscribed and prescribed, each productive of and calling forth specific assemblages of gestures, behaviors, attitudes, and feelings of belonging and an heightened awareness of danger. To be a refugee is to face loss of home, livelihood, kin, and a sense of the future. In the enclaves a similar sort of subjectivity takes hold as space and mobility shrink and loss becomes central to a sense of self. A shared narrative derived from the intimate and discernable continuities in the settler-colonial endeavor connects the Palestinian refugee community with the OPT in a world of loss, suffering, injustice, and an unforeseeable future. Palestinians are literally stranded in space, whether they are inside or outside of Palestine, in enclaves or camps.

As the writing of this book came to a conclusion in late 2015, a third intifada initially centered in Jerusalem seemed to be brewing. Triggered by Jewish-Israeli challenges to the status of al-Aqsa Mosque in Jerusalem's Old City, the vastly

unequal distribution of services, and a discernable uptick in Jewish-Israeli violence toward Palestinians, as well as relentless efforts to reduce the city's Arab
population, Palestinians have stabbed Israelis and run their cars into them.
Palestinians are confronted with limited choices: leave, submit to colonial rule
with its demands for political subjugation and servitude and compliance with
dehumanizing technologies of control and management, or form the political
means to resist. Conditioned as it is by a new assemblage of factors, particularly the decimation of an effective Palestinian resistance movement, it will not
resemble the previous two intifadas. Absent a unified and coherent leadership,
it may well feature spontaneous outbursts of individual violence, such as have
occurred throughout 2016. These decentralized, uncoordinated, seemingly lone-
wolf actions will suspend certainty and predictability for all living in this small
space. How does a regional power, with a well-equipped military confront such
an ungrounded, amorphous uprising? With a centrally unguided, seemingly in-
dividualized intifada, intelligence gathering becomes problematic as well for who
can provide information on spontaneous acts of violence. The question remains:
Can a viable anti-colonial movement emerge in this climate, and what shape will
it take?

Notes

Introduction

1. For late Ottoman and Mandate Palestinian population statistics, see McCarthy (1990).

2. The Balfour Declaration (1917), a letter from Arthur James Balfour, British foreign secretary, to Baron Rothschild, a leader of the British Jewish community, states, "His Majesty's government views with favour the establishment in Palestine of a national home for the Jewish people, and will use their best endeavours to facilitate the achievement of this object, it being clearly understood that nothing shall be done which may prejudice the civil and religious rights of existing non-Jewish communities in Palestine, or the rights and political status enjoyed by Jews in any other country."

3. Israel's unequivocal stance that it will retain the Jordan Valley makes it clear that any future Palestinian political entity or state will not share a border with an Arab neighbor. The Valley has been heavily colonized by Israelis; Palestinians, on the other hand, must have a permit to reside in their homes.

4. See, for example, Abu El-Haj (2001); Allen (2008); Elkins and Pederson (2005); Gordon (2008); Gregory (2004); Ochs (2011); Pappe (2006); Pateman and Mills (2007); Rodinson (1973); Shafir (1989); and Yiftachel (1998, 2005), among others.

5. For a discussion of Coetzee's work, see "In Focus: Cruelty, Suffering, Imagination: The Lessons of J. M. Coetzee," *American Anthropologist* 108 (2006): 84–87.

6. http://www.wboxi.com/www.israellandfund.com.html (accessed July 25, 2016). Maps in Netanyahu's book (1993) dissolve the Green Line and extend the border to the Jordan River. Israel's official tourism site does the same.

7. For many Palestinian refugees, return, or going to, is still imagined within the geographical space of Palestine, but the social relations and the political arrangements it entails have been reconfigured. They are not based on an unmediated, bucolically imagined past; rather, the experience of exile has re-created the world, expanding the boundaries of community and lines of inclusion, forging new social bonds and sentiments and new ways of locating oneself in the world. As a result, an ideological, as well as geopolitical, third space is identifiable: "Palestine/Israel" which implies recognition of both parties' presence in the same geographic space. Implicit in the term is the notion of "one state," in other words, a secular, democratic state rather than an exclusivist state in which citizenship is based on ethno-religious factors.

8. The Oslo (1993, 1995) interim agreements between Israel and the Palestine Liberation Organization include protocols for security and economic relations and fragment the West Bank into Areas A, B, and C, with differentiated levels of Israeli and Palestinian presence, control, and responsibility. They also established the Palestinian National Authority. I use the term "post-Oslo" to refer to the period since the second intifada in 2000, when it became clear to Palestinians that Israel would not abide by the Olso agreements.

9. http://visualizingpalestine.org/visuals/palestinian-israeli-peace-talks-settlements-oslo (accessed July 25, 2016).

10. See "A Clean Break: A New Strategy for Securing the Realm" (report by the Institute for Advanced Strategic and Political Studies, Jerusalem, Washington, DC, 1996). Prepared for Prime Minister Netanyahu following his 1996 electoral victory and based on discussions

among Richard Perle, James Colbert, Douglas Feith, and David Wurmser, among others, the report called for dropping the land-for-peace formula and seeking "peace for peace," whereby the Arabs unconditionally accept what are called Israel's territorial rights. Accessed July 25, 2016, https://web.archive.org/web/20140125123844/http://www.iasps.org/strat1.htm.

11. American celebrities have hired private Israeli security guards, a brand name that evokes toughness, competence, discretion, and experience. Connection with a state glosses the "mercenary" element. I would note that the Israeli military does more policing than actual combat in running checkpoints, guarding colonies, and quelling protests.

12. The Dahiya doctrine is a military strategy that targets civilian infrastructure and calls for a disproportionate use of force. Dahiya refers to the heavily Shia southern suburbs of Beirut targeted by the IDF in 2006; the strategy was subsequently used in Gaza in 2008–9 and 2014.

13. Security is performed in the media as well. For example, in reporting on rockets fired from Gaza into Israeli territory, both Western and Israeli leaders and the media, have consistently deployed the verb "rain": "Rocket fire rains on Sderot" or "Hamas is raining rockets on Israel." Rain implies steady, unlimited, and uncountable things, hardly relevant to these technologically crude weapons constructed with materials smuggled through tunnels (see Peteet 2016a).

14. For critical perspectives on the term "terrorism," see Beinin (2003); Esmeir (2006); and Whitbeck (2002).

15. "Israeli Military Leaders Agree: Separation from the Palestinians Is a Must," full-page ad, *New York Times*, December 4, 2015, 7. Sponsored by S. Daniel Abraham, Center for Middle East Peace.

16. The 2005 Israeli redeployment from Gaza, where the presence of around 8,000 colonists amid 1.4 million Palestinians meant that security had to be provided by military personnel, is an example of "colonial contraction" (Mansour 2011). Touted as a withdrawal, in reality the occupation continues in an even more brutal form, deploying high tech, remote-control mechanisms of surveillance and a punishing blockade. Israel withdrew troops, bases, and colonists but maintained control over Gaza's fenced borders and airspace and its civil registry, and still determines who can enter or exit. Redeployment and new surveillance technologies enabled a remote-control occupation. Redeployment had a clear demographic subtext: Israel rid itself of direct rule over 1.4 million Palestinians, reducing the demographic imbalance.

17. Knesset Members Yossi Beilin and Avshalon Vilan called for Eitam's prosecution for incitement and sedition. In his speech, Eitam included a call to "sweep the Israeli Arabs from the political system" (Khoury 2006).

18. The Allon Plan incorporated into Israel the Jordan Valley as well as an expanded Jerusalem area, and a strip of land along the Green Line.

19. Soffer and Bystrov (2005, 14) posit the income gap between Palestinians and Israelis as 17:1, the "largest economic gap in the world." There are no sources listed for this figure.

20. Soffer and Bystrov (2005) have a lengthy and detailed plan for winnowing the Arab Muslim and Bedouin population of Israel as well.

1. "Permission to Breathe"

1. See Yiftachel (1998) for a discussion of how Israeli land policies and planning generated ethno-class segregation between Ashkenazi Jews and the Mizrahis. He notes a "clear nexus connecting the de-Arabization of the country with the marginalization of peripheral Mizrahis, who have been positioned culturally and geographically between Arab and Jew, between Israel and its hostile neighbors, between a "backward" eastern past and a "progressive"

Western future. But the depth and extent of discrimination against Palestinians and Mizrahis have been quite different, with the latter included in the Zionist project as active participants in the oppression of the former." See also Lavie (2014).

2. Israel has no laws against miscegenation, perhaps because intermarriage and sexual relations between Palestinians and Israeli Jews are uncommon.

3. Curfews add to the chaos and unpredictability. Israel completely seals the West Bank and Gaza during Jewish holidays and when it makes certain announcements, such as the building of 1,600 new housing units in Jerusalem in March 2010.

4. See Lagerquist (2004) for a comprehensive history of the wall, its ideological foundations, and settler attitudes.

5. Egypt has been building an underground wall on its border with Gaza. Another notable wall is the seven-feet-high (two meters), double barbed-wire fence that separates Mellila, a Spanish exclave, from its border with Morocco. There is an electronic detection system built into the fence, and an alarm sounds if it is touched; anyone who manages to get through one set of barbed wire can be crushed by cables between the fences. The purpose of the fence is to prevent job-seeking Africans from entering Europe. By 2007, Saudi Arabia had begun constructing a 550-mile (885 kilometers) fence on its border with Iraq to deter the entry of terrorists, refugees, drugs, prostitutes, and weapons.

6. Sari Nusseibeh, president of Al-Quds, negotiated to have the wall rerouted in the areas around the university. As originally planned, the wall would have cut through the university's fields and sports areas.

7. *Courier-Journal* (Louisville, KY), January 25, 2010.

8. Graffiti and murals circulate globally on the web. Banksy's work, for example, is readily available on a number of websites. There is a website where, for a fee, it is possible to order a mural or graffiti and have it placed on the wall—a commodification of art and resistance; the profits go to local Palestinian organizations. Banksy writes on his website (https://www.youtube.com/watch?v=9LAChIoJQPg): "The segregation wall is a disgrace . . . The possibility I find exciting is you could turn the world's most invasive and degrading structure into the world's longest gallery of free speech and bad art."

9. Dov Weisglass, adviser to then Israeli prime minister Ehud Olmert, has been quoted as saying, "The idea is to put the Palestinians on a diet, but not to make them die of hunger." Urquhart, Conal "Gaza on Brink of Implosion as Aid Cut-Off Starts to Bite," *The Guardian*, April 15, 2006 (accessed July 12, 2016), http://www.guardian.co.uk/world/2006/apr/16/israel. Israeli has reportedly "relied on mathematic formulas which computed minimum nutritional requirements that would meet the basic needs of Gaza residents. Based on these formulas, the state determined the amount and volume of goods that were permitted to enter the Strip." Amira Hass, "Defense Ministry Ordered to Release Internal Documents on Gaza Policies," *Haaretz*, March 30, 2011 (accessed July 12, 2016), http://www.haaretz.com/print-edition/news/defense-ministry-ordered-to-release-internal-documents-on-gaza-policies-1.352768.

10. Some Palestinians personalize Zionist policy in the figure of Sharon, as the embodiment of the repressive nature of Zionism.

2. Mobility

1. Restricting Palestinian mobility is not a new phenomenon. After the *nakbah*, Israel carried out a census of the remaining Palestinians and issued them new identity cards. The Palestinians within Israel were governed by military rule until 1966, which included restrictions

on their mobility. With the 1967 occupation, Palestinians were once again subject to an Israeli census. East Jerusalem Palestinians were given Israeli-issued "residency" cards that enabled them to continue living in their homes. Syrian citizens in the Golan Heights were eventually accorded "residency" rights as well. Israel annexed the Golan in 1981 and offered the Syrians citizenship, which they refused, recognizing it as a tactic to legitimize occupation.

2. Curfews, anther means of immobilizing the population, are excluded from consideration here.

3. On immobilities, see Adey (2006); Urry (2007); Sheller (2008).

4. Within states, citizens may enjoy internal mobility, although not always equally, for example, in the United States, African Americans refer to the offense of DWB (driving while black) and in Saudi Arabia, women cannot drive.

5. Palestinian sociologist Elia Zureik (2001) details the history of various endeavors to define and count the Palestinian population since the Ottoman period. See Anderson (1991); Appadurai (1996); and Cohn (1996) on colonialism, the state, and the census.

6. In 1994, an American colonist, Baruch Goldstein, shot and killed twenty-nine Muslim worshipers and injured 125 in the al-Ibrahimi Mosque in Hebron and was then killed by other worshippers.

7. The Military Order is entitled "Order Regarding Prevention of Infiltration (Amendment No. 2) (Judea and Samaria) (No. 1650) 5769-2009.

8. The fingerprint and the signature were the earliest forms of biometrics. As vast numbers of people are on the move, security regimes have developed increasingly sophisticated means of identifying and documenting unique features of the body. The most unique human feature is DNA, but that is difficult to deal with on a mass and immediate scale; the retina, iris, and bone structure of the face (facial recognition) are individual, ostensibly fixed features of the body that can be captured and stored on magnetic cards.

9. See Torpay (2000) for a history of files in Europe. Biometric chips are being added to identity documents to ensure that the document and owner are the same person. The International Civilian Aviation Organization (ICAO) is responsible for airport security and sets the standards for machine-readable passports. A machine-readable zone (MRZ) is a space in which encryption can be read to ensure that a person and his documents match. This technology can read and process documents very quickly, facilitating the identification of hundreds of thousands of people moving through airports. Sometimes the chips can be read at a distance, before the holder even presents them at a scanner.

10. See Ayse Ceyhan (2008) for a history of biometrics; and Magnet (2011) for an examination of their limitations.

11. *Kunafeh* is a favorite Palestinian sweet made with cheese, shredded wheat, and syrup.

12. A neighborhood in Jerusalem just outside the walls of the Old City, Musrara was formerly populated by Palestinian Christians. It fell to the Israelis in the 1948 war and its inhabitants were denied return. Arab homes were subsequently occupied by Jewish immigrants.

13. See Bishara (2015); Dalakoglou (2010); Limbert (2010, 33–37); Pina-Cabral (1987); Selwyn (2001); Snead, Erickson, and Darling (2009); Roseman (1996); Stewart (1996).

14. See B'Tselem (2004, 26) for an account of a discussion with the Judge Advocate General and the IDF spokesperson on the legality of mobility restrictions. Israel claims the legal basis resides in Order Regarding Defense Regulation No. 387, from 1970, "which grants to the IDF . . . numerous powers." Section 88(a)1 of the order empowers the IDF to "prohibit, restrict, or regulate the use of certain roads."

15. In the late 1990s, settlers paved around 125 roads, totaling 111 miles, without government authorization (Zertal and Eldar 2007, 307). The Israeli government has constructed over

a thousand kilometers (621 miles) of roads, a number of which are used by only a very few colonists (Efrat 2006, 84).

16. Efrat (2006) details the topographical illogic of the road system.

3. Geography of Anticipation and Risk

1. The 1948 Universal Declaration of Human Rights, Article 13 (1) states, "Everyone has the right to freedom of movement and residence within the borders of each state." Article 12 of the International Covenant on Civil Rights and Political Rights reiterates this right.

2. Translated by Imad Elhaj. http://www.adab.com/modules.php?name=Sh3er&doWhat =shqas&qid=68413&r=&rc=94 (accessed April 20, 2014).

3. See Bornstein (2002, 2008); Braverman (2010); Hammami (2004, 2010); Havkin (2011); Jeganathan (2004); Tawil-Souri (2011).

4. For the "new mobilities paradigm," see Adey (2006, 90); Faulconbridge and Hui 2016; Shamir (2005); Thrift (2004); Urry (2007).

5. There was once a large shipping container at the site; hence the name "container." It is located at the end of Sawarha, a Palestinian section of East Jerusalem.

6. Israeli opinion, both among the public and the military, ranges from approval to serious critique of their efficacy and impact on Palestinian communities. See Grassiani (2009); Ben-Ari (2005).

7. See Joan Mandell (2009) for an insightful story about Bus 18.

8. Sources differ slightly on the width of the turnstile. See Machsom Watch, "List of Terms," September 29, 2009, http://www.en.machsomwatch.org/List-of-Terms.html (accessed July 24, 2016); Arbel, quoted in Weizman (2007); Braverman (2010), 5.

9. African Americans under the Jim Crow laws often faced similar situations in which deference was demanded (Davis, Gardner, and Gardner 1941).

10. This observation was confirmed by Machsom Watch activist Dorit Naaman (2006).

11. The Samaritans, an ethno-religious community, claim to be ancient Jews who remained in the land of Israel during the Babylonian exile. They have Israeli citizenship and West Bank identity cards.

12. See the Machsom Watch website for detailed records of their observations, http://www .en.machsomwatch.org/. They have been criticized for complicity in the checkpoint system (see Samera Esmeir 2006).

13. See Rosemary Esber, "The Tantura Massacre of 1948" (paper presented at the annual Middle East Studies Association meeting, Washington, DC, November 24, 2014).

14. The author of a master's thesis at the Hebrew University concluded that Israeli men do not rape Palestinian women because of racialized attitudes. Rapes did occur in 1948 (see Shalhoub-Kevorkian 2009, 128).

15. Norton, Ben, "Netanyhu Appoints Ayelet Shaked—Who Called for Genocide of Palestinians—as Justice Minister in New Government," *Mondoweiss*, May 6, 2015, http:// mondoweiss.net/2015/05/netanyahu-palestinians-government (accessed July 24, 2016).

16. Kashti, Or, "Israeli Professor's Rape as Deterrant Statement Draws Ire," *Ha'aretz*, July 22, 2014, http://www.haaretz.com/israel-news/.premium-1.606542 (accessed November 20, 2014).

17. For expressions of masculinity in Palestinian hip-hop music, see Greenberg (2009). For music and politics in the Middle East, see Levine (2011).

18. See, for example, the films *Omar*, *Lemon Tree*, *Rana's Wedding*, and *The Time That Remains*, among others.

4. Waiting and "Stealing Time"

1. See Bissell (2007) for cogent critique of the productivist and neo-Marxist approaches to waiting.

2. In the late 1980s, geographer David Harvey (1989, xii) wrote that social sciences usually "give time and history priority over space and geography." Although this was undoubtedly once true, time and space are now tackled as they intersect. See Lefebvre (2004) for a discussion of these entanglements.

3. El-Haddad (2009) is describing her attempt to enter Gaza after landing in Cairo on a flight from the United States. She and her two small children were detained in the Cairo airport for nearly three days before being put on a plane to the United States.

4. See Wick (2011) for an illuminating, ethnographically grounded account of waiting in Palestine.

5. Palestinian NGOs, especially those providing medical services, do use UN OCHA maps to navigate because they provide access to emergency medical services. OCHA prints large booklets of maps for NGO employees.

6. William Claiborne, "After All This Time, Can't 'Facts on the Ground' Be Overcome?" *Nieman Watchdog*, September 30, 2010, accessed November 25, 2012, http://www.nieman watchdog.org.

7. For critiques of biblical claims, see Abu El-Haj (2001); Sand (2010).

8. *From Time Immemorial: The Origins of the Arab-Jewish Conflict over Palestine*, authored by Joan Peters and later unmasked as a fraud by Norman Finkelstein ([1988] 2001), propagated this idea. A work of historical demography also undercut its argument (McCarthy 1990).

9. The narrative posits an unilinear progression through time and space that also elides two thousand years of Jewish diaspora. See Burg (2008); Zerubaval (1995).

10. The year 1948 is cast in the celebratory lens of statehood and even sexiness; "Israel: Still Sexy after 60 Years" was the advertising slogan used at the Georgetown Israel Alliance celebration of 1948. The 1967 "reunification" of Jerusalem is celebrated annually by Israeli Jews.

11. "Effects of Restrictions on Economy," Restriction of Movement, *B'Tselem*, January 1, 2011. accessed September 24, 2012, http://www.btselem.org/freedom_of_movement/economy.

12. Ibid.

13. Palestinian National Authority, "Health Conditions in the Occupied Palestinian Territory, Including East Jerusalem, and in the Occupied Syrian Golan" (report submitted by the PNA, Ministry of Health, to the World Health Organization, 65th Assembly, Geneva, May 21–26, 2012, A65/INF.DOC./4 6–7. February 2012.

14. Ibid., 9.

15. B'tselem, Statistic "Fatalities," accessed September 2012, http://www.btselem.org /statistics.

16. See "West Bank Movement and Access Update" (Report of United Nations Office for the Coordination of Humanitarian Affairs in the occupied Palestinian Territory, *Special Focus* August 2011, OCHA, accessed June 19, 2012, https://www.ochaopt.org/documents/ocha_opt _movement_and_access_report_august_2011_english.pdf.

17. The widespread circulation of stories of deliveries at checkpoints are indicators of a cruel occupation and reverberate with heightened fears and symbolic demographic meaning.

18. See "Infringement of the Right to Medical Treatment in the West Bank," B'Tselem: The Israeli Information Center for Human Rights in the Occupied Territories, http://www .btselem.org/english/Medical_Treatment/Index.asp accessed 1/27/2009; "The Issue of Palestinian Pregnant Women Giving Birth at Israeli Checkpoints" (annual report of the United

Nations High Commissioner for Human Rights and Reports of the Office of the High Commissioner and the Secretary-General, United Nations General Assembly A/HRC/7/44, February 1, 2008); BBC, "UN Fears over Checkpoint Births," September 23, 2005, accessed June 3, 2006, http://news.bbc.co.uk/2/hi/middle_east/4274400.

19. Quoted in Joseph Massad (2011).

5. Anti-Colonial Resistance in the Time of Closure

1. *Sumud* is the most common Palestinian response to occupation. A highly resonant word in the Palestinian lexicon, it means staying put, refusing to move in face of a machinery of dispossession and tactics to winnow the population. Indeed, the Palestinian organizer Mubarak Awad, who initiated a nonviolent movement, was accused of direct participation in the first intifada for authorizing the leaflets that guided the uprising and deported in 1988. The Palestinian Center for Study of Non-Violence drew Palestinian and Israeli adherents. Awad perceptively asked, "Is this the real reason for my deportation?" (quoted in King 2007, 162). For an excellent analysis of *sumud* see Meari (2014).

2. The Green Line is the 1949 Jordanian-Israeli Armistice Line separating the West Bank from Israel.

3. According to a study by Patrick O'Connor (2005), "The *New York Times* had published only three feature reports on Palestinian nonviolent resistance in the previous three years," despite hundreds of nonviolent protests.

4. During the first intifada, an estimated 160 Israelis (civilian and military) and 1,160 Palestinians were killed.

5. See Pallister-Watkins (2009) for a discussion of social movement theory, direct action, and protests in Palestine.

6. The Haram al-Sharif (Noble Sanctuary) dominates the panoramic skyline of Jerusalem's Old City. The third holiest site in Islam, it is the site of al-Aqsa Mosque and the Dome of the Rock.

7. See the ISM website, http://palsolidarity.org (accessed January 3, 2013). In 2004, the Palestinian Campaign for the Academic and Cultural Boycott of Israel asked academic associations to participate in the BDS campaign.

8. See Bayoumi (2010) for a detailed and comprehensive account of the flotilla and the Israeli response.

9. In the ISM protests and the Gaza flotilla, foreigners have been killed with impunity. ISM activist Rachel Corrie's death in 2003 by bulldozer sent a message to other young activists that Israel was ready to use lethal force to prevent protests, as did the death by sniper fire of British student and ISM activist Tom Hurndall in 2004. The summer 2010 flotilla killings of nine foreigners (eight Turks and one American Turk) shot by Israeli commandos again sent the message that protesters could face serious injury or possibly death.

10. DAM's 2012 video on the killing of Palestinian women by family members, often referred to as honor killings or femicide, was the subject of a heated debate on the Jadaliyya website in January 2013.

11. Jon Donnison, "British Palestinian Rapper Conducts a 'Musical Intifada,'" BBC News, Hebron, September 7, 2010, http://www.bbc.co.uk/news/world-middle-east-11215298. See also Ela Greenberg (2009).

12. Fatah formed in the late 1950s and early 1960s. A broad-based, secular, nationalist Palestinian organization once headed by Yasser Arafat, it assumed leadership of the PLO in 1969.

13. The localization of resistance preceded closure. With the PLO's 1982 withdrawal from its headquarters in Lebanon and a sense of abandonment by a leadership that had capitulated to the Oslo Accords and was highly corrupt were also factors in the shift toward local-level resistance.

14. The *jelabiyyeh* is a long, mono-colored, dress-like garment; on men it is usually white. On men, *abaya* functions as a cloak. Usually black or a camel color, it often has braided trim. The *hatta* or *kufiyyah* was once the standard headdress in villages and is still worn by the elderly. The *aghal* is a circular, braided black rope placed on the top of the *hatta* to keep it in place.

15. Sometimes touted as the Palestinian Mandela, Marwan Barghouti is a political activist and militant imprisoned for life in Israel.

16. See Kelly (2006) for an ethnographic account of Palestinian labor in Israel and the consequences of its retrenchment.

17. Sociologist Salim Tamari (1983, 42) writes, "The Leagues constituted the second historical attempt by the Zionist movement to establish a collaborative base among Palestinian peasants." The goal was to mobilize "the conservative peasantry against its own urban-based national movement."

18. Birthright Israel is an American organization that sends Jewish youth on free trips to Israel to strengthen their Jewish identity and solidarity with Israel. Birthright Unplugged organizes trips to Palestine and Israel from a social justice perspective.

19. Writer and activist Uri Avnery is a former member of the Knesset and a founder of Gush Shalom, an Israeli peace organization.

20. Percussion bombs are often better known as sound bombs. In summer 2008, Israeli forces began using the "Skunk" against demonstrators; it is an organic compound that when sprayed releases a stench that sticks to skin, clothes, and hair even after repeated washings. Its use, along with other innovations such as the "scream," which is a "large loudspeaker that sits on a truck and emits a dissonant and deafening sound," and sponge bullets, have led to characterizations of Bil'in and nearby Ni'lin as a "laboratory of experimentation" (Ben Shimon 2008, 4).

21. The Druze is a small sect thought to have origins in Shia Islam. They are a minority in Israel, but they do perform military service.

22. Later, Prime Minister Rabin, in the early and mid-1990s, "recognized that the iron wall of Jewish military power had achieved its purpose" and that negotiations were in order (Shlaim 2000, 504). Jabotinsky believed in negotiations only when the Palestinians conceded their weakness and Israel's "invincibility" (ibid., 599) and were obliged to submit to Israeli demands (ibid., 598). Shlaim writes that this is what has occurred: "The history of the state of Israel is a vindication of Jabotinsky's strategy of the iron wall" (ibid., 598–599). Shlaim perceptively notes that Jabotinsky did not envision a permanent wall but eventual peace, even if on unequal terms. In contemporary conceptualization of the iron wall, exemplified by current prime minister, Benjamin Netanyahu, it is seen as a means of separation and immisertion.

Conclusion

1. In 2014, the population of Jerusalem comprised 350,000 Palestinians in East Jerusalem, 300,000 Jews residing in West Jerusalem, and 200,000 Jews residing in colonies in occupied East Jerusalem.

2. See more at: http://mondoweiss.net/2014/08/knesset-genocide-against#sthash.Ns AmnX6h.dpuf.

Bibliography

Abowd, Thomas. 2014. *Colonial Jerusalem: The Spatial Construction of Identity and Difference in a Divided City*. Syracuse, NY: Syracuse University Press.

Abu El-Haj, Nadia. 2001. *Facts on the Ground: Archaeological Practice and Territorial Self-Fashioning in Israeli Society*. Chicago: Chicago University Press.

Abu-Zahra, Nadia. 2008. "Identity Cards and Coercion in Palestine." In *Fear: Critical Geopolitics and Everyday Life*, edited by Rachel Rain and Susan Smith, 177–191. Burlington, VT: Ashgate.

Adey, Peter. 2006. "If Mobility Is Everything Then It Is Nothing: Towards a Relational Politics of (Im)mobilities." *Mobilities* 1 (1): 75–94.

Agier, Michel. 2008. *On the Margins of the World: The Refugee Experience Today*. Cambridge: Polity Press.

Alexander, Michelle. 2010. *The New Jim Crow: Mass Incarceration in the Age of Colorblindness*. New York: New Press.

Allen, Lori. 2008. "Getting by the Occupation: How Violence Became Normal During the Second Palestinian Intifada." *Cultural Anthropology* 23 (3): 453–487.

———. 2013. *The Rise and Fall of Human Rights: Cynicism and Politics in Occupied Palestine*. Stanford, CA: Stanford University Press.

Aloni, Shulamit. 2007. "This Road Is for Jews Only: Yes, There Is Apartheid in Israel." *Counterpunch*, January 8, 2007.

Alsaafin, Linah. 2012. "How Obsession with 'Nonviolence' Harms the Palestinian Cause." *Electronic Intifada*, July 10. Accessed July 18, 2012. https://electronicinti fada.net/content/how-obsession-nonviolence-harms-palestinian-cause/11482.

Amoore, Louise, Stephen Marmura, and Mark Salter. 2008. "Editorial: Smart Borders and Mobilities: Spaces, Zones, Enclosures." *Surveillance and Society* 5 (2): 96–101.

Anderson, Benedict. 1991. *Imagined Communities*. London: Verso.

Appadurai, Arjun. 1996. *Modernity at Large: Cultural Dimensions of Globalization*. Minneapolis: University of Minnesota Press.

Appiah, Kwame Anthony. 1998. "Cosmopolitan Patriots." In *Thinking and Feeling Beyond the Nation*, edited by P. Cheah and B. Robbins, 91–114. Minneapolis: University of Minnesota Press.

Barber, Brian, Clea McNeely, Joseph Olsen, Carolyn Spellings, and Robert Belli. 2013. "Effect of Chronic Exposure to Humiliation on Wellbeing in the Occupied Palestinian Territory: An Event-History Analysis." *The Lancet* 382. Special issue S7 (December 5).

Barghouti, Omar. 2009. "Derailing Injustice: Palestinian Civil Resistance to the 'Jerusalem Light Rail.'" *Jerusalem Quarterly* 38 (Summer): 46–58.

Bauman, Richard, and Charles Briggs. 1990. "Poetics and Performances as Critical Perspectives on Language and Social Life." *Annual Review of Anthropology* 19: 59–88.

Bauman, Zygmunt. 1991. *Modernity and Ambivalence*. Ithaca, NY: Cornell University Press.

———. 2000. *Liquid Modernity*. Cambridge: Polity Press.

Bayoumi, Mustapha, ed. 2010. *Midnight on the Mavi Marmara: The Attack on the Gaza Freedom Flotilla and How It Changed the Course of the Israel/Palestine Conflict*. New York: Or Books.

Beinin, Joel. 2003. "The Israelization of American Middle East Policy Discourse." *Social Text* 21 (2): 124–139.

Ben-Ari, Eyal, Meirav Maymon, Nir Gazit, and Ron Shatzberg 2005. *From Checkpoints to Flowpoints: Sites of Friction Between the Israel Defense Forces and Palestinians*. Jerusalem: Harry S. Truman Research Institute for the Advancement of Peace, Hebrew University.

Ben-Ari, Eyal. 2008. "Human Security, the Militarized [Israeli] State: 'In-between organisations' at Checkpoints" In *The Visibility of Human Security*, edited by Monica den Boer and Jaap de Wilde, 126–148. The Netherlands: Amsterdam University Press.

Ben Shimon, Kobi. 2008. "Making a Stink." *Haaretz* online English edition, September 6, 2008. www.haaretz.com.

Berda, Yael. 2011. "The Security Risk as a Security Risk: Notes on the Classification Practices of the Israeli Security Services." In *Threat: Palestinian Political Prisoners in Israel*, edited by Abeer Baker and Anat Matar, 44–56. London: Pluto.

Bergmann, Sigurd. 2008. "The Beauty of Speed or the Discovery of Slowness: Why Do We Need to Rethink Mobility?" In *The Ethics of Mobilities: Rethinking Place, Exclusion, Freedom and Environment*, edited by Sigurd Bergmann and Tore Sager, 13–24. Aldershot, England: Ashgate.

Biehl, Joao, and Torben Eskerod. 2005. *Vita: Life in a Zone of Social Abandonment*. Berkeley: University of California Press.

Bishara, Amahl. 2015. "Driving While Palestinian in Israel and the West Bank: The Politics of Disorientation and the Routes of a Subaltern Knowledge." *American Ethnologist* 42 (1): 33–54.

Bisharat, George. 2007. "For Palestinians, Memory Matters, It Provides a Blueprint for Their Future." *San Francisco Chronicle,* May 13.

Bissell, David. 2007. "Animating Suspension: Waiting for Mobilities." *Mobilities* 2 (2): 277–298.

Blum, Ruthie. 2004. "One on One: It's the Demography, Stupid." Interview with Arnon Soffer. *Jerusalem Post*, May 20. http://www.ism-italia.org/wp-content/uploads/Jpost20040528-ONE-on-ONE-It%E2%80%99s-the-demography-stupid-An-interview-with-geographerdemographer-Arnon-Soffer-By-Ruthie-Blum.pdf.

Bodenhorn, Barbara, and Gabriele Vom Bruck. 2006. "'Entangled in Histories': An Introduction to the Anthropology of Names and Naming." In *The Anthropology of Names and Naming*, edited by Barbara Bodenhorn and Gabriele vom Bruck, 1–30. Cambridge: Cambridge University Press.

Bornstein, Avraham. 2002. *Crossing the Green Line Between the West Bank and Israel*. Philadelphia: University of Pennsylvania Press.

———. 2008. "Military Occupation as Carceral Society." *Social Analysis* 52: 106–130.

Bosmans, Marleen, Dina Nasser, Umaiyeh Khammash, Patricia Claeys, and Marleen Temmerman. 2008. "Palestinian Women's Sexual and Reproductive Health Rights in a Longstanding Humanitarian Crisis." *Reproductive Health Matters* 16 (31): 103–111.

Bourdieu, Pierre. 1977. *Outline of a Theory of Practice*. Translated by R. Nice. Cambridge: Cambridge University Press.

———. 1990. *The Logic of Practice*. Cambridge: Polity Press.

Bowker, Geoffrey, and Susan Starr. 1999. *Sorting Things Out: Classification and Its Consequences*. Cambridge, MA: MIT Press.

Bowman, Glenn. 2007. "Israel's Wall and the Logic of Encystations: Sovereign Exception or Wild Sovereignty?" *Focaal—European Journal of Anthropology* 50: 127–136.

Braverman, Irus. 2010. "Civilized Borders: A Study of Israel's New Crossing Administration." *Antipode*, September 22. Accessed November 19, 2010. doi/10.1111/j.1467 -8330.2010.00773.x/full.

Brenner, Lenni. 1984. *The Iron Wall. Zionist Revisionism from Jabotinsky to Shamir*. London: Zed Books Ltd.

Brink-Danan, Marcy. 2010. "Names That Show Time: Turkish Jews as 'Strangers' and the Semiotics of Reclassification." *American Anthropologist* 112 (3): 384–396.

Brooks, James. 2002. *Captives and Cousins. Slavery, Kinship and Community in the Southwest Borderlands*. Chapel Hill: University of North Carolina Press.

Brown, Wendy. 2010. *Walled States: Waning Sovereignty*. New York: Zone Books.

B'Tselem. 2004. *The Forbidden Roads: The Discriminatory West Bank Road Regime*. Jerusalem: B'Tselem.

Burg, Avraham. 2008. *The Holocaust Is Over: We Must Rise from Its Ashes*. New York: Palgrave Macmillan.

Butler, Judith. 1997. *Excitable Speech: A Politics of the Performative*. New York: Routledge.

Button, Gregory. 2009. "Family Resemblances Between Disasters and Development-Forced Displacement: Hurricane Katrina as a Comparative Case Study." In *Development and Dispossession: The Crisis of Forced Displacement and Resettlement*, edited by Anthony Oliver-Smith, 255–274. Santa Fe, NM: School for Advanced Research.

Calderia, Teresa. 1996. "Fortified Enclaves: The New Urban Segregation." *Public Culture* 8: 303–328.

Calhoun, Craig. 1994. "Social Theory and the Politics of Identity." In *Social Theory and the Politics of Identity*, edited by Craig Calhoun, 9–36. Oxford: Blackwell.

Campos, Michelle. 2011. *Ottoman Brothers: Muslims, Christians, and Jews in Early Twentieth-Century Palestine*. Stanford, CA: Stanford University Press.

Certeau, Michel de. 1984. *The Practice of Everyday Life*. Translated by Steven Rendall. Berkeley: University of California Press.

Ceyhan, Ayse. 2008. "Technologization of Security: Management of Uncertainty and Risk in the Age of Biometrics." *Surveillance and Society* 5 (2): 102–123.

Clarke, Richard. 2009. "Embodying Spaces of Violence: Narratives of Israeli Soldiers in the Occupied Palestinian Territories." In *Boundless World: An Anthropological Approach to Movement*, edited by Peter Kirby, 69–94. New York: Berghahn.

Coetzee, J. M. 1980. *Waiting for the Barbarians*. New York: Penguin.

Cohn, Bernard. 1996. *Colonialism and Its Forms of Knowledge: The British in India*. Princeton, NJ: Princeton University Press.

Collins, John. 2008. "Dromocratic Palestine." *Middle East Report* 248: 8–13.

Comaroff, John. 1998. "Reflections on the Colonial State, in South Africa and Elsewhere: Factions, Fragments, Facts and Fictions." *Social Identities* 4 (3): 321–61.

Cooper, Frederick. 2005. *Colonialism in Question: Theory, Knowledge, History.* Berkeley: University of California Press.

Crapanzano, Vincent. 1985. *Waiting: The Whites of South Africa.* New York: Random House.

Cresswell, Tim. 2006. "The Production of Mobilities: An Interpretive Framework." In *On the Move: Mobility in the Modern Western World,* edited by Tim Cresswell, 1–24. New York: Routledge.

Dalakoglu, Dimitrus. 2010. "The Road: An Ethnography of the Albanian-Greek Cross-Border Motorway." *American Ethnologist* 37 (1): 132–149.

Das, Veena. 2007. *Life and Words: Violence and the Descent into the Ordinary.* Berkeley: University of California Press.

Davis, Allison, Burleigh Gardner, and Mary Gardner. 1941. *Deep South: A Social Anthropological Study of Caste and Class.* Chicago: University of Chicago Press. Reprinted by the University of South Carolina Press in 2009.

Deeb, Lara. 2009. "Emulating and / or Embodying the Ideal: The Gendering of Temporal Frameworks and Islamic Role Models in Shia Lebanon." *American Ethnologist* 36 (2): 242–257.

Deeb, Lara, and Jessica Winegar. 2016. *Anthropology's Politics: Disciplining the Middle East.* Stanford, CA: Stanford University Press.

Deleuze, Gilles. 1995. *Negotiations: 1972-1990.* Translated by Martin Joughin. New York: Columbia University Press.

Dolphin, Ray. 2006. *The West Bank Wall: Unmaking Palestine.* London: Pluto.

Douglas, Mary. (1966) 1984. *Purity and Danger: An Analysis of the Concepts of Pollution and Taboo.* London: Ark Paperbacks.

Drobles, Mattityahu. 1980. *Master Plan for the Development of Settlement in Judea and Samaria (1979-1983).* Jerusalem: World Zionist Organiztion.

Dugard, John. 2007. "UN Rapporteur Compares Apartheid Israel to South Africa." *Electronic Intifada.* February 27. Accessed July 22, 2016. https://electronicintifada.net/content/un-rapporteur-compares-israel-apartheid-south-africa/6779.

Efrat, Elisha. 2006. *The West Bank and Gaza Strip: A Geography of Occupation and Disengagement.* New York: Routledge.

El-Haddad, Leila. "The Quintessential Palestinian Experience." *Electronic Intifada,* April 14. Accessed April 24, 2009. http:/electronicintifada.net/v2/article10463.shtml.

Elkins, Caroline, and Susan Pederson, eds. 2005. *Settler Colonialism in the Twentieth Century: Projects, Practices and Legacy.* New York: Routledge.

Esmeir, Samera. 2004. "Introduction: In the Name of Security." *Adalah's Review* 4: 2–9.

———. 2006. "On Making Dehumanization Possible." *PMLA: The Journal of the Modern Languages Association* 121 (5): 1544–1551.

Fabian, Johannes. 1983. *Time and the Other: How Anthropology Makes Its Other.* New York: Columbia University Press.

Falah, Ghazi. 2005. "The Geopolitics of 'Enclavization' and the Demise of a Two-State Solution to the Israeli-Palestinian Conflict." *Third World Quarterly* 26 (8): 1341–1372.

Fassin, Didier. 2001. "The Biopolitics of Otherness: Undocumented Foreigners and Racial Discrimination in French Public Debate." *Anthropology Today* 17 (1): 3–17.

Faulconbridge, James, and Allison Hui. 2016. "Traces of a Mobile Field: Ten Years of Mobilities Research." *Mobilities* 11 (1): 1–14.

Feldman, Ilana. 2008. *Governing Gaza: Bureaucracy, Authority, and the Work of Rule, 1917-1967.* Durham, NC: Duke University Press.

Finkelstein, Norman (1988) 2001. "Disinformation and the Palestine Question: The Not-So-Strange Case of Joan Peter's *From Time Immemorial.*" In *Blaming the Victim Spurious Scholarship*, edited by Edward Said and Christopher Hitchens, 33–70. London: Verso.

Fischback, Michael. 2003. *Records of Dispossession: Palestinian Refugee Property and the Arab-Israeli Conflict.* New York: Columbia University Press.

Foucault, Michel. 1979. *Discipline and Punish: The Birth of the Prison.* New York: Vintage.

Galili, Lily. 2002. "A Jewish Demographic State." *Ha'aretz*, June 28. Accessed December 14, 2005. www.bintjbeil.com/articles/en/-2-628-galili.htmil.

Giacaman, Rita, Laura Wick, Hanan Abdul-Rahim, and Livia Wick. 2005. "The Politics of Childbirth in the Context of Conflict: Policies or de Facto Practices?" *Health Policy* 72: 129–139.

Goffman, Erving. 1959. *The Presentation of Self in Everyday Life.* London: Penguin.

Gordon, Neve. 2008. *Israel's Occupation.* Berkeley: University of California Press.

Gordon, Neve, and Yinon Cohen. 2012. "The Demographic Success of Israel's Settlement Project." *Al-jazeera* (English), December 12, 2012. Accessed December 14, 2012. www.aljazeera.com/indepth/opinion/2012/12/2012.

Graham, Stephen. 2002. "Bulldozers and Bombs: The Latest Palestinian-Israeli Conflict as Asymmetric Urbicide." *Antipode* 34: 643–649.

Grassiani, Erella. 2013. *Soldiering under Occupation: Processes of Numbing among Israeli Soldiers in the al-Aqsa Intifada.* New York: Berghahn Books.

Greenberg, Ela. 2009. "'The King of the Streets': Hip Hop and the Reclaiming of Masculinity in Jerusalem's Shu'afat Refugee Camp." *Middle East Journal of Culture and Communication* 2: 231–250.

Greenberg, Hanan. 2010. "IDF Presents: 'Soldier-Free' Checkpoint Control." October 21. Accessed November 8, 2010. www.ynetnews.com.

Gregory, Derek. 2004. *The Colonial Present: Afghanistan, Palestine, Iraq.* Malden, MA: Blackwell.

Grossman, David. 1988. *The Yellow Wind.* Translated by Haim Watzman. New York: Picador.

Haggerty, Kevin, and Richard Ericson, eds. 2006. *The New Politics of Surveillance and Visibility.* Toronto: University of Toronto Press.

Halper, Jeff. 1999. "The 94 Percent Solution: A Matrix of Control." *Middle East Report* 216. doi:10.2307/1520209.

Hammami, Rema. 2004. "On the Importance of Thugs: The Moral Economy of a Checkpoint." *Middle East Report* 231, 26–34.

———. 2010. "Qalandiya: Jerusalem's Tora Bora and the Frontiers of Global Inequality." *Jerusalem Quarterly* 41: 29–51.

Hannerz, Ulf. 1996. *Transnational Connections: Culture, People, Places.* London: Routledge.

Harvey, David. 1989. *The Condition of Postmodernity.* Oxford: Basil Blackwell.

———. 2005. *A Brief History of Neoliberalism.* Oxford: Oxford University Press.

Havkin, Shira. 2011. "The Reform of Israeli Checkpoints: Outsourcing, Commodification, and the Redeployment of the State." Paris: SciencesPo / Centre d'Etudes et de Recherches Internationales.

Hoffman, Adina. 2009. *My Happiness Bears No Relation to Happiness: A Poet's Life in the Palestinian Century.* New Haven, CT: Yale University Press.

Jeganathan, Pradeep. 2004. "Checkpoint: Anthropology, Identity, and the State." In *Anthropology in the Margins of the State,* edited by Veena Das and Deborah Poole, 67–80. School of American Research Advanced Seminar Series. Santa Fe, NM: School of American Research Press.

Johnson, Penny, and Eileen Kuttab. 2001. "Where Have All the Women (and Men) Gone? Reflections on Gender and the Second Palestinian Intifada." *Feminist Review* 69: 21–43.

Johnson, Penny, Lamis Abu Nahleh, and Annelies Moors. 2009. "Weddings and War: Marriage Arrangements and Celebrations in Two Palestinian Intifadas." *Journal of Middle East Women's Studies* 5 (3): 11–35.

Jones, Martin. 2009. "Phase Space: Geography, Relational Thinking, and Beyond." *Progress in Human Geography* 33 (4): 487–506.

Judt, Tony. 2009. "Fictions on the Ground." *New York Times,* June 22. Accessed June 22, 2009. www.nytimed.com2009/06/22/opinion/22judt.html.

Kanaaneh, Rhoda. 2002. *Birthing the Nation: Strategies of Palestinian Women in Israel.* Berkeley: University of California Press.

Kandiyoti, Deniz. 1988. "Bargaining with Patriarch." *Gender and Society* 2 (3): 274–290.

Kelley, Robin. 2002. *Freedom Dreams: The Radical Black Imagination.* Boston: Beacon Press.

Kelly, Tobias. 2006. "Documented Lives: Fear and the Uncertainties of Law During the Second Palestinian Intifada." *Journal of the Royal Anthropological Institute* 12 (1): 89–107.

Khalidi, Rashid. 2004. *Resurrecting Empire: Western Footprints and America's Perilous Path in the Middle East.* Boston: Beacon Press.

Khalili, Laleh. 2010. "The Location of Palestine in Global Counterinsurgencies" *International Journal of Middle East Studies* 42(3): 413–433.

Khalili, Laleh. 2013. *Time in the Shadows: Confinement in Counterinsurgencies.* Stanford, CA: Stanford University Press.

Khoury, Jack. 2006. "Rightist MK Eitam: Expel Arabs from West Bank, Israeli Politics." *Ha'aretz,* September 11.

King, Mary Elizabeth. 2007. *A Quiet Revolution: The First Palestinian Intifada and Nonviolent Resistance.* New York: Nation Books.

Klein, Naomi. 2007. *The Shock Doctrine: The Rise of Disaster Capitalism.* New York: Metropolitan.

Kotef, Hagar, and Merav Amir. 2007. "(En)gendering Checkpoints: Checkpoint Watch and the Repercussions of Intervention." *Signs: Journal of Women and Culture in Society* 32 (4): 973–996.

Kruger, Martha. 2005. "Israel: Balancing Demographics in the Jewish State." Migration Information Source. Washington, DC: Migration Policy Institute.

Accessed June 12, 2010. www.migrationinformation.org/Feature/display.
cfm?ID=321.

Lagerquist, Peter. 2004. "Fencing the Last Sky: Excavating Palestine After Israel's 'Separation Wall.'" *Journal of Palestine Studies* 33 (2): 5–35.

———. 2008. "In the Labyrinth of Solitude: Time, Violence and the Eternal Frontier." *Middle East Report* 248. Accessed June 19, 2009. www.merip.org/mer/mer248/lagerquist.html.

Laurier, Eric, and Chris Philo. 2003. "The Region in the Boot: Mobilizing Lone Subjects and Multiple Objects." *Environment and Planning D: Society and Space* 21: 85–106.

Lavie, Smadar. 2014. *Wrapped in the Flag of Israel: Mizrahi Single Mothers and Bureaucratic Torture.* Brooklyn, NY: Berghahn Books.

Lefebvre, Henri. 1991. *The Production of Space.* Translated by Donald Nicholas-Smith. Oxford: Blackwell.

———. 2004. *Rhythmanalysis: Space, Time, and Everyday Life.* Translated by Stuart Elden and Gerald Moore. New York: Bloomsbury.

Levine, Mark. 2011. *Heavy Metal Islam: Rock, Resistance, and the Struggle for the Soul of Islam.* New York: Three Rivers Press.

Levy, Gideon. 2002. "Wombs in the Service of the State." *Ha'aretz*, September 9. Accessed July 23, 2016. http://www.haaretz.com/wombs-in-the-service-of-the-state-1.34696.

Li, Daryl. 2008. "Disengagement and the Frontiers of Zionism." *Middle East Report*, February 16. Accessed June 20, 2010. www.merip.org/mero/mero021608.html.

Limbert, Mandana. 2010. *In the Time of Oil: Piety, Memory, and Social Life in an Omani Town.* Stanford, CA: Stanford University Press.

Locke, Richard, and Anthony Stewart. 1985. *Bantustan Gaza.* London: Zed.

Lyon, David. 2006. "9/11, Synopticon, and Scopophilia: Watching and Being Watched." In *The New Politics of Surveillance and Visibility,* edited by Kevin Haggerty and Richard Ericson, 35–54. Toronto: University of Toronto Press.

Maalouf, Amin. 1984. *The Crusades Through Arab Eyes.* London: Al Saqi Books.

Magnet, Shoshana. 2011. *When Biometrics Fail: Gender, Race, and the Technology of Identity.* Durham, NC: Duke University Press.

Makovsky, David. 2004. "How to Build a Fence." *Foreign Affairs* 83 (2): 50–64.

Mamdani, Mahmood. 2001. *When Victims Become Killers: Colonialism, Nativism, and the Genocide in Rwanda.* Princeton, NJ: Princeton University Press.

Mandel, Ruth. 2008. *Cosmopolitan Anxieties: Turkish Challenges to Citizenship and Belonging in Germany.* Durham, NC: Duke University Press.

Mandell, Joan. 2009. "Bus #18." *Jerusalem Quarterly* 38 (Summer): 88–90.

Mann, Jonathan. 1998. "Dignity and Health: The UDHR's Revolutionary First Article." *Health and Human Rights* 3 (2): 31–38.

Mansour, Maha Samman. 2011. "Israeli Colonial Contraction: The Cases of the Sinai Peninsula and the Gaza Strip." In *Gaza-Palestine: Out of the Margins,* edited by M. Larudee, 77–111. Birzeit: Birzeit University Ibrahim Abu-Lughod Institute of International Studies.

Massad, Joseph. 2011. "Although Palestinian Children Endure Lives of Suffering, Obama's Love for Their Israeli Counterparts Knows No Limits," *Al Jazeera,*

May 30, 2011. http://www.aljazeera.com/indepth/opinion/2011/05/201152911
579533291.html.

Massey, Doreen. 1993. "Power-Geometry and a Progressive Sense of Place." In *Mapping the Futures: Local Cultures, Global Change*, edited by Jon Bird, Barry Curtis, Tim Putnam, and Lisa Tickner, 59–70. New York: Routledge.

McCarthy, Justin. 1990. *The Population of Palestine: Population History and Statistics of the Late Ottoman Period and the Mandate*. New York: Columbia University Press.

McClintock, Anne. 1995. *Imperial Leather: Race, Gender, and Sexuality in the Colonial Context*. New York: Routledge.

Meari, Lena. 2014. "Sumud: A Palestinian Philosophy of Confrontation in Colonial Prisons." *South Atlantic Quarterly* 113 (3): 547–578.

Memmi, Albert. 1965. *The Colonizer and the Colonized*. Translated by Howard Greenfeld. New York: Orion Press.

Meneley, Anne. 2008. "Time in a Bottle: The Uneasy Circulation of Palestinian Olive Oil." *Middle East Report* 248 (Fall): 18–23.

Merry, Sally Engle. 2000. *Colonizing Hawaii: The Cultural Power of Law*. Princeton, NJ: Princeton University Press.

Mirzoeff, Nicholas. 2011. *The Right to Look: A Counterhistory of Visuality*. Durham, NC: Duke University Press.

Morris, Tim. 2006. "Just a Wall?" *Forced Migration Review* 26 (August): 30.

Mufti, Burhan Al-. 2006. "Mixed Areas: A Dangerous Term." *Middle East Report* 239. http://www.merip.org/mer/mer239.

Munayyer, Yousef. 2012. "*When Settlers Attack*." Washington, DC: Palestine Center.

Munn, Nancy. 1992. "The Cultural Anthropology of Time: A Critical Essay." *Annual Review of Anthropology* 21: 93–123.

Naaman, Dorit. 2006. "The Silenced Outcry: A Feminist Perspective from the Israeli Checkpoint in Palestine." *National Women's Studies Association Journal* 18 (3): 168–180.

Nelson, Arthur. 2008. *Occupied Minds: A Journey Through the Israeli Psyche*. London: Pluto.

Netanyahu, Benjamin. 1993. *A Place among Nations. Israel and the World*. New York: Bantam Books.

Norman, Julie. 2010. *The Second Palestinian Intifada: Civil Resistance*. New York: Routledge.

Ochs, Juliana. 2011. *Security and Suspicion: An Ethnography of Everyday Life in Israel*. Philadelphia: University of Pennsylvania Press.

O'Connor, Patrick. 2005. "The Invisibility of Palestinian Nonviolent Resistance in the New York Times." *Electronic Intifada*, October 23. Accessed July 22, 2016. https://electronicintifada.net/content/invisibility-palestinian-nonviolent-resistance-new-york-times/5775.

Packer, Jeremy. 2008. *Mobility Without Mayhem: Safety, Cars, and Citizenship*. Durham, NC: Duke University Press.

Pallister-Wilkins, Polly. 2009. "Radical Ground: Israeli and Palestinian Activists and Joint Protest Against the Wall." *Social Movement Studies* 8 (4): 393–407.

Pappe, Ilan. 2006. *The Ethnic Cleansing of Palestine*. Oxford: Oneworld.

Parizot, Cedric. 2015. "From Stones to Nodes: For a Typology of the Separation Between Israelis and Palestinians." Paper presented at the conference "Palestine and

Self-Determination Beyond National Frames: Emerging Politics, Cultures, and Claims." Athens, Greece. September 24–25.

Pateman, Carol, and Charles Mills. 2007. *Contract and Domination.* Cambridge: Polity.

Peteet, Julie. 1991. *Gender in Crisis: Women and the Palestinian Resistance Movement.* New York: Columbia University Press.

———. 1994. "Male Gender and Rituals of Resistance in the Palestinian Intifada: A Cultural Politics of Violence." *American Ethnologist* 21 (1): 31–49.

———. 1996. "The Writing on the Walls: The Graffiti of the Intifada." *Cultural Anthropology* 11 (2): 1–21.

———. 1997. "Icons and Militants: Mothering in the Danger Zone." *Signs: Journal of Women and Culture* 23 (1): 103–129.

———. 2005a. *Landscape of Hope and Despair: Place and Identity in Palestinian Refugee Camps.* Philadelphia: University of Pennsylvania Press.

———. 2009. "Beyond Compare." *Middle East Report* 253. Assessed August 10, 2016. http://www.merip.org/mer/mer253/beyond-compare.

———. 2015. "Wall Talk: Palestinian Graffiti." In *Handbook of Graffiti and Street Art,* edited by J. I. Ross, 334–344. New York: Routledge.

———. 2016. "Enclaves and Camps: Palestine in the Time of Closure." *Journal of Refugee Studies* 28 (3): 1–22.

———. 2016a. "Language Matters: Talking About Palestine." *Journal of Palestine Studies* 45 (2): 24–40.

———. 2016b. "The Work of Comparison: Israel/Palestine and Apartheid." *Anthropological Quarterly* 89 (1): 225–260.

Pina-Cabral, Joao. 1987. "Paved Roads and Enchanted Mooresses: The Perception of the Past among the Peasant Population of Alto Minho." *Man,* n. s. 22 (4): 715–735.

Piterberg, Gaby. 2011. "Literature of Settler Colonial Societies: Albert Camus, S. Yizhar and Amoz Oz." *Settler-Colonial Studies* 1 (2): 1–52.

Rabinowitz, Dani. 2001/2002. "Borderline Collective Consciousness: Israeli Identity, 'Arabness' and the Green Line." *Palestine-Israel Journal of Politics, Economics and Culture* 8 (4) and 9 (1): 38–49.

Rapport, Nigel. 2006. "Anthropology as Cosmopolitan Study." *Anthropology Today* 22 (1): 23–24.

Rodinson, Maxime. 1973. *Israel: A Settler-Colonial State?* Translated by David Thorstad. London: Pathfinder Press.

Roseman, Sharon. 1996. "'How We Built the Road': The Politics of Memory in Rural Galicia." *American Ethnologist* 23 (4): 836–860.

Rosenfeld, Maya. 2011. "The Centrality of the Prisoners' Movement to the Palestinian Struggle against the Israeli Occupation: A Historical Perspective." In *Threat: Palestinian Political Prisoners in Israel,* edited by Abeer Baker and Anat Matar, 3–24. London: Pluto.

Rosen, Lawrence, ed. 1995. *Other Intentions: Cultural Contexts and the Attribution of Inner States.* Santa Fe, NM: School of American Research Press.

Rotenburg, Robert. 1992. "The Power to Time and the Time to Power." In *The Politics of Time.* Vol. 4, edited by Henry Rutz, 18–36. Washington DC: American Anthropological Association.

Roy, Sara. 1995. *The Gaza Strip: The Political Economy of De-development*. Washington, DC: Institute for Palestine Studies.

Sa'di, Ahmad. 2014. *Thorough Surveillance: The Genesis of Israeli Policies of Population Management, Surveillance and Political Control Towards the Palestinian Minority*. Manchester, England: Manchester University Press.

Sager, Tore. 2006. "Freedom as Mobility: Implications of the Distinction between Actual and Potential Travelling." *Mobilities* 1 (3): 465–488.

Said, Edward. 1984. "Permission to Narrate." *Journal of Palestine Studies* 13 (3): 27–48.

———. 2002. "Invention, Memory, and Place." In *Landscape and Power*, edited by W. Mitchell, 241–259. Chicago: University of Chicago Press.

Sand, Shlomo. 2010. *The Invention of the Jewish People*. Translated by Yael Lotan. London: Verso.

Sassen, Saskia. 2014. *Expulsions: Brutality and Complexity in the Global Economy*. Cambridge, MA: Belknap Press of Harvard University Press.

Schaeffer, Emily, and Jeff Halper. 2012. *Israel's Policy of Demolishing Palestinian Homes Must End: A Submission to the UN Human Rights Council by the Israeli Committee Against House Demolitions* (ICHAD). http://www.icahd.org/node/458#sthash .ILp3bvKk.dpuf.

Scheper-Hughes, Nancy. 2004. "Coming to Our Senses: Anthropology and Genocide." In *Annihilating Difference: The Anthropology of Genocide*, edited by A. Hinton, 348–381. Berkeley: University of California Press.

Scott, James. 1998. *Seeing like a State: How Certain Schemes to Improve the Human Condition Have Failed*. New Haven, CT: Yale University Press.

Selwyn, Tom. 2001. "Landscapes of Separation: Reflections on the Symbolism of By-pass Roads in Palestine." In *Contested Landscapes: Movement, Exile and Place*, edited by Barbara Bender and Margot Winer, 225–240. Oxford: Berg.

Shafir, Gershon. 1989. *Land, Labor and the Origins of the Israeli-Palestinian Conflict, 1882–1914*. Cambridge: Cambridge University Press.

———. 2005. "Settler-Citizenship in the Jewish Colonization of Palestine." In *Settler Colonialism in the Twentieth-Century: Projects, Practices, and Legacy*, edited by Caroline Elkins and Susan Pederson, 41–57. New York: Routledge.

Shalhoub-Kevorkian, Nadera. 2009. *Militarization and Violence Against Women in Conflict Zones in the Middle East: A Palestinian Case Study*. Cambridge: Cambridge University Press.

Shalhoub-Kevorkian, Nadera, Sarah Ihmoud, and Suha Dahir-Nashif. 2014. "Sexual Violence, Women's Bodies, and Israeli Settler-Colonialism." *Jadaliyya* 17 (November). Accessed November 19, 2014. https://alethonews.wordpress.com/2015/01/04 /sexual-violence-womens-bodies-and-israeli-settler-colonialism/.

Shamir, Ronen. 2005. "Without Borders? Notes on Globalization as a Mobility Regime." *Sociological Theory* 23 (2): 197–217.

Shehadeh, Raja. 2008. *Palestinian Walks: Forays into a Vanishing Landscape*. New York: Scribner.

Sheller, Mimi. 2008. "Mobility, Freedom and Public Space." In *The Ethics of Mobilities: Rethinking Place, Exclusion, Freedom and Environment*, edited by Sigurd Bergmann and Tore Sager, 25–38. Aldershot, England: Ashgate.

Shlaim, Avi. 2000. *The Iron Wall: Israel and the Arab World*. New York: W. W. Norton.

Shohat, Ella. 1988. "Sephardim in Israel: Zionism from the Standpoint of Its Jewish Victims." *Social Text* 19 (20): 1–35.

———. 1999. "The Invention of the Mizrahaim." *Journal of Palestine Studies* 29 (1): 5–20.

Sivaramakrishman, K. 2005. "Introduction to 'Moral Economies, State Spaces, and Categorical Violence': Anthropological Engagements with the Work of James Scott." *American Anthropologist* 107 (3): 321–330.

Snead, James, Clark Erickson, and J. Andrew Darling, eds. 2009. *Landscapes of Movement: Trails, Paths, and Roads in Anthropological Perspective*. Philadelphia: University of Pennsylvania Press.

Soffer, Arnon, and Evgenia Bystrov. 2002. "Demographics in the Israeli-Palestinian Dispute." Special Forum Report. Policywatch 370, 1–4, March 22. Washington, DC: Washington Institute for Near East Policy.

———. 2005. *Israel Demography 2004-2020 in Light of the Process of Disengagement*. Haifa, Israel: University of Haifa.

Solnit, Rebecca. 2009. *A Paradise Built in Hell: The Extraordinary Communities That Arise in Disaster*. New York: Penguin.

Stewart, Kathleen. 1996. *A Space on the Side of the Road: Cultural Poetics in an "Other" America*. Princeton, NJ: Princeton University Press.

Stoler, Ann Laura. 2002. *Carnal Knowledge and Imperial Power: Race and the Intimate in Colonial Rule*. Berkeley: University of California Press.

———. 2008. "Imperial Debris: Reflections on Ruins and Ruination." *Cultural Anthropology* 23 (2): 191–219.

———. 2009. *Along the Archival Grain: Epistemic Anxieties and Colonial Common Sense*. Princeton, NJ: Princeton University Press.

Suleiman, Yasir. 2004. *A War of Words: Language and Conflict in the Middle East*. New York: Cambridge University Press.

Tamari, Salim. 1983. "In League with Zion: Israel's Search for Native Pillar." *Journal of Palestine Studies* 12 (4): 41–56.

Tannen, Deborah. 1998. *The Argument Culture*. New York: Random House.

Taraki, Lisa. 2008. "Enclaved Micropolis: The Paradoxical Case of Ramallah/al-Bireh." *Journal of Palestine Studies* 37 (4): 6–20.

Tawil-Souri, Helga. 2011. "Qalandia Checkpoint as Space and Non-Place." *Space and Culture* 14 (1): 4–26.

Thompson, John. 2005. "The New Visibility." *Theory, Culture and Society* 22 (6): 31–51.

Thrall, Nathan. 2014. "Rage in Jerusalem." *London Review of Books* 36 (23): 19–21. November 21. Accessed November 28, 2014. http://www.lrb.co.uk/v36/n23/nathan -thrall/rage-in-jerusalem.

Thrift, Nigel. 2004. "Movement-Space: The Changing Domain of Thinking Resulting from the Development of New Kinds of Spatial Awareness." *Economy and Society* 33: 582–604.

Tilly, Charles.1998. *Durable Inequalities*. Berkeley: University of California Press.

Torpay, John. 1998. "Coming and Going: On the State Monopolization of the Legitimate 'Means of Movement.'" *Sociological Theory* 16 (3): 239–259.

———. 2000. *The Invention of the Passport: Surveillance, Citizenship and the State*. Cambridge: Cambridge University Press.

Turner, Brian. 2006. *Vulnerability and Human Rights.* University Park: Penn State University Press.

Turner, Victor. 1986. *The Anthropology of Performance.* New York: PAJ Publications.

Urry, J. 2003. *Global Complexity.* Cambridge: Polity.

———. 2007. *Mobilities.* Cambridge: Polity.

Virilio, Paul, and J. Armitage. 1999. "From Modernism to Hypermodernism." *Theory, Culture and Society* 16: 25–55.

Vitullo, Anita, Abdelnasser Soboh, Jenny Oskarsson, Tasneem Atatrah, Mohamed Lafi, and Tony Laurance. 2012. "Barriers to the Access to Health Services in the Occupied Palestinian Territory: A Cohort Study." *The Lancet.* Executive Summary. October 8, 2012. http://www.thelancet.com/pb/assets/raw/Lancet/abstracts/palestine/palestine2012-12.pdf.

Wacquant, Loic. 2004. "Ghetto." *International Encyclopedia of the Social and Behavioral Sciences.* Amsterdam, Netherlands: Elsevier.

Walker, Alice. 2009. "The Best Place One Could Be on Earth." *Electronic Intifada,* July 24. Accessed July 26, 2009. http://electronicintifada.net/v2/article10675.

Warschawski, Michael 2006. "The 2006 Israeli Elections: A Drive to Normalcy and Separation." *Journal of Palestine Studies* 35 (4): 44–53.

Weizman, Eyal. 2007. *Hollow Land: Israel's Architecture of Occupation.* London: Verso.

———. 2011. *The Least of All Possible Evils: Humanitarian Violence from Arendt to Gaza.* London: Verso.

Whitbeck, John. 2002. "'Terrorism': The Word Itself Is Dangerous." *Global Dialogue* 4 (2): 59–65.

Wick, Livia. 2011. "The Practice of Waiting Under Closure in Palestine." *City and Society* 23 (51): 24–44.

Wick, L. N. Mikki, R. Giacaman, and H. Abdul-Rahim. 2005. "Childbirth in Palestine." *International Journal of Gynecology and Obstetrics* 89: 174–178.

Willem, Sarah. 2010. "Citizens, 'Real' Others, and 'Other' Others: The Biopolitics of Otherness and the Deportation of Unauthorized Migrant Workers from Tel Aviv, Israel." In *The Deportation Regime: Sovereignty, Space, and the Freedom of Movement,* edited by Nicholas de Genova and Nathalie Peutz, 262–294. Durham, NC: Duke University Press.

Wittgenstein, Ludwig. 1953. *Philosophical Investigations.* Translated by G. E. M. Anscombe. New York: Macmillan.

Wolfe, Patrick. 2006. "Settler Colonialism and the Elimination of the Native." *Journal of Genocide Research* 8 (4): 387–409.

———. 2013. "Recuperating Binarism: A Heretical Introduction." *Settler Colonial Studies* 3 (3/4): 257–279.

Yiftachel, Oren. 1998. "Democracy or Ethnocracy: Territory and Settler Politics in Israel/Palestine." *Middle East Report* 207: 8–13.

———. 2005. "Neither Two States nor One: The Disengagement and 'Creeping Apartheid' in Israel/Palestine." *Arab Geographer / Le Geographe du monde arabe* 8 (3): 125–129.

Zertal, Idith, and Akiva Eldar. 2007. *Lords of the Land: The War over Israel's Settlements in the Occupied Territories, 1967-2007.* Translated by Vivian Eden. New York: Nation Books.

Zerubavel, Eyal. 1995. *Recovered Roots: Collective Memory and the Making of Israeli National Tradition*. Chicago: University of Chicago Press.

Zinn, Howard. 2002. *You Can't Be Neutral on a Moving Train: A Personal History of Our Times*. 5th ed. Boston: Beacon Press.

Zureik, Elia. 2001. "Constructing Palestine Through Surveillance Practices." *British Journal of Middle Eastern Studies* 28 (2): 205–227.

Index

JULIE PETEET is Professor of Anthropology at the University of Louis-
ville. She is author of *Landscape of Hope and Despair: Palestinian Refugee
Camps* and *Gender in Crisis: Women and the Palestinian Resistance
Movement.*

www.ingramcontent.com/pod-product-compliance
Lightning Source LLC
Chambersburg PA
CBHW050349270326
41926CB00016B/3662